THE
$\mathcal{B}$EVERAGE
BOOK

THE
$\mathcal{B}$EVERAGE
BOOK

Andrew Durkan & John Cousins

Hodder & Stoughton

A MEMBER OF THE HODDER HEADLINE GROUP

British Library Cataloguing in Publication Data

Durkan, Andrew
  Beverage Book
  I. Title   II. Cousins, John A.
  641.2

  ISBN 0 340 60484 0

First published 1995
Impression number   10 9 8 7 6 5 4 3 2 1
Year   1999 1998 1997 1996 1995

Typeset by Wearset, Boldon, Tyne and Wear.
Printed in Great Britain for Hodder & Stoughton Educational, a division of Hodder Headline Plc, 338 Euston Road, London NW1 3BH by The Bath Press, Avon.

CONTENTS

—

ACKNOWLEDGEMENTS

—

The authors and publishers would like to thank all those who have assisted in the preparation of this work and the provision of photographs. In particular The Courage Brewery; Croners Catering, Croner Publications; Food and Wine from France; The German Wine Information Service; Griersons Wine Merchants; Gonzales Byass; The Hotel and Catering Training Company; International Coffee Organisation; The Italian Trade Centre; Merrydown Cider; The School of Hospitality Studies at Thames Valley University; The Sherry Institute.

INTRODUCTION

—

The aim of this book is to cover the basic knowledge and skills for those involved or likely to be involved at a variety of levels in beverage service. This is an introductory text for students and practitioners. It also provides a framework on which to acquire further knowledge and skills.

In preparing this book we have taken into account the various changes in examination syllabuses and in particular the National Vocational Qualification standards. The book is specifically intended to cover the knowledge and skill required by those wishing to be assessed up to level three. However, the book has also been written to meet the broader study requirements of a range of other programmes such as HCIMA, BTEC and degree courses.

In writing this book we have taken a new approach to the presentation of the material. Traditional approaches have been product-led, in that they have presented information based on the type of beverages that are available. The approach taken for this text, mainly in recognition of changes in approaches to the teaching of the subject, has been to take a generic view of drinks.

We begin by providing information on the processes for making wine and other drinks. Two scene-setting introductory chapters introduce the licensed trade (chapter 1) and alcohol (chapter 2), then fermentation, brewing and distillation each have chapters (chapters 3, 4 and 5) devoted to them. This is followed by a look at the methods of making other drinks (chapter 6).

After covering the basic knowledge about wine and drinks, we have then provided information on wine and drink lists (chapter 7), purchasing, storage and control of beverages (chapter 8) and food and wine harmony (chapter 10). Chapter 9 provides information, in an A to Z listing, of all wine regions and chapter 11 deals with the sales and service of beverages and cigars.

In our experience the general knowledge of wine and drinks among customers has increased tremendously. New World wines in particular, with their simple names and clear identification of grape varieties, have demystified wine for many. There are also now some wine lists emerging which are categorised according to grape varieties. Reasonably priced, good quality wines are freely available in supermarkets and off-licences and wine consumption is generally growing.

With this background, service staff have needed generally to improve the level of professionalism in the selling and service of wine and drinks. This book is solely aimed at assisting this process.

1

THE LICENSED TRADE

THE HOTEL AND CATERING INDUSTRY

The hotel and catering industry is now becoming more widely known as the hospitality industry. In addition, the industry is also referred to as the hotel and food service industry. Beverages are sold throughout the industry, but alcoholic beverages are sold selectively in only some sectors.

Licences are required to sell intoxicating liquor in Britain. These licences govern the type of liquor which can be sold, the extent of the market which can be served, and the times of opening (or permitted hours). There are also regulations on measures and restrictions on sales to young persons. These restrictions are made by the Government and penalties for infringement are applied not only to the licensee but also to the customer.

Table 1.1 provides a summary of the sectors of the food service industry and an indication of the licensing arrangements available.

Table 1.1 *Summary of the licensing arrangements available in different sectors of the hospitality industry*

SECTOR	PURPOSE OF SECTOR	LICENSING
Hotels and other tourist accommodation	Provision of food and drink together with accommodation	Generally licensed but may be restricted (see page 5)
Restaurants including: conventional specialist carveries	Provision of food and drink generally at high price with high levels of service	Generally licensed but may be restricted (see page 5)
Popular catering including: cafés, pizza, Wimpy, grills, specialist coffee shops, Little Chefs, steak houses	Provision of food and drink generally at low/medium price with limited levels of service	Limited Licensing at present
Fast Food including: McDonalds, Burger King	Provision of food and drink in highly specialised environment characterised by high investment, high labour costs and vast customer throughput	Unlicensed
Take-away including: ethnic, spuds, KFC, snacks, fish and chips, sandwich bars, kiosks	Provision of food and drinks quickly	Unlicensed
Retail stores	Provision of food and drink as adjunct to provision of retailing	Licensing varies
Banqueting conferences/exhibitions	Provision of food and drink on large scale, usually pre-booked	Usually licensed
Leisure attractions such as theme parks, galleries, theatres, airline terminals	Provision of food and drink for people engaged in another leisure pursuit	Licensing varies
Motorway service stations	Provision of food together with retail and petrol services for motorway travellers, often in isolated locations	Unlicensed
Industrial catering either in-house operations or provided by catering contractor	Provision of food and drink to people at work	Licensing varies
Welfare including: hospitals, schools, colleges, universities, forces, prisons, other welfare	Provision of food and drink to people through social need, primarily determined by an authority	Licensing varies
Licensed trade including: public houses, wine bars, licensed clubs, members clubs	Provision of food and drink in environment dominated by licensing requirements	All licensed
Transport including: railways, airlines, marine	Provision of food and drink to people on the move	Usually licensed
Outdoor catering ('off premises' catering)	Provision of food and drink away from home base and suppliers	Licensing varies

CAREERS IN BEVERAGE SERVICE

From the wide range of sectors given in table 1.1, it is obvious that there is a wide range of opportunities for those wishing to work in beverage service. Opportunities exist for both part- and full-time employment. Some of the range of positions are outlined below.

Positions

Bar staff   Employed on a part- or full-time basis. The hours of work are usually those of the licensing requirements plus periods before and after permitted (opening) hours for duties such as stocking and cashing up. The changes that took place in permitted hours (up to 12 hours per day, see page 6) have also opened up the possibility for straight shift work.

Cocktail bar staff   This role is similar to general bar staff but requires additional skills because of the specialisation in cocktails.

Bars manager   This position can be found in a variety of sectors. The bar manager is usually responsible for all the beverage operations within an establishment. This includes the purchasing, storage and control of the beverage operations, as well as the employment and training of staff.

Head sommelier (or head wine waiter)   This person is usually a professional making a career in beverage service. The job is generally found in medium- to full-priced restaurants which require a specialist in the purchasing, care and knowledge of wine. In larger establishments an **assistant sommelier** (wine waiter) and/or a **commis du vin** (assistant wine waiter) may also be employed.

Publican   This person could be a proprietor of a public house, a manager in a managed house or a tenant in a tenanted house (see page 4).

In addition to these specific roles, beverage service is also of concern to food and beverage managers, restaurant proprietors, and a range of food service staff who should at least have a basic knowledge of the beverage product and the service associated with it.

Opportunities for advancement in beverage service are many. Progression is possible through experience and there are opportunities to pursue careers throughout the world.

General attributes of beverage service personnel

The following are some of the principal attributes required in good beverage service personnel:

- a high standard of personal hygiene;
- good product knowledge;
- good technical skills in service techniques;
- good social skills;
- the ability to work as part of a team;
- honesty;
- sobriety.

LIQUOR LICENSING

The information on licensing below is as it stands in 1994. There are reforms being considered by the Government which essentially relate to three issues.

The first is changes in the grounds on which licensing justices decide on applications. This includes consideration of the suitability of the licensee, the premises and the likelihood of public nuisance or threat to public safety. This might also include taking into account the number of licenses already granted for a particular area.

The second is for a system, similar to that already operational in Scotland, whereby accompanied young people (under 14 years of age) may be allowed in a bar where a Children's Certificate is held for the purposes of a family meal up to 8 p.m.

The third is for a new category of licence which would allow the sale of alcoholic drinks in café-style premises without a bar counter, provided that food and non-alcoholic drinks were on sale at the same time. Again it is considered that accompanied young people should be allowed into such places.

Alcoholic beverages are sold in two main types of establishment: free houses and tied houses.

Free house   This is a licensed premises which is privately owned and has no attachment to one particular source of supply.

Tied house   This is a licensed premises which is either tenanted or managed and is linked (or tied) to a particular source of supply.

- Tenanted: The tenant leases the property from a brewery and is tied to that brewery for the purchase of beer and perhaps other drinks. The tenancy agreement lays down the conditions of operation.
- Managed: A manager is paid a salary to run the premises for the brewery.

Types of licence

The various types of licence available in Britain are described below. The definitions for the licences quoted here apply to England and Wales. In Scotland the licensing pattern is similar, although there are differences in the definitions and in the permitted hours. Licensing definitions in Northern Ireland are similar to those in England and Wales.

FULL ON-LICENCE

This allows the licensee to sell all types of intoxicating liquor for consumption on and off the premises. However, there are a few examples of On-licences where the type of alcohol is restricted, such as beer only or beer and wine only.

RESTRICTED ON-LICENCES

Restaurant Licence   This applies to the sale of alcoholic liquor to persons taking main meals only.

Residential Licence   This applies to the sale of alcoholic liquor to persons residing on the premises or to their private friends who are being genuinely entertained at the guests' expense.

Combined Licence   This is a combined Restaurant and Residential Licence.

CLUB LICENCES

Licensed Club   Normally this is a licence to run a club, which is operated by individuals or a limited company as a commercial enterprise. The sale of alcoholic liquor is to members only.

Members' Club   A licence to run a club, normally by a committee of members, as a non-profit making organisation. The members own the stock of liquor and sale is to members only.

OFF-LICENCE

A licence authorising the sale of intoxicating liquor for consumption off the premises only.

OCCASIONAL LICENCE

This is granted to holders of On-, Restaurant or Combined Licences, enabling them to sell alcoholic liquor at another place for a specified time. For example, a licensee may be able to set up a bar for a local village hall function.

OCCASIONAL PERMISSION

This is similar to an Occasional Licence but may be applied for by non-licence holders. For example, a charity may apply for Occasional Permission in order to sell alcoholic drink at a specific fundraising event.

MUSIC AND DANCING LICENCES

These licences are not liquor licences but are required for public music and dancing. The licences are granted by local councils and the law varies from place to place. Licences are not required where radio, television and recorded music are used or where there are no more than two live performers, although if dancing takes place a licence is required.

Permitted hours

Currently permitted hours are as follows in England and Wales and Scotland.

Weekdays	11 a.m. to 11 p.m.
	8 a.m. to 11 p.m. at off-licences
Sundays ⎫	
Good Friday ⎬	12 noon to 3 p.m.
Christmas Day ⎭	and 7 p.m. to 10.30 p.m. at on-and off-licences

Within these permitted hours the licensee can choose when and for how long to close the premises.

EXCEPTIONS TO PERMITTED HOURS
The following exceptions apply to permitted hours in England, Wales and Scotland:

- the first 20 minutes after the end of permitted hours is for consumption only;
- the first 30 minutes after the end of permitted hours for those taking table meals is again for consumption only;
- residents and their guests may be (but do not have to be) served at any time as long as only the resident makes the purchase.

EXTENSIONS TO PERMITTED HOURS

Special Order of Exemption   This is available for specific occasions, such as weddings, dinner dances or carnivals.

General Order of Exemption   This applies to an area where a particular trade or calling is going on, for example market day or food markets which are operating early in the morning.

Supper Hour Certificate   This allows for an additional hour at the end of permitted hours for licensed restaurants.

Extended Hours Certificate   This is an extension for establishments which already hold a Supper Hours Certificate and provide some form of entertainment. The extension is until 1 a.m.

Special Hours Certificate   This allows for extensions of permitted hours to premises which are licensed, hold a Music and Dancing Licence and provide substantial refreshment. The extension can be until 3 a.m. in the West End of London and until 2 a.m. elsewhere.

Young persons

It is an offence for persons under 18 to be served in a licensed bar. It is also an offence to allow persons under 18 to consume alcoholic beverages in a bar. Similarly, it is an offence for the person under 18 to attempt to purchase or to purchase or consume alcoholic beverages in a bar. The position regarding young persons is summarised in table 1.2.

Table 1.2   *Licensing restrictions on young persons*

AGE	PURCHASE IN A BAR	CONSUME IN A BAR	ENTER A BAR	PURCHASE IN A RESTAURANT	CONSUME IN A RESTAURANT
Under 14	No	No	No	No	Yes[1]
Under 16	No	No	Yes	No	Yes[1]
Under 18	No	No	Yes	Yes[2]	Yes

[1] As long as the alcoholic beverage is bought by a person over 18
[2] Beer, cider and perry only

Note: tobacco should not be sold to persons under 16 years old.

Weights and measures

Beer and cider   Unless sold in a sealed container, beer and cider may only be sold in measures of ⅓ or ½ pint, or multiples of ½ pint. This does not apply to mixtures of two or more liquids such as a shandy.

Spirits   For whisky, gin, vodka and rum where these are sold by the measure, the traditional measure was ¼, ⅕ or ⅙ of a gill or multiples thereof (a gill is ¼ pint). From 1st January 1995, the law was changed so that spirits have to be sold in 25 ml or 35 ml measures and multiples thereof. Other measures may be changed, based on the spirit requirements as they are now. A notice must be displayed in the establishment indicating the measure that is being used. This restriction does not apply to mixtures of three or more liquids, e.g. for cocktails.

Table 1.3 gives examples of the number of measures, for control purposes, that may be obtained from the following bottles.

Table 1.3   *Examples of measures per bottle*

	BOTTLE SIZE	METRIC MEASURE	IMPERIAL MEASURE
Spirits	75 cl	30 × 25 ml	32 × 6 out
Spirits	70 cl	28 × 25 ml	29 × 6 out
Spirits	65 cl	26 × 25 ml	27 × 6 out
Vermouths	75 cl	15 × 50 ml	16 × 3 out
Fortified wines	75 cl	15 × 50 ml	16 × 3 out

Liqueurs   These are usually sold in six-out measures. Under the new legislation this is likely to be in measures of 25, 30 or 35 ml.

Wines   Wines sold open in carafes must be sold only in measures of 10 or 20 fl oz, 25, 50 or 75 cl or 1 litre. For wine by the glass, 11 measures are identified: 100, 125, 150, 175, 200 and 250 ml and 4, 5, 6, 6⅔ and 8 fl oz. However, it is still legal to serve wine by the glass in any measure if no specific measure is advertised. Part of the code of practice covering wine measures has become law and requires wine by the glass, in bars, to be sold in 125 ml or 175 ml measures.

ADDITIONAL LEGAL REGULATIONS

Within beverage operations there are also a number of situations that are the subjects of legal regulations. These are highlighted below. It should, however, be borne in mind that these are highly summarised guidelines and that many of the issues highlighted are affected by the particular circumstances at the time.

Provision of services

Hotel and catering operations are under no obligation to provide services unless the operation is an establishment covered by the Hotel Proprietors Act (1956) and the customers seeking services are classed as bona fide travellers. Establishments may refuse to serve people who do not meet the dress requirements of the establishment, for example the wearing of jackets or not wearing beachwear. Additionally, licensed establishments may refuse to serve people who are drunk or quarrelsome.

Establishments are, however, under the obligation to ensure that they do not breach the Sex Discrimination Act (1975) and the Race Relations Act (1976). These Acts, amongst other things, legislate against discrimination on the grounds of sex, race, creed or colour. Under these Acts, establishments may not refuse services, provide inferior services or set unreasonable conditions on the basis of these characteristics.

Refusing to pay

Under the Sale of Goods Act (1979) the customer can refuse to pay or demand a replacement if:

- the goods supplied do not correspond to the description;
- a displayed item is not what it seems;
- the food is inedible or the drink undrinkable.

Additionally, the Trades Description Acts (1968/1972) make it a criminal offence to misdescribe goods or services.

Unable to pay

If the guest for some reason is without the means to pay and this is a pure mistake, then the establishment can seek proof of identity and take the customer's name and address. However, if fraud is suspected, then the police may be called in. The bar or restaurant may not take personal items as security unless the guest is staying in an hotel covered by the Hotel Proprietors Act (1956). In this case the proprietor has the 'right of lien'; in other words, the guest's luggage may be taken pending payment.

Personal property and the guest

If an establishment is covered by the Hotel Proprietors Act (1956) then it is liable for the security of the guests' property whilst staying there. Other than this, there is no automatic liability unless the damage to or loss of the guests' property has resulted from negligence on behalf of the establishment, which would have to be proved.

Under the Health and Safety legislation (1974 and others) there is a duty on the part of the establishment to care for all lawful visitors, and negligence is a criminal offence. Establishments are, therefore, legally bound to look after their guests' health and safety whilst they are on their premises.

Price lists, service, cover and minimum charges

Restaurants are required to display food and drink prices (Price Marking Order 1979) so they can be seen before entering the premises or, in the case of a complex, before entering the dining area.

Under the Food Labelling (Amendment) Regulations (1989) there is a requirement for the alcoholic strength (given as a percentage of alcohol by volume) of a representative sample of dispensed drinks to be displayed on price lists, wine lists and menus. Exemptions from this requirement are drinks which are less than 1.2% alcohol by volume, and cocktails. The number shown need not exceed six in the case of EU controlled wines or 30 in the case of other alcoholic drinks. Wines sold in bottles are not covered as the alcoholic strength should be shown on the label.

In 1989, Part III of the Consumer Protection Act (1987) came into force. This part of the Act deals with misleading prices and, among the provisions, it states that it is an offence to give misleading price information. It recommends that, where the customer has to pay a non-optional charge, this should be incorporated into the total price or should not be charged at all. It also states that cover charges and minimum charges should be prominently displayed. Compliance with these provisions is not obligatory, but failure to do so could be used as evidence by the Office of Fair Trading that an offence has been committed. If service and cover charges are stated on menus and price lists, then they should be paid unless, in the case of service charges, the guest considers that the service has been poor. All bars are required to show price lists.

2

ALCOHOL

—

INTRODUCTION

Alcohol is a volatile mobile fluid obtained by fermenting a liquid containing sugar, the strength of which can be further increased by distillation. The name is derived from the Arabic *al-kohl*. *Kohl* is a black, very fine staining powder which is used cosmetically – once for staining the eyelids of harem beauties. Later the name was applied to highly refined chemical powders and essences and then to spirits produced by distillation and rectification.

Although there are various kinds of alcohol, the main ones are methyl alcohol (methanol) and ethyl alcohol (ethanol). Whilst methanol is used for some industrial purposes it becomes a powerfully dangerous poison if drunk. Ethyl alcohol (C_2H_5OH), sensibly consumed, is a beneficial alcohol. It has a faint but pleasant ethereal smell and it is the alcohol we shall be dealing with throughout this book.

Although alcohol must be treated seriously, it is only a problem to those who abuse it. It is not the direct cause of any disease nor will it, on its own, cure any. But it is often used medicinally as part of the treatment for certain physical conditions. There is a very small proportion, 0.003%, in the blood of each human being – yes, even in life-long abstainers – and (after the urine of a healthy person) it is regarded as the world's second oldest disinfectant.

Origins of alcoholic beverages

Fermented

grapes (wine)	table wines, sparkling, fortified, aromatised, vins doux naturels
apples	cider
pears	perry
honey	mead
agave or maguey	pulque

Brewed

grain	lager, beer, ale, stout, porter
rice	sake

Distilled

grapes (wine)	cognac, armagnac, other brandies
grain (beer)	whisky, vodka, kornbranntwein
sugar cane (molasses)	rums: light, dark, full-bodied
dates, palm sap	arrack
agave (pulque)	tequila

Fruit brandies

apples	calvados
plums	slivovitz, mirabelle, quetsch
cherries	kirsch, cherry brandy
pears	eau-de-vie de poire
strawberries	eau-de-vie de fraise
raspberries	eau-de-vie de framboise

Compounded flavoured spirits

grain, molasses	gin
grain, potatoes	aquavit
grapes	pastis – Pernod, Ricard, ouzo
aromatic fruits	bitters
fruit, grapes, grain	liqueurs

Benefits of alcohol

When drunk in moderation, alcohol can be good for you. It can even be considered as a food because it creates heat and is a source of nutriment and energy. In the form of a variety of drinks it can be an appetiser, an accompaniment to and an enhancer of food flavours and an aid to digestion. It accentuates sensory perception, sharpens memory and gives some protection to the heart and blood vessels by raising the level of good cholesterol. It also depresses centres of anxiety, relieving tension and stress. It exhilarates the spirit and can, on occasions, produce a magnificent glow.

Abuses of alcohol

Alcohol should be treated with great respect. Long-term heavy drinking can lead to serious illness, including liver cirrhosis, the hastening of age and the deterioration of the nervous system. Heavy drinking impedes the speed and quality of performance and can lead those who indulge to become a danger to themselves and others, especially when driving or operating machinery. In extreme cases, people who become addicted to alcohol may undergo personality changes and become extremely unpleasant and unreliable. Sometimes they will be unfit for work and become an embarrassment and a general burden to their families and friends.

Safe, sensible drinking

Most of the alcohol consumed passes into the bloodstream and is rapidly absorbed. The absorption will be slowed down if drink is accompanied by food. Almost all the alcohol is burnt up by the liver and what remains is discharged in urine or perspiration.

   The liver is like a car with one gear; it can only burn up one unit of alcohol per hour and if it has to cope with too much alcohol over a very long period it will suffer damage. If we are to avoid damage to our health, expert medical opinion suggests that our alcoholic intake should be limited to:

21 units a week for men (spread throughout the week)
14 units a week for women (spread throughout the week)

1 unit = ½ pint of ordinary beer or lager
            or a glass of sherry (⅓ gill or 50 ml)
            or a measure of vermouth or other apéritif (⅓ gill or 50 ml)
            or a glass of wine (125 ml)
            or one measure of spirits (⅙ gill or 25 ml)

Note: in Scotland, an ordinary spirit measure is ⅕ of a gill or 1¼ units. In Ireland, it is ¼ of a gill or 1½ units. Extra strength lagers and beer have sometimes two or three times the strength of ordinary beers. Remember too that many low calorie drinks contain more alcohol than their ordinary equivalents.

Drinking and driving

Some alcohol remains in the bloodstream for up to 18 hours after consumption. This should be considered in relation to the UK legal limit set in 1989 which states that the limit for car drivers is 80 mg of alcohol in 100 ml of blood. The number of units required to reach that level varies between individuals but it can be as little as three units.

Hangovers

Every pleasure has a price, so if you over-indulge most likely you will get a hangover too. A hangover is a headache and makes you feel awful all over. It results from:

- dehydration of the body caused by excess consumption of alcohol;
- the presence of congeners (additives etc.) in the drink;
- and a lack of good sound sleep.

If you want to avoid a hangover, prevention is better than cure: control your alcohol intake.

Sensible drinking requires a mature outlook. However, if occasions or situations weaken your resolve, the best advice is to:

- eat well before an evening of drinking; food lines the stomach and acts as a buffer against the alcohol;
- avoid mixing drinks; stick to one style if possible, such as beer or wine;
- avoid concoctions such as laced drinks, dubious punches, weird wine cups and cheap nasty wine;
- drink lots of water, milk or fruit juice before, during and after a heavy drinking session.

CORRECTIFS
Should you still feel 'under the weather' next morning, try a Prairie Oyster (see page 287) or one of the proprietary bitters such as Fernet Branca or Underberg (see pages 87–8).

Calories in alcohol

There are about 100 calories in a single unit of alcohol. The amount of calories adds up quickly and can increase weight. However, replacing food with alcohol as a source of calories denies the body essential nutrients and vitamins.

A guide to the number of calories found in a variety of drinks is given in table 2.1. The number of calories in different brands of drinks can vary significantly, so the following information is only given as a rough guide.

TASTE AND SENSORY EVALUATION OF DRINK

It is estimated that taste may be at least 80% smell. As proof, try tasting when you have a heavy cold. We taste mainly to savour the product, to assess quality and relate it to price. We also taste to check and record the drink's condition, to monitor

Table 2.1   *A guide to the number of calories found in drinks*

QUANTITY	DRINK	CALORIES
Fortified wines		
sherry 50 ml (⅓ gill)	dry	55
	medium	60
	sweet	65
Wines		
113 ml (4 fl oz) glass	dry, white or red	75
	rosé	85
	sweet	100
Spirits		
25 ml (⅙ gill)	gin, whisky, vodka, rum, brandy	50
Beers, lagers and cider		
284 ml (10 fl oz)	lager, low alcohol	60
	light or mild ale	70
	brown ale	80
	lager	85
	bitter	90
	cider, dry	95
	cider, sweet	110
Non-alcoholic drinks		
250 ml (9 fl oz)	tonic water	35
250 ml (9 fl oz)	low calorie tonic water	0
180 ml (6 fl oz)	orange juice	80
330 ml (11.5 fl oz)	can of coke	130
330 ml (11.5 fl oz)	diet coke	0

progress and to determine its potential. Ideally, serious tasting should be done in perfect conditions such as:

- good natural daylight;
- in a room with north-facing windows where the light is not subject to variations;
- where there is no possibility of competing with distracting, pungent odours;
- where conditions are comfortable and where there is sufficient space to manoeuvre without being jostled.

Stemmed glasses   These are best for tasting and the International Standards Organisation (ISO) tasting glass is a good example. The sherry copita or the paris goblet or the tulip glass are also considered suitable shapes. These are broad at the base and narrow at the top so as to concentrate the smell as the drink is being swirled to release its bouquet.

Tasting glasses   These should be washed in plain hot water – detergents leave an odour – and dried and polished to a brilliance with fresh, clean cloths. Dirty cloths leave rancid odours and nowadays there is a trend for guests in restaurants to smell the empty wine glass before the wine is actually served. They do so in order to detect if there are any off odours which would adversely affect the aroma and taste of the wine.

Wine taster's glass

The tongue: an arbiter of taste

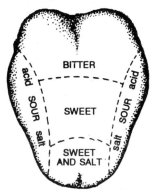

Taste is detected on different parts of the tongue

The taste of a drink is detected in different parts of the mouth but most essentially on the tongue. Sweetness is detected at the tip and centre of the tongue, acidity on the upper edges, saltiness on the sides and tip, and bitterness at the back. When tasting a drink, consider the following characteristics:

- **Sweetness** and **dryness** will be immediately obvious.
- **Acidity** will be recognised by its gum-drying sensation, but in correct quantities acidity provides crispness and liveliness to a drink.
- **Astringency** or **tannin content**, usually associated with some red wines, will give a dry coating or furring effect especially on the teeth and gums.
- **Body** is the weight or feel of the drink in your mouth.
- **Flavour** is the essence of the drink, and the longer tasting the flavour the better.
- **Aftertaste** is the finish of the drink on your palate.
- **Overall balance** is determined by the evaluation of all the above elements, which hopefully are in correct proportions. Balance is particularly important in terms of acidity and sugar when assessing white wine and in terms of tannin and fruit when appraising red wine.

Colour, aroma and taste

Whatever the drink, these three factors govern its appreciation. Beer drinkers, especially real ale enthusiasts, take their beer tasting or 'sampling' seriously. They have evolved some 250 terms to describe the balance of characteristics and taste of their special brews. Many beers, however, taste as their style suggests – bitter, light, mild, cream and so on.

Spirits, such as whisky, rum and brandy, because of their high alcohol content, are often professionally judged 'on the nose' (by smell) and by sight. A little of the spirit is put into a glass and sniffed or rubbed into the palm of the hand and nosed. Liqueurs and some fortified wines, such as sherry, may be treated in the same way but more often they are sipped and savoured then spat out into a receptacle.

Of all the drinks, wine seems to generate the most passion. A glass of wine seems to send some people into a frenzy of emotive words and highly colourful phrases. That is their prerogative, but it is best to remember that wine was made to be drunk and enjoyed. Of course, conversation and discussion regarding the merits of a wine can be enjoyable and beneficial especially at wine tastings and social occasions, but keep it simple and be true to your own opinions.

Wine tasting procedures

As with all drinks, the three factors which govern the appreciation of wine are colour, aroma and taste. About 50 ml (2 fl oz) is poured into the glass which allows sufficient room for the wine to be swirled so that the bouquet can be enhanced and appreciated.

Colour   Hold the glass by the stem, tilt it against the light or a white background. Look at the wine both at the centre and the miniscus (the edges) in order to observe the brilliance, limpidity and intensity of the colour. Healthy wine should be clear and gleaming – star bright – never faded, cloudy or dull.

Red wine   This usually starts its life purple but gradually, through the ageing process, it changes to brick red or mahogany.

White wine   This ranges in colour from very pale with green tinges to deep gold or amber. Beware of browning at the rim as this may indicate that the wine has become oxidised.

Rosé wine   This can have the colour of onion skin or be light, medium or deep pink. It should always look bright and brilliant in the glass.

AROMA

Swirl the wine, get your nose right into the glass and take a gentle but good, deep smell. Aroma or bouquet is very personal and relies on one's own imagination. It can also be associated with other previously experienced smells. Many tasters associate grape aroma to that of other fruits, as in table 2.2.

Table 2.2   *Grapes and their associated aromas*

GRAPE	ASSOCIATION
Cabernet Sauvignon	blackcurrants
Chardonnay	ripe melon, fresh pineapple
Chenin Blanc	apples
Gewürztraminer	tropical fruits, such as lychees
Merlot	plums, damsons
Nebbiolo	prunes
Pinot Noir	strawberries, cherries, plums (depending on where grown)
Riesling	apricots, peaches
Sauvignon Blanc	gooseberries
Syrah	raspberries
Zinfandel	blackberries, bramble, spice

Other aroma associations can be as diverse as pine trees, resin, vanilla, coffee, tea, herbs, smoke, toast, leather, cloves, cinnamon, nutmeg, ginger, mint, truffles, oak, figs, lilac and jasmine.

TASTE

The aroma of the wine has promised a certain taste and the palate should now confirm this. When tasting more than five wines it is usual, for obvious reasons, to spit the wine out rather than swallow it. Take a small amount of the wine in the mouth together with a little air and roll it around so that it reaches the different parts of the tongue. Now lean forward so that the wine is nearest the teeth and suck air in through the teeth. This practice helps to highlight and intensify the flavour. At this stage, and when you spit out the wine, the impressions made must be carefully noted otherwise you can get muddled and confused.

OBSERVATIONS

To help you analyse and make judgements on what you are tasting, the following descriptive words may be helpful.

Describing colour

brilliant	Showy with striking appearance
clear	Well defined, no obscuration
cloudy	Looks in a state of gloom; may be due to the wine being badly made or badly stored or handled; perhaps it has been affected by too drastic a change in temperature
dull	Lacks exciting tinges and interesting contrasts
faded	Rich appearance has disappeared due to old age or bad storage
jolie robe	French term to describe a wine with an attractive appearance; well turned out
impeccable	Faultless appearance
legs	Tears of wine on the inside of a glass due to the viscosity of alcohol and glycerine
limpidity	Cleanness and clarity of a wine
sumptuous	Rich, opulent looking

Describing aroma

acetic	Smells of vinegar; beware, it will probably taste the way it smells
clean	The wine has no smells it should not have
deep	Full, rich bouquet
dumb	It does not tell you anything
fruity	Smells of a particular fruit, such as apple, blackcurrant, strawberry
flowery	Fragrance of flowers, such as roses, violets, elderflowers
green	Young, even precocious, lacking maturity with acidity predominant
peppery	Sharp, indicating that all the components have not, as yet, harmonised; further maturing is necessary
piquant	Agreeably pungent with a pleasing acidity
sulphury	A slight smell of bad eggs which may result from stale air that has lodged between cork and wine during maturation in the bottle

woody	Associated with wines which have been part or fully matured in unseasoned casks
volatile	A good word when you cannot think of any other. Almost uncomplimentary but not quite so; mercurial

Describing taste

acid	An acid taste is essential for the 'bite' of a wine but the degree varies from wine to wine and between the same wine at different stages of maturity. The acid you do not want is acetic acid which is vinegar (*vin aigre* = sour wine)
bite	A refinement of acid, acknowledging the tannic acid of which too much is undesirable
clean	No faults, straightforward flavour
cloying	Hangs around in the mouth
delicate	Devoid of coarseness, light in flavour
depth	The tastes of the wine are discernible but still they are thoroughly blended
finish	The taste does not fade into lesser flavours; personality remains right to the end
full-bodied	A small sip fills the mouth with flavour; shows wine is at optimum maturity
green	Still too young
harsh	Undesirable character of wood tannin
heavy	Fuller than full bodied
length	The flavours that remain after swallowing; the longer they remain, the better the wine – usually
light	Light in body and in alcohol
luscious	Sweet, creamy, soft, rich and fruity
medium	Can be medium dry or medium sweet or medium quality
mellifluous	Smooth flowing, rich in flavour, almost honey-sweet
oaky	Slightly sweet vanilla flavour resulting from the wine maturing in oak casks
rich	Not necessarily sweet but splendid
robust	A good honest mouthful, strong in alcohol
silky	Very smooth on the palate
soft	Usually applied to red wines; lovely balance of blending and maturity
tannin	Acid derived from grapeskins, pips and stalks; the mouth is inclined to screw up if there is too much of it but tannin is essential in young red wines if they are to age well
tart	Bitter, acid taste
unctuous	Softly winning; it grows on you
vinosity	Vinous strength of a wine as it relates to its grape
well-balanced	Has all the desirable constituents in agreeable proportions

SUMMING UP

There are three main considerations:

- **Quality:** Is the wine a good example of its style or is it disappointing?
- **Maturity:** Is it ready to drink now, could it benefit by keeping longer or is it past its best?
- **Value:** Is the wine priced right in terms of value? How does it compare with other wines in the same price band.

Judgement should be noted immediately when tasting wine seriously. A marking system is well worthwhile. A sample tasting sheet often includes a column for the food dishes the wine might best accompany (see below).

Name, vintage and shipper of wine	Clarity Max 2	Colour Max 3	Aroma Max 5	Taste Max 10	Total	Food dishes	Conclusion
Date		**Location**				**Time of day**	

Wine tasting sheet

ALCOHOLIC STRENGTH

Beer was first taxed in Britain in 1660. The 'ale conners' wore leather trousers and that was their equipment when deciding whether beer was 'strong' or 'small'. The ale conners would sit in a puddle of beer on a bench or wooden chair and the rate of duty then depended on the extent to which they stuck there. Traditionally, duty was paid according to the original gravity, that is the gravity of wort (the sugary liquid obtained after mixing hot liquor and grist in the brewing process) at the start of fermentation. Since 1st June 1993, beer duty is based on the final alcoholic strength of a brew.

Long before distillation became a science, the early distillers had a unique and entertaining method of testing alcoholic strength. They mixed equal quantities of spirit and gunpowder and applied a flame to it. If the mixture failed to ignite, the spirit was too weak; if it exploded or burned too brightly, it was too strong, but if it burned evenly with a mild blue flame, it was 'proved' suitable and safe to drink (potable). Hence, the word 'proof'.

This primitive method was superseded by a man called Clarke who very late in the seventeenth century invented a weighted float. When this was dropped into a spirit, the depth to which it sank revealed the density of the liquor and from that knowledge the alcoholic strength could be calculated. He was then able to calibrate a particular strength as 'proof' and any with a greater or lesser concentration of alcohol was 'overproof' or 'underproof' respectively.

Further sophistication came when Board of Excise man Bartholomew Sykes introduced his now famous Sykes hydrometer in 1816. The apparatus was adopted by the Exchequer under the Hydrometer Act in 1818. Sykes determined that 100° was proof and that pure alcohol was 175° (75° overproof). On this scale, the figure for pure alcohol is 1¾ times the figure accorded to proof spirit. In other words, 100° proof equals 57.1% alcohol and 42.9% water. The system became traditional throughout the United Kingdom where spirits were sold at a potable strength of 70° proof (30° underproof). So to convert the British proof into percent by volume of alcohol, you simply multiply the proof by four and divide by seven.

$$\frac{70 \times 4}{7} = 40\%$$

A French chemist Joseph Gay-Lussac (1778-1850) invented a system which was much easier to understand and which was adopted throughout mainland Europe. The Gay-Lussac or GL system was logic itself with 0° the absence of alcohol and 100° pure alcohol. Thus, degree equals percentage.

Meanwhile, the Americans introduced their own system which was reasonably logical when they decided that proof spirit was an exact balance of alcohol and water and that pure alcohol should be 200°. Each degree of proof equals one-half percent of alcohol. So, a spirit marketed at 90° proof would contain 45% of alcohol by volume.

Note: The United Kingdom no longer uses the Sykes system. The new system, the *Organisation Internationale de Métrologie Légale* (OIML), expresses alcoholic strength as a percentage by volume of alcohol. It is very similar to the Gay-Lussac system except OIML measures strength at 20°C while Gay-Lussac does so at 15°C which gives a slightly higher reading. The difference is almost negligible except when deciding excise duty on very large quantities of drink.

The top ten favourite British drinks are:

1	White wine	6	Cider
2	Lager	7	Gin
3	Bitter	8	Vodka
4	Red wine	9	Stout
5	Whisky	10	Liqueurs

Approximate strengths of drinks

Alcohol by volume

- alcohol-free   not more than 0.05%
- de-alcoholised   not more than 0.5%
- low alcohol   up to 1.2%
- cider   4–6% but 'specials' up to 8%
- beer   3–6%, some go up to 8% even 10%
- light wines (table wines)   8–15%, more usually 10–13%
- sparkling wines   10–13%
- fortified wines (liqueur wines) such as sherry   16–22%
- aromatised wines such as Vermouth   14–20%
- vins doux naturels such as Muscat de Beaumes-de-Venise   15–18%
- spirits such as whisky, brandy   most sold at 40%, some at 45%
- white spirits such as vodka   sold at 37½% upwards
- liqueurs   17%–55%

3

FERMENTATION

—

INTRODUCTION

The chemistry of fermentation is basic to the making of all alcoholic beverages. Yeast reacts on sugar and converts the sugar into alcohol and carbon dioxide and then, if the liquid is not protected from air, into vinegar. Alcoholic beverages are obtained from ingredients containing sugar, for example grape juice, apple juice and pear juice. They are also obtained from ingredients such as grain, cereals and potatoes which have no sugar but which have sugar potential because they are rich in starch. Once the starch is converted into fermentable sugars, mainly maltose, yeast is introduced and fermentation begins.

Although it has always been known that certain sugar-containing liquids would ferment when exposed to air that phenomenon was not fully understood for a long time. Then in 1857 the great French biologist Louis Pasteur (1822–95) – famous for his work on pasteurisation and fermentation – explained scientifically the principle of vinous and malt fermentation. We now know that fermentation is the breaking down of organic substances by enzymes (ferments) which have been secreted by yeast cells, resulting in chemical changes as follows: one molecule of sugar is split into two molecules of ethyl alcohol and two molecules of carbon dioxide. The chemical formula for fermentation is:

$$C_6H_{12}O_6 \rightarrow 2CH_3CH_2OH + 2CO_2 + \text{HEAT ENERGY}$$

Yeast

There are two main categories of yeast: natural yeast and cultured yeast.

NATURAL YEASTS

Innumerable yeasts, moulds and bacteria are all around, hovering and floating in the air, eventually settling on or being carried onto ripe fruit, grapes and grain husks either by insects and more specifically by the fruit fly drosophila. They simply teem down and it is known that a single grape before fermentation will harbour on its skin (cuticle) 100,000 wine yeasts, 100,000 moulds and up to ten million wild yeast. They adhere to the pruina, a waxy substance formed on the grape skin, and this dull whitish haze of yeasts and micro-organisms is known as 'bloom'.

CULTURED YEASTS

These are pedigree strains of natural yeasts cultivated in a laboratory. They are used because they are efficient in converting sugar into alcohol and are less susceptible to sulphur in the fermenting process. Sometimes they are selected to do a specific job because they are more reliable than natural yeasts for that particular job. They can also be used in situations where natural yeasts have been washed away by heavy rain or when some of the yeasts have been brushed off in transit. There are up to a thousand varieties of yeast, but the name is normally associated with a type of unicellular fungi called *Saccharomyces* of which four varieties are important regarding the production of alcohol.

Saccharomyces cerevisiae   This is the traditional beer and ale yeast which ferments at the top of the brew. There are different strains of the yeast and most brewers propagate their own special cultures in laboratories, although some brewers still rely on airborne yeasts. The yeasts are fermented at a warmer temperature than Continental yeasts. As beer reveals its flavour better at the temperature of its fermentation, that is possibly the reason why British beers were traditionally served on the warm side.

Saccharomyces carlsbergensis   This is the lager yeast. It is a bottom fermenter because it ferments at the base of the brew. Fermentation is kept at a much lower temperature and lasts much longer than for the British style of beer. Even then the lager is 'stored' in a conditioning tank for up to six months before being released for sale. In German, lager means store. Brewing is dealt with in chapter 4.

Saccharomyces apiculatus   Known as 'wild yeasts' or 'starter yeasts' in the making of wine, although these start the fermentation they are feeble fermenters and are only active up to 4% of alcohol. At that concentration they are killed and wine yeasts take over the fermentation. Wild yeasts are aerobic – only able to work in the presence of oxygen – and they impart an 'off-flavour' and delay the action of the true wine yeasts. In modern wine-making they are usually dispensed with and, as they have only limited tolerance to sulphur dioxide (SO_2), a strictly controlled quantity of SO_2 is added to the grape juice before fermentation. Not only does this kill the wild yeasts, it also destroys undesirable bacteria, principally the Acetobacter, which in the presence of oxygen would attack the alcohol in wine and turn it into vinegar.

Saccharomyces ellipsoideus   This is the true wine yeast. It is much more tolerant to SO_2 and it is also anaerobic – able to work in the absence of oxygen. There are many varieties of the species, each suited to its native wine district or region. Most wine regions have yeasts that cling to each other and the fermenting vessel, and this clinging property assists the wine-maker to clear the wine and make it star bright. Champagne yeasts, on the other hand, do not cling to each other or the containing vessel, which facilitates the operation known as *remuage* prior to disgorging the exhausted yeast to clear the wine. Depending on the amount of sugar in the grape juice, wine yeasts are rapid workers fermenting quickly up to 13% alcohol and then more slowly up to 16% of alcohol. At that concentration, they are destroyed by the very alcohol they have worked so hard to produce.

Fermentation temperatures

Wine yeasts can only work between 5°C and 35°C. Once it starts, fermentation must be continuous and complete although it can be artificially stopped for a specific style of wine. The fermenting process causes a rise in temperature so every effort is made to ensure that the activity of the yeast does not stall, or worse, stop altogether. Incomplete fermentations are a problem and may be due to too high or too low a fermenting temperature or to the use of poor quality grapes or even to the use of inferior yeasts with a low alcohol tolerance. Ideally white wines are fermented slowly and cooly between the temperatures of 15°C and 20°C (59–68°F) to impart delicacy and fragrance. Red wines are fermented more quickly and at a higher temperature between 25°C and 30°C (75–85°F) which helps to extract colour and body for the wine. Modern wine-makers favour a slow, cool fermentation as they consider it helps to preserve aroma and intensifies flavour. Very high temperatures cause imperfect fermentations resulting in loss of bouquet and the development of the vinegar microbe *Asceti mycodermae*.

Malolactic fermentation

This is a secondary fermentation which most wines go through. It usually takes place in the spring following the vintage and results in the harsh malic acid being converted into the softer lactic acid and carbon dioxide (CO_2). There is no increase of alcohol only a lowering of the total acidity of the wine, making it softer and rounder on the palate.

Chaptalisation

Sometimes, due to poor summer weather, grapes do not ripen properly and the Baumé reading (a scale of measurement used to indicate the sugar content of grape *must*) indicates a lack of sufficient sugar. This can sometimes happen, especially in the cooler climates of northern France, Germany and Britain. The remedy is to add sugar or concentrated *must* to the grape juice before fermentation. This secures a higher final alcohol content, although the resulting wines will never be considered great. They should never be marketed as vintage wines but at least they will have lost their thinness and weakness. The term for this sugaring is Chaptalisation and it is named after Dr Jean Antoine Chaptal, Minister of Agriculture to Napoleon I, who authorised the practice in 1801. In Germany it is called *Verbesserung*, meaning 'improvement', but in reality only the alcohol content is improved.

Macération carbonique

This is associated usually with the product of light, fragrant, fruity red wine such as Beaujolais. Whole grapes are put into a closed vat or container; those at the bottom get crushed by those above and the free-run juice begins to ferment. Then carbon dioxide gas is pumped in, causing fermentation to take place inside the uncrushed grapes. As fermentation finishes, the grapes burst and release their juices, which are now coloured. These are run off and the remaining mass is pressed. The resulting juice is either kept separate or added to give body and tannin to the new wine.

THE VINE

The vine belongs to the Ampelidaceae family, as does the Virginia creeper and other climbing berry-bearing growths (but not common ivy). It is only the genus Vitis (vine) that interests the wine-maker. There are five families of wine-producing vines: *Vitis vinifera*, *Vitis riparia*, *Vitis rupestris*, *Vitis labrusca* and *Vitis berlandieri*. Of those, *Vitis vinifera* (wine-bearing vine) produces all the noble grapes associated with the production of classic wine. The vinifera vines were once only associated with European vineyards but are now used throughout the world, with just a few exceptions. These are in the east coast of America and Canada where other species are cultivated because they are more suited to the terrain and climatic conditions.

Vineyard scene

Composition of the vine

The vine consists of:

Roots   These are for anchorage and for absorbing nutrients and moisture from the earth. The root system is large and can reach to a depth of about 12 m (13 yds).

Leaves   Chlorophyll is the green matter in the leaves and is necessary for photosynthesis. When sunlight falls on them, carbon dioxide is absorbed from the atmosphere through the leaves into the plant where it combines with water, absorbed through the roots, to make sugar. The sap which is circulating in the vine takes the sugar and stores it within the grape. Leaves also shade the grapes in very hot climates.

Flowers   Vine flowers are very small. They self-pollinate from May to June in the northern hemisphere and from November to December in the southern hemisphere. Flowering lasts about ten days when, hopefully, the weather remains warm and dry. Frost is the great enemy – if it arrives during the flowering, unprotected vines will not bear grapes. Frosts can be combatted by smoke and heat devices and by spraying the vines with water.

Grapes   The grapes form after pollination. At first they are small, hard and green, but as they ripen, they swell out and change colour in August and September. They should be fully ripe 100 days after flowering. A ton of grapes produces 675 litres (148 gallons), equivalent to 960 bottles of wine.

Composition of the grape

The grape is made up of a stalk, skin, pips and pulp.

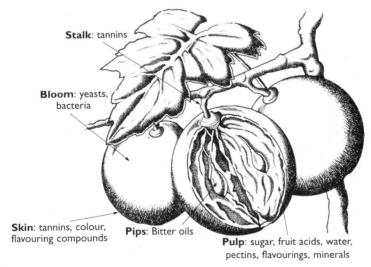

Stalk: tannins

Bloom: yeasts, bacteria

Skin: tannins, colour, flavouring compounds

Pips: Bitter oils

Pulp: sugar, fruit acids, water, pectins, flavourings, minerals

Section through a grape

Stalk   When the stalk is used it imparts tannic acid to wine. It is mostly used in the making of big, flavoursome red wine and is not used when making white and light wines. Tannin is a necessary ingredient as it acts as a preservative and antioxidant. If over-used, it makes the wine astringent and nasty. It is recognised on the palate by its tongue-furring properties.

Skin   The outer skin or cuticle has a whitish downy or cloudy coat known as bloom. This waxy substance contains wild yeasts and wine yeasts, millions of minute enzymes which contribute to the fermentation process. It also contains other micro-organisms such as bacteria, principally the acetobacter which is a potential danger to wine. If uncontrolled, it can turn wine into vinegar. The inside of the skin imparts colour which is extracted during fermentation.

Pips   Crushed pips impart tannic acid, oils and water. If left uncrushed, they do not contribute to vinification.

Pulp   The flesh of the grape provides the juice, also known as *must*, which is essential for fermentation. The *must* contains:

- 78–80% water;
- 10–25% sugar;
- 5–6% acids.

As we can see, water makes up the bulk.

Sugar is formed in the grape by sunlight and is of two kinds: grape sugar (dextrose and glucose) and fruit juice (levulose and fructose). They are found in about equal quantities.

Tartaric, malic, tannic and citric acids in the *must* help to preserve wine and to keep it fresh, brilliant and give it balance. Esters are formed when the acids come in contact with alcohol and it is these that give wine its aroma or bouquet.

The *must* (unfermented grape juice) will also have trace elements of nitrogeneous compounds such as albumen, peptones, amides, ammonium salts and nitrates, as well as potassium, phosphoric acid and calcium, all of which have an influence on the eventual taste of the wine.

Vine training and pruning

Training will relate to the type of pruning employed. The main purpose of vine training is to ensure no cane goes into the ground (i.e. roots back into the soil) thereby avoiding the dangers of phylloxera. Pruning and training also prevents hybrids forming and ensures the purity of the stock. Pruning concentrates the vigour of the vine and controls yield and quality. The method of training is influenced by conditions of soil, aspect and climate.

Some vines are trained high to escape the hazard of ground frost. Others are trained low to maximise on the reflected heat given by some soils such as stone and slate. Vines may also be trained wide apart to benefit from sun and to minimise the effects of humidity. By contrast other vines may be trained in the shape of a canopy or pergola so that the foliage prevents too much sun getting to the grapes in very hot climates.

Vines are trained according to one or other of three classical methods: the Cordon, the Gobelet, the Espalier, or by variations of these, such as the Pergola.

The Cordon system, of which the Dr Guyot method is a prime example, uses a permanent stump of vine. From this, one horizontal and two vertical shoots are cultivated. At the end of each season the horizontal shoot which has produced the crop is cut away and one of the vertical shoots is bent over to replace it as the fruit-yielding shoot for the next year. The remaining vertical shoot is pruned to produce two vertical replacement shoots. This system curtails the growth of unnecessary vegetation and encourages a maximum yield of good fruit. These vines are normally trained along wire strand supports.

There is also a double Dr Guyot training system which will give two horizontal fruiting shoots and three vertical shoots. This system increases quantity but is inclined to reduce quality.

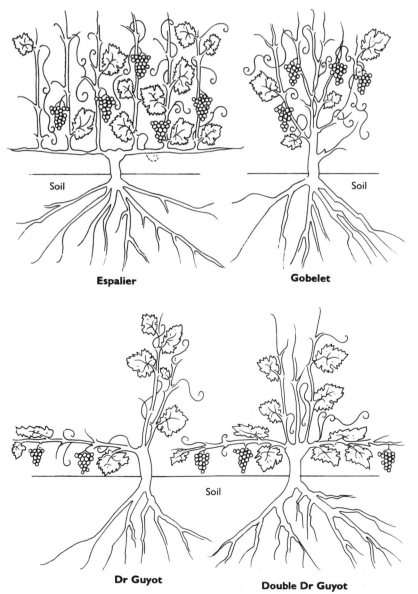

Training and pruning systems for vines

The Gobelet system cultivates the vine in one vertical trunk. The branches rise and spread from it to form the shape of a goblet. Vines pruned by this system are normally self-supporting. The free-standing Bush system is a variation.

The Espalier system grows the vine as a fan based on vertical shoots rising upwards from two horizontal arms. The shoots are usually trained on wire supports or on trellises.

Annual cycle of work in the vineyards in the northern hemisphere

January   The year starts with pruning the vines and general maintenance to walls, posts and the wire used for vine training

February   Pruning, to regulate quality, continues and cuttings are taken for grafting. Machinery is cleaned, oiled and put in good working order.

March   Pruning is completed and ploughing begins to aerate the soil. This allows roots to breathe and facilitates free drainage of water to the roots. Bench grafting takes place. That means American root stock and *Vitis vinifera* scions are joined together in a nursery rather than a vineyard.

April   Ploughing is completed, weeding continues and year-old cuttings are planted out.

Traditional harvesting

May   Vines are treated with copper sulphate against mildew. Vine suckers are removed.

June   The vines flower and treatment (spraying) continues.

July   Weeding and spraying continues. Overlong green shoots are pinched back.

August   Weeding as before and trimming of the vines to allow maximum sunshine to the grape bunches. Wine-making aparatus is prepared. Grapes swell and begin to change colour.

September   Grapes continue to swell and colour deepens. White grapes change to yellow-green. Black grapes change from yellow-green to violet or deep purple. Sunshine is badly needed now to finish the ripening. Refractometers are taken into the vineyards to gauge the sugar level within the grapes. That, and the acidity level, will decide when the harvest can begin. Traditionally the grapes should be perfectly ripe and ready 100 days after flowering. Bands of pickers will be contracted and the vintage usually starts about the third week in September, depending on location.

October   The cellarmaster finishes making the wine. Fermentation can take from six days to six weeks depending on the style of wine. Vineyards are deep ploughed and fertilised with chemicals to compensate for any deficiencies.

Mechanical harvesting

November   More fertilising. Long shoots are cut off and the base of the vines are 'hilled up' with soil for protection against snow and frost.

December   Wine equipment is cleaned and stored away. Deep ploughing of soil continues. Minor pruning commences and the cycle of work begins again.

FACTORS AFFECTING QUALITY

Soil

Vineyards usually thrive where other crops struggle. Poor soils rich in minerals are best for the vine as they provide nutrients such as phosphate, iron, potassium, magnesium and calcium – all of which contribute to the final taste of the wine. Favoured soils are chalk, limestone, slate, sand, schist, gravel, pebbles, clay, aluvial and volcanic. These soils have good drainage and moisture retention to keep the vine roots healthy. Drainage is especially important, as the vine does not like having wet feet. Soil is analysed annually and any chemical deficiency is compensated for.

Climate

The vine needs a good balance of moisture and heat. Temperature should average 14–16°C (57–60°F). The lowest annual average temperature necessary for the vine to flourish is 10°C (50°F). It is estimated that the vine needs about 68 cm (27 in) of rain per year – mainly in winter and spring – and at least 1,400 hours of sunshine. The main climatic types are as follows.

Arid   Desert landscape, no rain for all or most of the year. Very hot summers, mild winters.

Semi-arid   No rain for more than half the year; rivers dry in the summer. Very hot summers, cold winters.

Continental   Hot summers, cold winters, rain for more than six months of the year.

Temperate   Rain all the year round, hot summers, cold winters, wet springs and autumns.

Maritime   Rain all the year round, high humidity, cooling breezes.

Micro-climate

A micro-climate is a particular and usually beneficial weather pattern which prevails in a single vineyard or a group of vineyards or within a small region. It could be to do with hills or mountains protecting the vines from heavy winds, or even a break in the mountain range allowing the air to freshen and fan the vines in very hot weather.

Sometimes the angle of the sun, especially the clear brilliant morning sun, will strike one vineyard more favourably than another. The rise and fall of the terrain will also have an effect, as will location beside water for ground moisture and reflected heat. These subtle differences in atmospheric conditions, allied to the quality of the soil and the grape variety used, are the reason why some vineyards have such outstanding reputations.

Bio-climate

This is the relationship of soil and climate in a specific vineyard. Such knowledge can be used to obtain stable yields of high-quality grapes.

Aspect

Vineyards are ideally planted on south-facing slopes where they point at the sun and benefit from maximum sunshine and good drainage. Siting is of prime importance to capture the sunlight for photosynthesis and good ripening. Some vineyards are sited up to 243 m (266 yds) or more on mountainsides, while many of the great vineyards are located in river valleys and along lakesides benefitting from humidity and reflected heat.

Grape

The grape must be in harmony with the soil, the location of the vineyard and local climatic conditions. It must also be reasonably disease resistant, give a good yield and produce the best quality wine possible. Wine is produced from either varietal grapes, usually a classic single grape like the Riesling, or from hybrids, which are a cross such as Riesling × Silvaner = Müller-Thurgau. Grapes behave differently in different soils which is why, for example, Pinot Noir is a classic in Burgundy and a disaster in Bordeaux.

Viticulture

Viticulture denotes how the vine is cultivated. An overworked vineyard without compensatory treatment or a neglected vineyard will only produce second rate wine, so the farming of the vineyard is of prime importance. It involves:

- vine selection;
- keeping the vineyard healthy;
- ploughing to aerate the soil;
- weeding;
- fertilising;
- pruning to regulate quality;

- training the vines;
- spraying to combat diseases;
- harvesting.

Vinification

The making of the wine encompasses:

- the pressing of the grapes;
- the treatment and fermentation of the *must*;
- maturing the wine and occasionally topping it up to keep the air out;
- racking, fining and filtration to make the wine star bright:

  Racking: running the clear wine off its lees or sediment from one cask to another.

  Fining: a further clarification of wine usually before bottling. A fining agent such as isinglass is added and this attracts the sediment suspended in the wine, causing it to coagulate and fall to the bottom of the container.

  Filtration: the final clarification before bottling. It removes any remaining suspended matter and leaves the wine healthy and star bright in appearance.

- blending – compensatory or otherwise;
- bottling for further maturing or for sale.

Luck of the year

In some years, everything in the vineyards and cellars go well, combining to produce a wine of excellence – a vintage wine. In other years, there can be great disappointments brought on by an excess of sun, rain, snow, frost and the dreaded hail, which will produce either poor wine or worse. So the wine-grower can never be confident, but must always be vigilant.

Enemies of the vine

Phylloxera   Unfortunately, vinifera vines have one great weakness – they have no resistance to the aphid phylloxera (Greek word for dry leaf). These small yellow insects puncture the roots of the vine and form galls on the underside of the leaves. The larvae sticks to the roots and sucks the sap which kills the vine roots. Once it feeds on the sap, the aphid multiplies at lightning speed to continue to lay waste the vineyards. The louse is native to North America and it is thought it was brought to Europe on bunches of table grapes or on vines imported from America for the purpose of experiment in the treatment of oidium (see page 37). It was first noticed in 1863 in the vinery at Kew Gardens and then in Provence in the same year. For the next 30 years it devastated most of the world's vineyards – Austria and Hungary 1868, Bordeaux 1869, Beaujolais and the Rhône Valley 1870, Switzerland 1872,

Germany and Australia 1874, Spain, Portugal and Madeira 1876, Burgundy 1878, Italy 1879, South Africa 1886, Algeria 1887, Champagne and California 1890. When almost all the vineyards were destroyed, it was found that the vines on the east coast of America – *Vitus rupestris,* for example – were immune to the ravaging aphids. The solution was to graft the European vinifera scion (shoot cut for grafting) onto the American root stock. Phylloxera is still prevalent in the soil and without the American root stock the native vine would die within three years. There are, however, some pockets of vineyards resistant to phylloxera, either due to geographical isolation or to the fact that the vines are planted on sandy soil which the louse finds impossible to penetrate.

Oidium   Known as powdery mildew, this forms patches of dusty mould on the grapes and leaves, causing the grapes to split and shrivel. Treatment: sulphur powder.

Mildew   Mildew develops in damp areas. It is a very common vine disease which is noticeable when yellow patches appear on the leaves. When the leaves wither, the grapes become deprived of nourishment. Treatment: spraying with copper sulphate.

Grey Rot (*Pourriture grise*)   This can be malevolent or benevolent. In most regions, and at a certain time of year, it produces, in humid conditions, a grey mould which destroys colour pigmentation in black grapes and gives an unpleasant taste to wine. Treatment: anti-rot spraying. However, the very same fungus, known as *Botrytis cinerea*, in certain areas produces wonderful sweet wines when conditions are favourable (see Sauternes, page 168).

Coulure   This happens when there is a soil deficiency or too much rain or uneven temperature. The flowers on the vine are infertile, resulting in a disappointing yield of grapes. Treatment: use good fertilisers.

Chlorosis   Too much limestone in the soil causes yellowing, even death of the plant. Treatment: iron sulphate.

Pyralis, Endemis and Cochylis   These tiny butterfly moths pierce the grapes and destroy the crop within hours. Treatment: spray with insecticides.

Frost   Especially in spring, frost stunts the formation of the buds which greatly reduces yield. Treatment: fire heat, spraying with water.

Hail   Hail is a particular danger, especially just before the vintage when the grape skins are very thin and the grapes are very vulnerable. Hail can easily puncture the skins and ruin the crop. Treatment: pray it doesn't happen.

Discovering wine and the spread of the vine

The farming of the vineyards (viticulture) and the making of wine (vinification) has been well documented since history was first recorded. Although it has been suggested that honey was the first liquid to be fermented, we know that the grape was one of the sustaining foods of prehistoric peoples. It is thought that the secret of wine-making originated in Asia Minor where the wine-bearing vine *Vitis vinifera* was cultivated in Caucasia – south of the Black Sea and west of the Caspian Sea – some 6,000 years BC. However, the origin of wine itself remains a mystery. We must rely on fable to give us a clue. Apparently King Jamshid of Persia was very fond of grape juice and ordered his staff to store the juice in jars so that he could enjoy it throughout the year. When winter arrived, the king tasted the juice, but found it had become quite bitter and horrible. He marked the jars 'poison' and dispatched them to a store. A lady in his court, finding herself out of favour with the king, became so depressed she decided to end her life by drinking this poison. She became drowsy and all her cares and anxieties disappeared. Returning later to the comforting liquid, her conduct became so remarkable she was once again noticed by the king and he too tasted the juice which had now fermented to become wine. He was so impressed he called the new drink 'medicine for kings'.

APPROXIMATE TIMETABLE OF THE SPREAD OF THE VINE

6000 BC	Israel and neighbouring countries, Caucasia, around the Caspian Sea
4000 BC	Mesapotamia
3000 BC	Phoenicia
2800 BC	Egypt
1600 BC	Greece, Crete
1000 BC	Sicily, Italy, North Africa
600 BC	Persia
500 BC	France, Spain, Portugal
140 BC	China
100 BC	North India
AD 100	Other Balkan countries, north of France, Germany, England
AD 1520	Mexico, Japan
AD 1560	Argentina, Chile
AD 1580	Peru
AD 1652	South Africa
AD 1770	United States, California
AD 1788	Australia, New Zealand

HOW WINE IS MADE

Presses

Presses are necessary in wine-making to extract juice from the grapes. Modern presses are usually enclosed and mechanically controlled for maximum efficiency. Nowadays the French Vaslin press is perhaps the most widely used. This horizontal, stainless steel press has chains attached to metal hoops to rough up the grapes. As the press

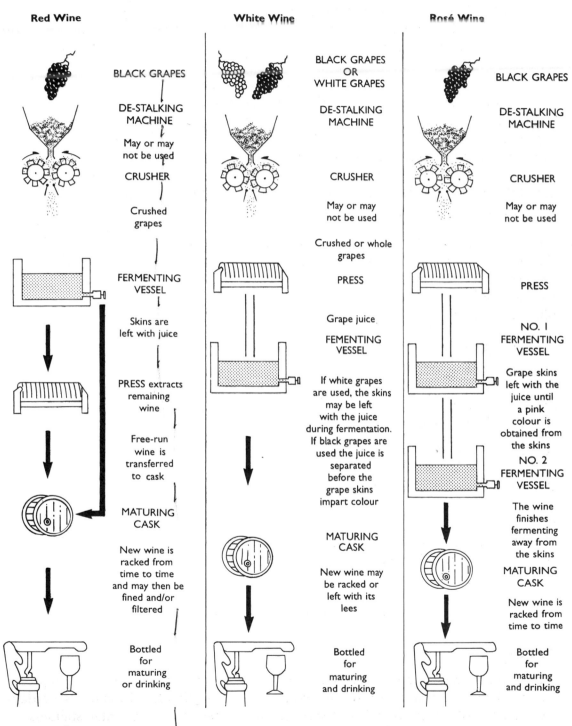

Red Wine

BLACK GRAPES

DE-STALKING
MACHINE

May or may
not be used

CRUSHER

Crushed
grapes

FERMENTING
VESSEL

Skins are
left with juice

PRESS extracts
remaining
wine

Free-run
wine is
transferred
to cask

MATURING
CASK

New wine is
racked from
time to time
and may then be
fined and/or
filtered

Bottled
for
maturing
or drinking

White Wine

BLACK GRAPES
OR
WHITE GRAPES

DE-STALKING
MACHINE

CRUSHER

May or may
not be used

Crushed or whole
grapes

PRESS

Grape juice

FEMENTING
VESSEL

If white grapes
are used, the skins
may be left
with the juice
during fermentation.
If black grapes are
used the juice is
separated
before the
grape skins
impart colour

MATURING
CASK

New wine may
be racked or
left with its
lees

Bottled
for
maturing
and drinking

Rosé Wine

BLACK GRAPES

DE-STALKING
MACHINE

CRUSHER

May or may
not be used

PRESS

NO. 1
FERMENTING
VESSEL

Grape skins
left with the
juice until
a pink
colour is
obtained from
the skins

NO. 2
FERMENTING
VESSEL

The wine
finishes
fermenting
away from
the skins

MATURING
CASK

New wine is
racked from
time to time

Bottled
for
maturing
and drinking

Wine-making process

slowly rotates, the two end plates move towards one another, squashing the grapes. The juice is then extracted under pressure and removed by centrifugal force.

Another popular press is the Wilmes or Pneumatic press consisting of a horizontal, stainless steel cylinder with a strong rubber bladder or balloon in the centre. The cylinder is loaded with grapes and air is pumped in to inflate the bladder. The grapes are forced against the slatted sides and the juice is released.

The continuous hydraulic and Archimedes screw presses are also frequently used, especially in very large wineries.

Grapes going into a wine press

RED WINE

Red wine is made from black grapes. Modern wine-making calls for a wine without too much tannic acid so it is now the custom to de-stem all the grapes or include only a small percentage of stems, depending on the wine style. The grapes are crushed in the wine press.

The *must* – a combination of juice, skins and pips – is put into fermentation vats. A small amount of sulphur dioxide is added to kill off wild yeast and undesirable bacteria and to protect against oxidation. The juice remains with the skins from 10 to 30 days to extract colour and tannin; the lighter the colour required, the less time it needs with the skins.

Fermentation

The new flowing wine

During fermentation, the yeast transforms the sugar into alcohol and carbon dioxide. This action also generates heat so the temperature has to be carefully controlled. When fermentation is completed, most of the liquid will be run off. This is known as free-run wine or *vin de goutte*. The remaining pulp is pressed again, resulting in a very dark, tannic wine known as press wine or *vin de presse*. These are matured separately, classically in oak casks, where they undergo a malolactic fermentation (see page 26).

They are racked several times. This means that they are transferred into fresh casks, leaving the lees or sediment behind. With each racking, the wine becomes clearer. Before bottling, the wine is fined to get rid of unwanted solid particles held in suspension which cause cloudiness. Isinglass, egg whites, gelatine, dried albumen and bentonite are particularly good fining agents as they drag the dregs down to the

Vats in a traditional cellar

bottom of the casks leaving behind brilliantly clear wine. The free-run wine and the press wine are now blended and may be fined or filtered or both before being bottled.

WHITE WINE
White wine can be made from white grapes or black grapes.

From white grapes   After pressing, the *must* may or may not be left with the skins. The *must* will usually be treated with sulphur dioxide and then passed through a centrifuge to be cleansed of suspended matter such as pips and skin pieces. Most likely, fermentation will take place in large temperature-controlled, stainless steel tanks. Cultured yeast may be added and a slow, cool fermentation takes place which lasts a month or more and gives the wine greater intensity of flavour. After fermentation, the new wine is matured in casks for a short time. It will be racked and later it may be fined and stored in sterilised tanks or casks to await bottling. Sometimes a little concentrated grape *must* is added if a sweeter wine is required.

From black grapes   The grapes are pressed to separate the clear juice from the skins. Speed is of the essence because the liquid must not contain any dyes from the skins.

Some white wines are matured *sur lie* – on the lees – which means they are not racked or filtered before being bottled. This practice gives a greater depth of flavour to the wine and an enhanced freshness and liveliness.

Rosé wine

Classically made from black grapes, the *must* is left to macerate with the skins for about one day or until the correct degree of colouring has been achieved. Then the *must* is removed to continue fermenting at a low temperature elsewhere. Rosé wines can also be made by mixing red and white wine to the desired colour.

Blush wine

An American invention, blush wine is a pale pinky-blue wine made from black grapes. The skins are only in contact with the *must* for an hour or two during fermentation.

Sparkling wine

There are four ways to add sparkle to wine.

The champagne method   In the *méthode champenoise*, also known as *méthode traditionnelle* or *metodo classico*, yeast and sugar are added to dry wine and bottled immediately. The second fermentation takes place inside the sealed bottle and as the CO_2 is unable to escape, it becomes chemically bonded in the wine. See champagne, page 175.

Méthode cuve close or charmat method   This was invented by a Frenchman Eugène Charmat in 1909. Also called the bulk method or closed tank method, the wine undergoes a secondary fermentation in a sealed tank and then is filtered and bottled under pressure.

Transfer method (méthode transvasement)   The second fermentation takes place inside the bottle which is then chilled and disgorged into a pressurised tank. There the wine is filtered and then bottled under pressure.

Méthode gazifié   In the injection method, known also in France as *méthode pompe bicyclette*, the CO_2 is pumped into the chilled wine under pressure. It is the quickest and cheapest method of all. The resulting large bubbles soon disappear once the wine is poured into a glass.

Organic Wines

These are wines made from grapes grown without the aid of artificial insecticides, pesticides or fertilisers. These wines will not be adulterated in any way except for a minimal amount of the traditional preservative sulphur dioxide.

Alcohol free wines

These contain a maximum of 0.05% alcohol. De-alcoholised wines contain a maximum of 0.5% alcohol. Low alcohol wines contain a maximum of 1.2% alcohol. Reduced alcohol wines contain a maximum of 5.5% alcohol. These wines are made in the normal way and then the alcohol is removed by one of two methods.

The hot treatment   Using distillation, this method unfortunately removes most of the flavour as well.

The cold treatment   Known as reverse osmosis or fine filtration, the alcohol is removed by mechanically separating or filtering out the molecules of alcohol through membranes made of cellulose of acetate. The wine is repeatedly passed through the membranes which filter out the alcohol and water, leaving behind a syrupy wine concentrate. To this, water and a little grape *must* is added, the latter to preserve the flavour and mouthfeel of the original wine.

VINS DOUX NATURELS
These are sweet wines which have their fermentation stopped by the addition of alcohol to retain the sweetness. The wines are muted when the alcohol level reaches 5–8%. They usually have a final strength of 17% alcohol by volume.

FORTIFIED OR LIQUEUR WINES
These wines are strengthened by the addition of alcohol, usually brandy. This is done either during fermentation (as in port) or after fermentation (as in sherry).

AROMATISED WINES
These wines are flavoured and fortified. Examples are vermouth, Commandaria, Dubonnet, Punt-e-Mes.

Wine faults

Because wine is a living thing, faults or bottle sickness occasionally occur. Sometimes the faults are very obvious and the wine tastes terrible, looks awful and smells worse. Sometimes, however, there is only a hint or slight suspicion that something may be wrong. In all these situations, and even if you doubt the complaint, it is best to remember that the customer always gets the benefit of any doubt. Here are the more obvious faults found in wines.

Acetification   The wine has been affected by acetobacters through over-exposure to air. The vinegar microbe develops a film on the surface of the wine which produces acetic acid. The wine tastes sour, resembling vinegar (*vin aigre* = sour wine).

Cloudiness   This may be caused by extremes in storage temperature, excess protein, contact with metal or bacterial action or an unwanted continuation of fermentation.

Crystalline deposits   Tartaric acid is soluble in water but not in alcohol, so an excess of potassium bitartrate may precipitate in very cold temperatures as crystals. The sugar-like crystals, or minute flakes, spoil the appearance of the wine although it is otherwise sound to drink.

Corked wine   This is a wine affected by a diseased cork. The wine will have a musty, rancid, fungal smell and taste. The term should not be confused with cork residue – little harmless bits of cork which may splinter into the wine on opening.

Excess sulphur dioxide (SO₂)   Sulphur is added to keep wine healthy. It must be used with restraint otherwise it will be perceptible to nose and palate. If noticed on the nose, leave the wine for a few minutes and the stink will disappear.

Fermentation   This may happen when the wine is not fined or filtered properly. Traces of sugar and yeast remain in the bottled wine. An unwanted fermentation occurs causing bubbles to appear, usually accompanied by a nasty aroma and taste. This must not be confused with the healthy and predetermined styles of refreshing wines such as those of pétillant and spritzig character.

Foreign contamination   This may be caused when wine has been put into previously used bottles which have not been hygienically cleaned or sterilised – faulty bottling machinery may also cause glass to splinter and get into the wine. Wines may also be adversely affected if they are stored in a badly kept cellar at incorrect temperatures or stored next to strong odours such as petrol, vinegar or fish.

Oxidation or maderisation   There are degrees of oxidation ranging from an off-smell to a darkening or browning of the colour. It is caused by too much absorption of air either before bottling or when bottled (loose cork). The wine may also have been stored in much too warm conditions. The wine tastes flat and musty, having lost its fruit and brilliance. It slightly resembles a badly made Madeira, hence the term.

Weeping   This seeping of the wine from the cork can be caused by a too small or faulty cork or when a secondary fermentation pushes the cork loose.

Wine that 'does not travel'   In the old days, this was a fairly common occurrence. Sometimes the wine was not correctly balanced – too much acidity and too little alcohol. The wine might also have been roughed up by being badly handled or have undergone too many extremes of temperature on the journey. Nowadays all wines travel happily, mostly in refrigerated tanks, without being noticeably impaired. Problems may arise if the wine is too young or too old when shipped. In all cases, wine should be given an acclimatising or resting period before being offered for sale.

4

BREWING

—

INTRODUCTION

Long before it became the heady mix of science, secrets and nature that it is today, brewing was probably stumbled on by accident. Very likely some nomadic tribes in the Middle East, once they decided to stop roaming, would cultivate some land with corn. In some years they would be rewarded by a bumper crop and would store the surplus grain, keeping it in reserve for the occasions when the harvest would fail. Inevitably the crude stores would allow moisture to permeate and the grain would start to sprout and germinate. In order to salvage something from the spoilt grain a porridge would be made. By natural occurrence, enzymes would be released and these would convert the starch in the porridge into maltose, resulting in a sweet-tasting porridge. If this was stored in the open, yeasts from the atmosphere would soon settle to feed on the sugars, converting them into alcohol and carbon dioxide. We can presume that this accidental, crude brew was enjoyed, leading to experimentation and more rewarding results.

A modern computerised brewery

By 6000 BC, brewing was well established in Babylon. The Egyptians, Greeks and Romans all produced beer of acceptable quality. The Normans are credited with bringing their brewing skills to England.

Ingredients for brewing

WATER

Water is the main ingredient for beer – in brewing parlance it is called liquor. It must be biologically pure and its mineral content assured. It can be softened or hardened. Hard water is ideal for lager and soft water more suitable for heavier beers like bitter. Historically, brewers have depended for their supply on local wells where the mineral composition of the water has come through from natural sources.

BARLEY

Varieties of *Hordeum sativum* are used, and the styles chosen for brewing are those with a low protein content such as Maris Otter and Pipkin. Protein causes cloudiness. Barley is very rich in starch and in the enzyme called diastase. It is diastase which converts the starch into sugar so vital for fermentation. Barley in its malted form gives unrivalled taste to beer. Other grains such as maize, wheat and rice used in conjunction with barley are introduced to add some balance, but in total would not amount to more than 10% of the grain content.

HOPS

Hops come from the mulberry family, specifically from the *Humulus lupulus* species. Outstanding varieties are the English Fuggles, Golding and Northern Brewer, the

Czech Saaz, the American Cascade and the German Hallertau and Hersbruck. The hop is a herbaceous, perennial, climbing plant. Only the flower or the cone part of the female hop vine is used, and when they are harvested in September they are taken to oast houses to be dried, then cooled and stored until required.

Hops were first introduced to British brewing by Flemish traders in 1525. The hopped 'biere' was not immediately popular, but eventually the value of hops was recognised by the native brewers who previously specialised in 'unhopped ale'. Through their oils and resins, hops impart a bitter flavour, aroma and a biological preservative which prevents microbial spoilage as well as aiding longevity.

Yeast
Individual brewers specialise in particular strains of cultured yeast to maintain the characteristic of their brews. Some brewers have cultivated the same strain for over 50 years. There are two main types used. *Saccharomyces cerevisiae* is used for the production of ales and beers. This floats on the surface during fermentation and protects the brew from air and harmful bacteria. The lager yeast *Saccharomyces carlsbergensis* ferments at the bottom of the fermenting vessel, leaving the liquid unprotected from air, and for that reason lager fermentation takes place only in an enclosed vessel.

Sugar
The sugar used is the invert variety which facilitates fermentation. In the form of a priming sugar it is also used to add sweetness to some brown ales and sweet stouts before they leave the brewery.

Finings
Finings are used simply to clarify beer. Isinglass, the bladder of the sturgeon, is the traditional classical fining agent. It is very expensive so some synthetic fining agents may also be used. A carefully measured quantity of the fining is injected into each cask prior to the beer leaving the brewery.

The brewing process

Malting
Malted barley is required for brewing. Malting has three distinct steps.

Steeping   After screening the barley to remove any extraneous matter it is put into a large tank and steeped in water to a moisture content of about 45%. This is simply an accelerated version of the absorption of water which would normally occur over several weeks in the soil. The grain absorbs water and oxygen which leads to germination.

Germination   This is the commencement of growth when the food reserves in the grain – namely starch and protein – are broken down into sugars and amino acids. The initiating step in germination is the release of hormones from the embryo, which in turn trigger the production of enzymes. The key step of germination is the destruction by enzymes of the insoluble walls around the starch particles in the bulk of the grain known as the endosperm. The moist grain is spread onto a malting floor which is air-conditioned. It is frequently turned to regulate growth and temperature and provide oxygen to assist germination. Each grain sprouts tiny rootlets and at the same time the enzymes begin to convert the starch into sugars. The main fermentable sugar obtained is maltose, with small amounts of glucose, lavulose and fructose. Non-fermentable dextrins like maltotriose and more complex carbohydrates remain to go through to the finished beer.

Kilning   After about five days, when germination has reached the desired stage, further development is stopped by kilning. The grain is gently dried by hot air and the moisture content reduced to 4.5%. It is imperative that the kilning temperatures used do not destroy the very important enzymes which have developed during germination. Depending on the intensity and duration of kilning, different coloured malts are produced.

- **Pale malt**: the lightest kilned malt, this retains the maximum amount of sugar. It is used for many of the lighter beers.
- **Lager malt:** this is lightly roasted and suited to lager production.
- **Crystal malt:** medium roasted and deep golden in colour, this is used in the production of deeper-coloured and fuller-bodied beers.
- **Chocolate or black malt:** deep roasted with a chocolate colour and flavour, this is used to produce stout and porter.

BEER

Malted barley is lightly crushed by passing it through a mill which produces a coarse powder called grist. At this stage, other cereals can be introduced, such as wheat, unmalted barley, rice and flaked maize to give more subtle characteristics of flavour and colour to the finished brew. But there will still be about 90% of malted barley in the blend. The grist is transferred to a very large vessel called a mash tun where it is mashed with hot water. The temperature is kept at 65°C (150°F), allowing the enzymes formed during malting to degrade the soluble starch in the grain, producing a sweet brown liquid known as wort (pronounced wert) to be run off. The wort is now taken to a copper, a sort of massive kettle usually made of stainless steel, where hops and sugar are added and boiled for an hour and a half.

The sweet, hopped wort together with the hops are taken to the hop back: a large tank where the hops settle and form a compact filter bed to clarify the wort as it goes through. The wort is pumped through to a paraflow (heat exchanger) where it is cooled to a temperature of 15°C (60°F). It is now ready for fermentation. At this point the Customs and Excise used to come to test the original gravity for the purpose of assessing duty. Since 1st June 1993, beer duty is based on the final alcoholic strength of the brew.

Cooperage

The wort is put into a fermenting tun and 'pitched' with yeast. The yeast absorbs the nutrients and feeds on the sugars, converting them into alcohol and carbon dioxide. Over the first three days the yeasts utilise up to 80% of the sugars and the yeast will form a rocky and then a cauliflower appearance as it increases fourfold to a depth of up to 1 m (1 yd) on the surface. The surplus yeast is skimmed off. Some is stored in a cold room for the next brew. The rest is sold to farmers for cattle or pig food. A final yeast head is formed on the brew which protects the new beer from airborne infection. Fermentation takes seven or eight days to be fully completed.

The beer is now racked into casks, which clears some of the debris left after fermentation. Isinglass finings are injected into each cask before dispatch to further clarify the beer. However, there will be still some viable yeast remaining to feed on the residual sugars, producing alcohol and carbon dioxide which give the finished beer its 'natural condition'.

The term 'brewery-conditioned beers' refers to bottle beers and keg beers. Bottled beers are conditioned in large tanks. The beer is then carbonated and filtered. It is pasteurised which protects it against microbial spoilage and stabilises it for a longer shelf-life of about three months. Keg beers are matured for a short period in the brewery and then filtered and kegged into bulk containers. Keg beer has a longer life than cask-conditioned beer, making it ideally suited for premises whose nature of business is irregular, such as outdoor catering.

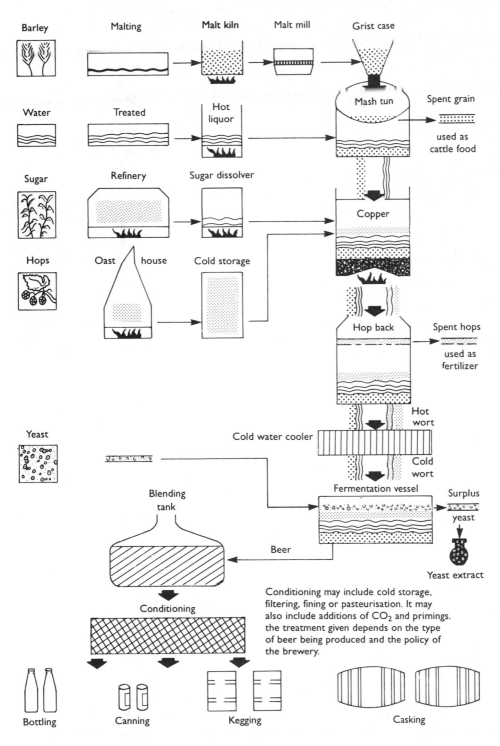

Barley
Malting
Malt kiln
Malt mill
Grist case

Water
Treated
Hot liquor
Mash tun
Spent grain
used as cattle food

Sugar
Refinery
Sugar dissolver
Copper

Hops
Oast house
Cold storage

Hop back
Spent hops
used as fertilizer

Yeast
Cold water cooler
Hot wort
Cold wort

Blending tank
Fermentation vessel
Surplus yeast
Yeast extract

Beer

Conditioning may include cold storage, filtering, fining or pasteurisation. It may also include additions of CO_2 and primings. the treatment given depends on the type of beer being produced and the policy of the brewery.

Conditioning

Bottling
Canning
Kegging
Casking

Brewing process

Six steps to beer-making – Summary

1   Barley is steeped in water and the grain is left to germinate and become malt. This releases the enzyme diastase to convert the starch in the grain into fermentable sugars, mainly maltose.

2   When the malt has reached the desired stage, germination is stopped at a precise moment by kilning. The longer and more intense the kilning, the darker and more flavoursome the beer.

3   The malt is milled and the crushed grain, grist, is mixed with hot water in a mash tun to extract the sugars. This results in a sweet wort.

4   Hops are added, mixed thoroughly and boiled to extract the oils and resins from the hops which impart bitterness, aroma and preservatives. This produces a sweet, hopped wort.

5   This is allowed to cool to a fermentable temperature and yeast is added. The strain of yeast used will be determined by the style of beer being produced: ale, top-fermenting yeast, lager, bottom-fermenting yeast.

6   Fermentation begins and lasts for seven days. The sugar is converted into alcohol and carbon dioxide using yeast as the catalyst. The result is beer.

Reduced alcohol beer

There are two categories of beer with reduced alcohol levels:

- **Non-alcoholic beers (NABs):** by definition, these must contain not more than 0.5% alcohol by volume
- **Low alcohol beers (LABs):** by definition, these must contain not more than 1.2% alcohol by volume

Beer is firstly made in the traditional way and then the alcohol is removed. The two favoured processes for removing the alcohol are vacuum distillation and reverse osmosis.

Vacuum distillation   In vacuum distillation, the alcohol and other volatile compounds are removed by passing the beer down a heated column under conditions of vacuum. This lowers the temperature needed to evaporate off the alcohol; the lower the temperature the better the flavour of the ensuing product.

Reverse osmosis   Reverse osmosis, also known as *cold filtration*, is carried out at low temperature. The beer is passed through a system of cellulose membranes which permit small molecules of alcohol to pass through.

Both of these techniques can be used to produce non- and low-alcohol products. It is also possible to produce low-alcoholic products by arresting fermentation at the appropriate point. This, however, tends to give a strongly flavoured product which is not particularly close to the flavour of a finished beer.

Beer strength

The average strength of beer is 4% alcohol by volume, but this figure varies with the type of beer produced. Table 4.1 illustrates different types and makes of beer available, classified in terms of their strength.

Table 4.1   *Beers classified by strength*

Super strength (8–11% alcohol by volume)

Lager	*Ale*
Tennent's Super (9%)	Gold Label Strong Ale (10.9%)
Carlsberg Special Brew (9%)	

Premium strength (4–6% alcohol by volume)

Lager	*Ale*	*Stout*
Stella Artois (5.1%)	Worthington White Shield (5.6%)	Guinness Extra (4.3%)
Harp Premier (5%)	Ruddles County (5%)	Draught Guinness in cans (4.1%)
Foster's (5%)	Marston's Pedigree (4.5%)	Marston's Stout (4%)
Beck's Bier (5%)	Stones Best Bitter (4.1%)	Murphy's (4%)
Grolsch (5%)		Beamish (4%)
Harp Extra (4.5%)		
Miller Lite (4.2%)		
Tennent's (4%)		
Carling Black Label (4%)		

Standard strength (3–4% alcohol by volume)

Lager	*Ale*
Castlemain XXXX (3.6%)	Tetley Bitter (3.6%)
Tennent's Pilsner (3.5%)	Whitbread Best (3.5%)
Harp (3.5%)	Flowers Bitter (3.4%)
Heineken (3.4%)	Worthington's Special (3%)

Low alcohol (0.5–1.2% alcohol by volume)

Lager	*Ale*
Tennent's LA (1%)	Whitbread White Label (1.2%)
Swan Light (0.9%)	Bass LA (1%)
Dansk LA (0.9%)	John Smith's LA (1%)
McEwan's LA (0.9%)	

Alcohol free (not more than 0.05% alcohol by volume)

Lager	*Ale*
Kaliber (0.05%)	Smithwick's AFB (0.05%)

Beer-producing countries

The top ten beer producing countries are:

1 USA
2 Germany
3 China
4 Japan
5 UK
6 Brazil
7 Mexico
8 Spain
9 South America
10 Canada

Beer types

Draught beer in cans   These draught-flow beers have been the success story of the brewing industry in the last decade. The system uses a plastic chamber in the bottom of the can. The can is filled with beer containing dissolved gas and it is then sealed. When it is eventually opened the pressure pushes the beer down, then up through a small hole in the chamber which releases a very fine stream of bubbles. As you finish pouring, a pub-style, smooth, creamy head will have formed. The great benefit is that you can now enjoy your favourite draught beer in the comfort of your own home. Best selling brands are Guinness, Murphy's, Boddingtons, Draught Bass, Theakstons and Castle Eden.

Steam beer   This style of beer originated in California and it is the trademark of the Anchor Brewery of San Francisco. It is an interesting hybrid of beer and lager. It uses bottom-fermenting lager yeasts at top-fermenting temperatures, which results in a bright sparkling beer with an alcoholic strength of 5%. The name may have derived from the time when breweries were steam-powered.

Weissbier   Also known as *Weizenbier* in Germany, this cloudy, 'white' beer is made from wheat instead of barley. Belgium also makes a good style called Hoegaarden (pronounced 'who garden').

Bitter   Pale, amber-coloured beer served on draught, this may be sold as light bitter, ordinary bitter or best bitter (the latter usually being the brewer's premium brand).

Mild   Mild can be light or dark depending on the colour of the malt used in brewing. It is sold on draught and has a sweeter and more complex flavour than bitter.

Burton   A strong, dark, draught beer, this is especially popular in winter when it is often mulled or spiced and offered as a winter warmer.

Old ales   These are brown, sweet and on the strong side. Again, they are ideal for mulling and spicing or for simply drinking on their own.

Strong ales   These vary in colour between pale and brown, in alcohol between strong and very strong, and in taste between dry and sweet.

Barley wine   Traditionally an all-malt ale, barley wine is sweet, strong and swift to have effect. It is sold in stubby bottles or nips (equivalent to 190 ml (⅓ pint)). The alcoholic strength is about the same as a double whisky.

Stout   Made from scorched, very dark malt and generously flavoured with hops, stout has a smooth, malty flavour and creamy consistency. It is sold on draught or in bottles, with traditionalists favouring it being served at room temperature.

Porter   This ale gets its name from its popularity with porters working in Dublin and London. It is brewed from charred malt, could be described as a cross between stout and bitter, and is highly aromatic and flavoursome.

Lager   This beer gets its name from the German *lagern*, meaning 'to store', and was originally made in central Europe. During production, the yeast (*Saccharomyces carlsbergensis*) ferments at the bottom of the fermenting vessel. The beer is stored at low temperatures for up to six months after fermentation in order to condition and mature it before it is sold either in bottle or on draught. The long storage period also helps the beer to withstand variations of temperature without clouding.

Bottle-conditioned beers   Also known as sediment beers because, by their very nature, these beers throw sediment in bottle where their conditioning takes place. After fermentation, the inactive yeast remains and forms a sediment. Such beers require care in both storing and pouring. Prime examples of the style include Worthington White Shield and Guinness Extra (in bottles, not cans).

Other bottled beers   Light ales, brown ales and export ales are pasteurised beers, free of sediment. They have an affinity with ordinary bitter, mild ale and best bitter respectively.

Beer measures

Nips	22.72 cl (7–8 fl oz)
Half Pint	28.40 cl or 0.284 litres (10 fl oz)
Pint	56.80 cl or 0.568 litres (20 fl oz)

Draught beer containers

1 pin	20.457 litres (4½ gallons)
1 firkin	40.914 litres (9 gallons)
1 keg	45.46 litres (10 gallons)
1 kilderkin	81.828 litres (18 gallons)

1 barrel	163.656 litres (36 gallons)
1 hogshead	245.484 litres (54 gallons)
2½ barrel tanks	205 litres (45 gallons)
5 barrel tanks	410 litres (90 gallons)

CIDER

Cider is usually classified as a beer. In reality, however, it has a greater affinity to wine, being made from fruit and not from grain. Ideally, cider is fermented apple juice but it can also be legally made from a mixture of apple juice and up to 25% pear juice. It came to prominence in England after the Norman conquest. At first it was a simple cottage industry with orchard owners making cider for their own needs and selling off any surplus. Gradually it developed into a substantial modern industry, although it will never vie with beer or wine in the commercial chase for business. Cider is made in many countries such as France – especially Normandy – Spain, Germany, Italy, Switzerland, Canada, New Zealand, South Africa, Australia and America where it is known as hard cider. Just as table grapes do not make good wine, eating apples will not, on their own, make good cider. What is needed is a balance of flavours and characteristics. Dessert apples give sweetness, cooking apples acid, and cider apples, through their tannin content, give bitterness and preserving qualities. In England, cider apples are cultivated principally in the south-west in Hereford, Devon, Dorset,

Cider apples

Somerset, Gloucester and Worcester. Cooking and dessert apples are the main crop in the south-east counties of Kent, Sussex, Norfolk and Suffolk. Some cider companies also use concentrated apple juice from France and Germany.

Making cider

Apples in prime condition are machine-gathered in September through to October. They are water-sprayed clean and taken to a mill where they are reduced to a pulp known as pomace. The pulp is wrapped in coarse cloth to form a 'cheese' which is

Old Merrydown cider press

pressed and the resulting juice fermented. Fermentation lasts for about one month and the new cider is then put through a centrifuge. This device spins the liquid to get rid of suspended solid particles which otherwise would cause cloudiness. Before reaching its point of sale, the cider may also be fined and filtered to make it brilliant in appearance.

Styles of cider

Draught cider   This may be dry and still or slightly sweet and sparkling. The sweetness is added in the form of sugar or concentrated apple juice. The sparkle is induced by adding yeast and sugar to the cask. Draught cider is usually unfiltered and it will have a hazy appearance as a result. When completely dry, it is often called scrumpy or farmhouse cider.

Keg cider   These are pasteurised, filtered ciders, star bright in appearance. They are usually sweetened and carbonated.

Bottle ciders   These ciders are pasteurised and filtered, and brilliant in appearance. Many are sparkling, which may be due to carbon dioxide being injected or through an addition of yeast and sugar. This may be added to the cider in a closed tank or in bottle where it goes through a classic second fermentation. This produces what used to be known as champagne cider. The term can no longer be used but an equivalent standard is marketed as pomagne. Many bottled ciders are sold as 'special' or 'vintage'. These are high quality ciders, the product of one year.

Cider strengths may vary between 1.14% and 8.5%. Beyond that strength, the product, for the purpose of tax, becomes an apple wine and is taxed as for British wine.

PERRY

Perry is the fermented juice of pears. It is made in a similar way to cider and the producers are even allowed to use up to 25% apple juice in the blend. The most popular styles of perry are carbonated, either through the injection of carbon dioxide or by the inducement of a second fermentation which takes place in a sealed tank. Before being bottled it will be filtered under pressure.

SAKE

Sake is a high strength (18%), slightly sweet rice beer, the result of a double fermentation. It gets its name from Osaka, the Japanese city where it was first made.
Before service, sake is put into a porcelain jar called a *tokkuri* or *chosi*. This is placed in a bowl of hot water to warm the drink which is then served from small porcelain cups called *sakazuki*. Sake may also be served chilled.

5

DISTILLATION

—

INTRODUCTION

The first distillers were probably perfume makers who made distillates – not from fermented liquids but from flowers, scents and water. Prior to the Christian era the Chinese made a crude spirit from rice beer. Arak was being distilled from sugar cane and rice in the East Indies as early as 800 BC. Physicians such as Hippocrates of Cos (469–339 BC) and other Greek Medics used boiled-down wine and wine concentrates as part of the medical treatment to cure sores and heal wounds. It is thought that the Arab physicians learned the art of distillation from the Greeks. Certainly the Arabs advanced the technique further and fashioned for us words such as alcohol, alembic (still) and elixir. Even the word distillation is attributed to Albukassen, an Arabian alchemist of the tenth century. In the Middle Ages, spirit was known as *aqua vitae*, water of life. In France it was referred to as *eau-de-vie* and the Celts of Ireland called it *uisge beatha*.

In the eleventh century, the Italian distillers were making brandy from wine. By the twelfth century, *uisge beatha* (whiskey) was being made in Ireland from barley beer. The twelfth century also saw the emergence of *zhiznennia voda* or water of life – later to be called vodka – in Russia and Poland.

In the fourteenth century, brandy was distilled in France and by the fifteenth century whisky-making was well established in the Scottish Highlands. Rum was first made in the West Indies in the sixteenth century and about the same time calvados was first distilled in Normandy, France. Gin started life as a medicine in Holland in the seventeenth century, while the eighteenth century saw the development of whiskey distilling in America.

To make a potable spirit, that is a spirit which is safe for humans to drink, it is first of all necessary to have a fermented alcoholic liquid. Of these, beer (without hop flavours) seems to be the most versatile, as it is the base for whisky, gin, vodka and korn. Molasses comes next because, although it is traditionally associated with rum, it can also be used to make gin and vodka. Wine when distilled becomes brandy. Cider is the base for calvados and apple jack 'brandy', pulque is the base for tequila and perry the base for eau-de-vie de poire. What distinguishes the individual spirit is the method of distillation employed and the flavouring and aroma elements – the small amounts of higher alcohols, solids and minerals – that differ in the base material of vegetable, fruit, cane and grain.

Distillation

The principle of distillation is that ethyl alchohol vaporises at a lower temperature than water – 78°C (172°F) against 100°C (212°F). The distillation of alcoholic spirits depends on three factors:

1   Ethyl alcohol vaporises, becomes a gas, when a temperature of 78°C (172°F) is

reached. Water boils at 100°C (212°F). The still is the apparatus which allows the separation of water and alcohol to be carried out.

2 Water is constantly vaporising to some extent so every distillation will contain water

3 The minor constituents, or congeners, which include higher alcohols (fusel oils) aldehydes, ethers, esters, volatile acids and organic compounds, give the product its distinctive, individual character of taste and aroma. These are obtained either in the vaporising process or by extraction from the residue and are further enhanced as the spirit ages in wood. Aldehydes, produced from a combination of alcohols and air, are particularly important for the character of a spirit. Esters result from a combination of acids and alcohol and form the volatile substance that contributes to the aroma of a spirit.

Stills

There are two main types of still in general use today: the pot still and the patent still.

THE POT STILL

The Pot Still originated in the Middle Ages and is based on the alchemist's alembic. It is associated with separate, slow, low-temperature distillations. As a result, the end product contains a good proportion of congeners – the flavour and aroma agents – which give individual spirits their character and appeal. All the heavy, highly flavoursome spirits such as brandy, malt whisky, dark rums, tequila and fine Calvados are pot still products.

The pot still is shaped like a giant onion and consists of two parts: a still and a worm condenser. The still is made of copper, which is a good conductor of heat and also builds up a good resistance to the effects of acids which are normally capable of dissolving metal. The worm condenser is a spiral tube also made of copper and this is connected to the still by a copper pipe. The worm passes through a jacket or condenser, which speeds up the condensation of the alcohol-rich vapours. The pot still is time consuming and costly to operate. It needs to be cooled, cleaned and refilled after each distillation, but it produces spirits of remarkable individuality, quality and flavour.

How it works The fermented liquid is placed in the still and slowly heated over a naked flame. When the temperature reaches 78°C (172°F) the alcoholic vapours rise and are led through a system of piping called the worm to a cooling apparatus – the condenser – and consensed into a liquid containing about 30% alcohol. This is re-distilled. The first part of the distillate to emerge is known as the heads or foreshots and contains a high proportion of methanol, which can be toxic and very unpalatable. This is put to one side to be dealt with later. The central portion or the heart of the distillation – the best part – has an alcoholic strength of about 80% and is channelled into the spirit receiver and ultimately into maturing casks. The final part of the distillation, known as tails, feints or after-shots, is weak in alcohol and contains the nauseating fusel oils and other impurities. This is now added to the reserved heads and sent back to be re-distilled and refined. The new spirit may be reduced in strength to 63% by the addition of deionised water, which does not react with the chemical elements of the spirit.

The spirit now requires resting, maturing, blending, reducing in strength and perhaps colour enhancement before being bottled for sale. Spirits only improve whilst maturing in porous containers such as wood, although they can also develop in earthenware crocks where the spirit mellows through oxidation. Spirits do not improve in glass containers. Once bottled, their quality remains unchanged.

THE PATENT STILL

The patent still or Coffey still was named after Aeneas Coffey, a Dublin excise officer who patented the still in 1831. It employs the principle of distillation by steam and uses rectification to make the end product as pure and congener-free as possible. It produces a continuous flow of high strength – about 90% – alcohol. It is cheaper than the pot still to operate as it is lighter on fuel. Because its system of operation is continuous, it does not require the labour-intensive tasks of emptying, cleaning and refilling. The patent still is associated with all the light spirits such as vodka, gin, white and light rums and grain whiskies which are later used for blending.

How it works   The patent still consists of two columns each about 18 m (19 yds) high. One column is called the analyser, whose role is to separate the constituent parts. The other column is the rectifier which raises the strength of and purifies the spirit, and condenses the alcoholic vapours. Each column is sub-divided horizontally into chambers by perforated copper plates which have a drip pipe leading to the chamber underneath. Both columns are preheated by steam and the fermented liquid or wash enters at the top of the rectifier and gradually descends through it inside a pipe.

By the time the wash reaches the bottom of the rectifier it is almost at boiling point. It is then pumped into the analyser where it gradually makes its way downwards through perforated plates and bubble caps. As it descends, it is met by a current of raw steam which has been injected under pressure into the bottom of the analyser. On contact, the steam boils the wash and produces alcoholic vapours. These rise and are channelled by a pipe into the bottom of the rectifier. The spent wash is removed at the bottom of the analyser.

Meanwhile inside the rectifier, the alcoholic vapours pass through a series of perforated plates. As they rise they meet, at certain points, the cold wash being carried down the rectifier by the wash coil. Partial condensation takes place – the vapours getting cooler and the wash, on its way to the analyser, getting hotter. When the spirit vapours reach two-thirds of the way up in the rectifier, they hit a cold spiral plate or water frame and precipitate. The first liquid to emerge – the heads or foreshots – is removed and sent back to the analyser because it is pungent and needs further refining. The comparative pure spirit which follows is guided into a spirit receiver. This will be reduced in strength by deionised water and matured for a short time before being treated (or flavoured as in the case of gin) according to style.

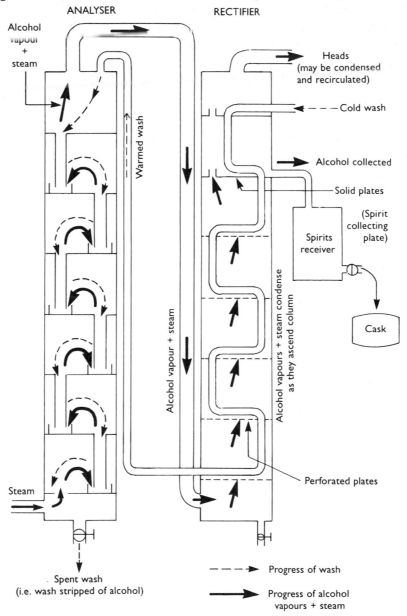

Coffey still

BRANDY

Cognac

Cognac is recognised as one of the world's great drinks. It is made north of Bordeaux in the departments of the Charente and the Charente Maritime in south-west France.

The geographical region of production was defined by decree on the 1st May 1909 and was divided into six zones known by the following appellations or *crus*:

- Grande Champagne
- Petite Champagne
- Borderies
- Fins Bois
- Bons Bois
- Bois Ordinaires

The zones form concentric rings around the town of Cognac. The soil is soft and chalky, rich in phosphates, but becomes progressively less chalky as you leave the highly prized champagne zones. Then, earthier and sandier soils take over and the vine is less in harmony. The main vines cultivated are Ugni Blanc (also known as St Emilion), Folle Blanche and Colombard. Their grapes are picked when barely ripe to produce a thin harsh wine, low in alcohol and high in acidity – the perfect wine for distilling.

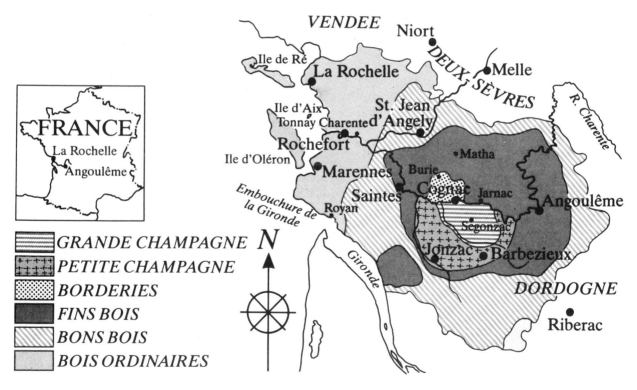

In the late seventeenth century, Dutch and Scandinavian salt merchants doing business through the port of La Rochelle liked this coarse wine and decided to boil it down for ease of transport, but mainly to avoid the tax levied on volume. They called the product *brantwijn* – burnt wine – and found they liked the new spirit better than the old wine. By the nineteenth century, many Cognac trading houses were established and after 1830 Cognac was exported in bottle as well as barrel.

MAKING COGNAC

Cognac is distilled in copper pot stills (alambic charentais). It is twice distilled but only the heart of the run is taken off each time, leaving the heads and tails, which contain impurities and little alcohol, to be put back in the still for re-distilling. The first distillation produces the *brouillis* (boiling up), which will have an alcohol strength of around 30%. The second distillation known as the *bonne chauffe* (good heat) becomes a raw, fiery, colourless Cognac with an alcohol content of up to 72%. It is estimated that it takes ten bottles of wine to make one bottle of Cognac. The new spirit is put to mature in weathered oak casks. The wood, matured for 75 to 100 years, comes from the forests of Limousin and Tronçais. The raw spirit, by its interaction with the wood, extracts tannin, colour and flavour. Simultaneously the porous wood allows a slow oxidation critical to the development of the unique finesse associated with Cognac. The rate of oxidation is relative to the humidity in the cellars, but during the ageing process 2–3% of alcohol is lost through evaporation per year. This proportion is known locally as 'the angels' share'.

Cognac only improves whilst maturing in cask. Once bottled, its age is arrested and its quality remains constant. It will eventually be bottled at an alcohol strength of 40% – the reduction in strength can come naturally over very long ageing in cask or by the addition of distilled water.

LABEL LANGUAGE

There is no regulation concerning names and ages appearing on a Cognac label. Producers are at liberty to call their products what they like, but the great producers adhere to the following standards.

Grande Fine Champagne   This is a Cognac made exclusively from grapes grown in the classic Grande Champagne zone. The word champagne here has nothing to do with the famous sparkling wine champagne but in this case means 'level open countryside'.

Fine Champagne   Made from grapes grown in the Grande Champagne and Petite Champagne zones, this must contain at least 50% Grand Champagne grapes in the blend.

Fine Maison   Brandy of the house, usually a quickly matured Cognac, which is smooth, delicate and offering good value.

Three Star/VS (very special) Blended Cognac   The younger brandy in this blend must have spent at least three years maturing in cask. However, these qualities will usually have spent five to nine years in cask.

VSOP (very superior old pale) VO (very old) Réserve   These are known as liqueur or fine quality Cognacs. They are not sweet but are finely matured, having spent at least ten years maturing in cask, usually 14–17 years.

Old Liqueur Cognacs   Cognacs such as XO (extra old) Grande Réserve, Extra Vielle, Hors d'Age and Extra are Cognacs of great age and refinement, the finest products of the Cognac houses. They will have matured in cask for 20, 30, 40 or even more years.

Napoleon Brandy   This is a myth. Napoleon I died in 1821, and as Cognac only improves in cask the name cannot be taken seriously.

BRANDS
Well known brands of Cognac are:

- Bisquit
- Camus
- Courvoisier
- Hennessy
- Hine
- Martell
- Rémy Martin
- Otard

Armagnac

Armagnac is produced in the Gers department in south-west France. The region was delineated in 1909 and the method of production established to preserve the individuality and status of Armagnac. There are three separate zones of grape production.

Bas Armagnac   Produced around its capital Eauze, this area has a predominance of sandy soil with some clay, producing full, supple brandies with a bouquet of prunes and plums.

Ténarèse   This region surrounds the capital Condom, where clay soil with some chalk produces fast-maturing brandies which are light in body and have a scent of violets.

Haut Armagnac   Around the capital Auch, this is the largest area and has the classic chalky soil but produces poor quality brandy, much of which is used as a base for liqueurs or for the local speciality – prunes in Armagnac.

The following are the principal grape varieties used for Armagnac: Folle Blanche, Ugni Blanc, Picpoul, Jurançon and Colombard.

MAKING ARMAGNAC
The traditional still of the region is a modified version of the continuous still. It produces a spirit of low strength – around 53% – which retains a high proportion of flavouring elements, even impurities. It is this combination that gives Armagnac its

acknowledged earthy character and rustic charm. The pot still, which was banned in 1936, was back in favour in 1972 and, despite reservations, the overall character has not been eroded or significantly changed. The age date of Armagnac starts on the 1st September after the harvest.

The young spirit is put into Monlezun oak which is noted for its fast maturing capabilities. Armagnac is aged as follows: three star indicates three years maturing in casks; VSOP, VO and Hors d'Age will have been matured more than five years in cask. Some houses offer vintage Armagnacs which are the product of just one outstanding year. They may also specialise in only BAS Armagnac blends, a fact they are eager to emphasise on the label.

Great producers of Armagnac are Janneau, Marquis de Montesquiou and Sempé.

Marc

Marc (pronounced Marr) is a brandy distilled from the pomace or grape husks left after the pressing of the grapes. Also known as eau-de-vie de Marc, it is made from the residue of black grape skins in many parts of France. The styles Marc de Bourgogne and Marc de Champagne are particularly well appreciated. In Italy and California an equivalent spirit is known as *grappa* – grape stalk – an apt description. The Spanish equivalent is *aguardiente* (fire water) and the Portuguese style is called *bagaçiera*. All are an acquired taste.

Pisco

Pisco is a distillation of Muscat wine and is native to Chile and Peru. This brandy is delicious on its own but as part of a Pisco Sour it is superb.

Other well-known brandies

Asbach Uralt	Germany	Vecchia Romagna	} Italy
Christian Brothers	}	Stock	
Korbel	} USA	Oude Meester	South Africa
Paul Masson	}	Cambas	} Greece
Fundador	}	Metaxa	
Lepanto	}	Anglias	
Conde de Osborne	} Spain	Five Kings	} Cyprus
Bobadilla 103	}	Peristiani VO 31	

CALVADOS

Calvados takes its name from *El Calvador*, one of the galleons of the Spanish Armada wrecked on the coast of Normandy in 1588. One of the villages adopted the name and after the French Revolution the name was also applied to the local apple brandy: Calvados. Since 1946 the region of production has been defined. The best region is the appellation Pays d'Auge, around and inland from the town of Lisieux. Whereas other regions may use the continuous still as a method of production, in Pays d'Auge the pot still method of double distillation is used. As we already know, the pot still leaves more congenerics – flavouring agents – with the final product.

How Calvados is made

The apples are mashed into a pulp and the juice is fermented into cider. The cider is distilled and only the best or middle part, *alcools de coeur*, is kept. This is distilled a second time and, once more, only the middle part is retained; the rest goes back for redistillation. The raw fiery young Calvados is aged from three to six years, usually in Limousin oak casks but sometimes also in sherry and port casks. It is carefully appraised and blended before sale.

Calvados is a *digestif* and served as for brandy. In northern France it is sometimes drunk during a meal between the fish and meat course. It is drunk in one gulp to whet the appetite or make a hole for the rest of the meal – hence the expression *trou Normand* – the Norman holemaker.

About 48 varieties of apples are used, graded from tart to sweet. Fine examples of Calvados are Busnel, Père Magloire, Boulard, Dauphin and Gilbert.

WHISKY

The name whisky comes from the first word of the Gaelic expression *uisge beatha*, meaning water of life. The earliest record of the spirit indicates that it was first made in Ireland in the twelfth century from barley beer. Irish monks brought the craft of distillation with them when they settled in Scotland. Thereafter the Scots set about making whisky the most internationally enjoyed spirit, helped, of course, with input from the Irish, American and Canadian producers. The big breakthrough came in 1831 with the invention of the Coffey still which revolutionised the whisky industry. Previously only barley-based, highly flavoured pot still products were available. Now much lighter and more delicate flavoured whiskies could be made from other grains such as maize, milled oats and rye using the new still. The Scots saw the possibility of blending the products of the pot still and Coffey still so that the blend of the component parts became more generally appreciated than any single part. A huge market for blended whisky resulted and this was helped enormously by the virtual cessation of brandy production in the 1870s due to the spread of the vine disease phylloxera. Canny salesmanship saw to it that Scotch whisky filled the gap.

Scotch whisky

The success and renown of Scotch whisky is based on five factors.

1   The shape of the pot still which retains maximum flavour and aroma in the spirit.

2   The quality of the soft spring water which must be of unquestionable purity yet contain the essential minerals so necessary to the character of the whisky.

3   The quality of the malt which uses peat to impart the traditional reek or smoky flavour.

4   The attention to detail as the whisky matures in casks.

5   The art of the blender.

Scotland produces two very different styles of whisky:

- Malt whisky: the star product, this may be sold as it is or used for blending.
- Grain whisky: used, almost always, to be blended with the malt product.

MALT WHISKY

How malt is made   Malting is the germination and subsequent drying of the barley. Barley is soaked in water tanks known as steeps. It is left for two or three days, drained and then spread out on concrete floors up to 60 cm (2 ft) deep. The combination of moisture and warmth causes the grain to germinate. The grain sprouts rootlets and gives off heat as it absorbs oxygen and gives off carbon dioxide. To avoid matting, the grain must be turned daily by the maltmen who use long handled shovels called skips. Modern distilleries use mechanical revolving forks or stirrers. The barley secretes the enzyme diastase, making the starch in the grain soluble and capable of producing sugars for conversion into alcohol.

After four or five days, the rootlets will have withered and the barley is considered malted. Germination is stopped by spreading the green malted barley on layers of perforated plates. Underneath is a peat fire which gives off a pungent, earthy, swirling smoke that gives the barley its special fragrance or 'peat reek'. Coal and anthracite is later added to the fire to increase the heat and completely dry the barley to a crisp and crumbly finish. The withered roots are removed and sold for cattle food. The grain is milled and becomes grist.

The grist is mixed with hot water in a mash tun and churned violently to reactivate and extract the enzyme diastase from the grain. This is completed in three or four washings. The first two washings give a semi-transparent sweetish liquid called wort. The remaining washings, called 'sparge', go back to be used with the next batch of grist.

Fermentation   The wort is transferred to deep wooden or steel vessels called wash tuns where cultured yeast is added. The enzymes convert the maltose in the wort to dextrose and then to alcohol and carbon dioxide. After about 36 hours a liquid called wash, with an alcoholic strength of 7–10%, emerges – in essence a crude beer without the flavouring of hops.

Distillation   Malt whisky is made only in pot stills (see below). In Scotland these are known as wash stills and spirit stills. The wash is put into a wash still and heated until the alcohol vaporises and rises through the neck of the still to the water-cooled condenser where it precipitates as 'low wines'. The second distillation of the low wines is carried out in a spirit still. This distillation will produce heads or foreshots, the centre part known as hearts, and the final part known as tails or feints.

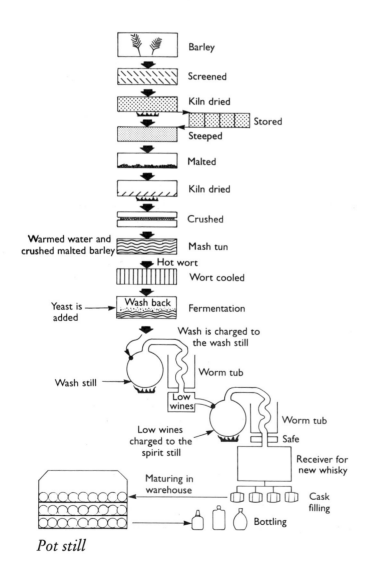

Pot still

The foreshots and feints are pungent, crude and undesirable, without further refinement, for whisky. They are held over to be added to the oncoming low wine. The heart is raw, colourless whisky with a powerful aroma and an alcoholic strength of 70%.

Maturing   The young whisky is pumped into sherry casks or American oak or rum casks where it matures for a minimum legal requirement of three years, but usually for much longer. The whisky is matured in bonded warehouses under excise supervision. As the whisky rests, air penetrates through the pores of the wood to mellow the raw whisky. The location of the warehouse will also influence maturation. Damp conditions will reduce the alcohol content and slightly increase the volume. Dry atmosphere greatly reduces volume and to a slight extent strength. Cask age mellows the whisky and adds colour and character. Malts are aged between 15 and 20 years. There is a danger that prolonged ageing will impart an unfavourable woody flavour. The age appearing on a label must indicate the age of the youngest whisky in the blend.

Blending   If distilling is a craft, then blending is an art. The blender is a person of great judgement and experience, showing the extra, essential qualities of imagination and flair. The skill is to combine whiskies from many distilleries,whether malt whiskies or a combination of malt and grain whiskies. All the whiskies will have their own special characteristics to impart. The art is to ensure that each whisky contributes to the blend without any being dominant and that the whole will be better than the sum of the parts. The other reason for blending is to ensure a consistent brand taste year after year. There may be as many as 30 to 40 whiskies blended to make one brand. After blending the whisky is rested and the components marry together. Although new whiskies pick up some colour from their maturing casks, the final blend will require some colour enhancement so as to maintain a standard, acceptable shade – very important to the eye of the consumer. This is done at the time of blending by adding minute quantities of caramel-based colouring. Soft water is added to reduce the alcohol to a potable strength – 40% by volume. The whisky is filtered before bottling.

GRAIN WHISKY

The cereals used to make grain whisky are maize, wheat, millet, some barley plus a little malted barley. Maize is usually the main ingredient and when ground it is cooked under steam pressure in a converter to burst the starch cells and make it amenable for fermentation later. The maize is mixed with hot water and a little green malt. Wort is extracted, yeast is added and after fermentation 'low wines' result, which have a slightly lower alcohol strength than the wash used in the pot still product. The patent or Coffey still is used to make grain whisky. Its operation is detailed on page 62, but basically it is a continuous process based on the principle of distillation by steam. The process removes most of the congenerics – flavouring and aroma agents – which results in a much milder, less assertive product, ideally suited for blending.

STYLES OF SCOTCH WHISKY

Blended whisky

This accounts for almost 90% of all Scotch sold. These whiskies are produced from a blend of malt and grain whisky, usually on a 50/50 basis. Blends using a higher proportion of malt are known as deluxe whiskies. These are usually matured for much longer in cask and are consequently smoother and inevitably more expensive. If there is an age showing on the label it will reflect the number of years the youngest whisky in the blend has matured in cask. Like all spirits, whisky only improves whilst maturing in cask. Some examples of blended whiskies include:

Blended whiskies	Deluxe blends
Ballantine	The Antiquary
Bells	Chivas Regal
Black and White	Haig's Dimple
Cutty Sark	Johnnie Walker Black Label
Hankey Bannister	Old Parr
Teachers	Red Hackle
VAT 69	Usher's Deluxe

Malt whisky

This is made entirely from malted barley.

Single cask malt: known in the trade as 'specials', this is an exceptionally high quality whisky put to mature in a particular cask for a number of years. It is usually sold in commemorative bottles to mark a special occasion or event.

Single malt: sometimes known as straight malt, this is the unblended product of one single distillery.

Vatted malt: a marriage of single malts from different distilleries.

Main malts and their regions

Highland malts: these big, prestigious malts are produced north of the line drawn from Greenock to Dundee. Many of the famous distilleries are concentrated around the river Spey. Fine examples are Blair Athol, Dufftown, Glenfarclas, Glenfiddich, Glengrant, Glenlivet, Glenmorangie, Knockando, Macallan, Singleton and Tormore.

Lowland malts: produced south of the highland line, these are the gentlest of malts and tend to mature quite young, between eight and ten years. Good examples are Auchentoshan, Glenkinchie and Rosebank. Because of their gentle character, these malts are often used as blenders.

Campbeltown malts: produced in and around Campbeltown in the Mull of Kintyre, once known as the whisky capital of Scotland. These heavy, smoky malts are best exemplified by Springbank and Longrow.

Island or seaside malts: there are many fine malts made in the Islands. The better known are:

Islay: Bunnahbhain, Lagavulin and Laphroaig
Jura: Isle of Jura
Mull: Tobermory
Orkney: Highland Park and Scapa
Skye: Talisker

Irish whiskey

Bushmill's stillhouse

When King Henry II invaded Ireland in the twelfth century, he found the natives drinking *uisge beatha*. By the mid 1500s there was so much drunkeness that the Government passed a law against it – whiskey makers were considered an undesirable species of humanity. Tax was imposed on the 1228 distillers operating at the time. Very soon there was only a quarter of that number in business and the numbers continued to diminish, either through closure or amalgamation. By 1887 there were only 28 distilleries in Ireland and in 1966 the Irish Distillers Company was formed to merge three giants of the business together – John Jameson, John Power and Cork Distillers who owned Paddy's, Murphy's and Dunphy's. Old Bushmills, the oldest registered whiskey distillery in the world (1608), joined the group in 1972 but continued to operate on the bank of the river Bush in County Antrim. The other group members operate from very modern distilleries in Middleton, County Cork.

Here the pot still and the Coffey still work side by side, but the individual character of each brand is carefully preserved. Most Irish whiskey is a blend of the pot and Coffey still products. The one exception is Bushmills, who make a fine ten-year-old malt as well as traditional blends. Irish whiskey is made from malted and unmalted barley and very small quantities of other grain. It is triple distilled and as a result it has less congenerics – flavouring elements – which makes it light and easy on the palate. By law, it must be matured for at least five years in oak casks – sherry casks and charred American barrels, even Bourbon barrels, are often used – which gives it a distinctive and smooth finish.

Brands to look out for include Bushmills Black Bush, Bushmills Malt, Jameson, Paddy, Power's Gold Label, Tullamore Dew and the ultimate Irish whiskey, the distinctive and brilliant Middleton Rare which was launched in 1984.

American whiskey

The skill of distilling was brought to America by Irish and Scottish immigrants who settled in Pennsylvania, Maryland and Virginia. The product became so popular that in 1791 George Washington imposed a tax on it. This led to the whiskey rebellion of 1794. The temperance movement and others had it banned by the notorious Fourteenth Amendment of November 1920. This led to Prohibition which lasted 13 long years, ending in 1933. In 1964 the 38th Congress of the United States codified the various types of whiskey.

Rye whiskey   Rye whiskey is made from a mash containing not less than 51% rye. Most comes from Pennsylvania and Maryland and there is a wide variety of quality and styles. There are some straight ryes, but the majority are blended with other whiskies or neutral spirit.

Corn whiskey   Made from a mash containing 80% maize, this gets little ageing and has a fiery flavour.

Straight whiskey   Unblended and made from one type of grain, this is aged for at least two years in charred oak casks.

Bottled in bond whiskey   These are straight whiskies matured in cask in Government Bonded Warehouses for four years. They are bottled at 100° USA proof, equivalent to 50% alcohol.

Blended whiskey   This is a combination blend of straight and neutral spirits.

Bourbon whiskey   The classic American whiskey, this was named after Bourbon County, Kentucky where it was first made. In 1789 the Reverend Elijah Craig, a Baptist Minister, set up a still beside a limestone creek in the Blue Grass Mountains of Kentucky and sold his product as Kentucky Bourbon Whiskey. It is produced from a mash containing at least 51% maize (corn) but more usually the mash contains up to 70% maize. Famous examples of this quality whiskey are Jim Beam, Old Crow, Old Forrester, Old Grandad, Wild Turkey, Four Roses and Maker's Mark.

Sour mash bourbon   This is made from a mash which is fermented by using yeast from a previous fermentation. Typical examples are Maker's Mark and Eagle Rare.

Jack Daniels   This is not truly a Bourbon as it is made in Lynchburg, Tenessee; it is, however, America's biggest seller by far in the United Kingdom. The producer's motto is 'every day we make it, we'll make it the best we can'. It has real star quality.

Most American whiskies are matured in charred oak barrels. No one really knows why, but the charring probably came about as a means of cleaning the inside of a cask. It certainly gives whiskey a distinctive flavour.

In making Bourbon, these casks are only used once, but there is a great demand for the used casks wherever whiskey is made. The Americans and the Irish spell their product with an 'e': whiskey. All other countries leave out the 'e'.

Canadian whisky

Canadian whisky, noted for its fine, clean taste, is made from a mixture of grains: corn, wheat, malted barley and rye. It is mostly made in multi-column, continuous operation patent stills and aged in charred oak casks. It is somewhere between Scotch and Bourbon to taste, being light in body and flavour and slightly sweet. It is a very good mixer and is used frequently in cocktail recipes.

Special brands are:

Hiram Walker: Canadian Club
Seagram: Crown Royal
Schenley: Golden Wedding
Corby: Royal Reserve
Gilbey: Black Velvet
Wiser: Deluxe

GIN

Medical science created gin. Credit for its discovery goes to a Dutch Professor of Chemistry, Franciscus de la Boe (1614–72), who became known as Sylvius when he adopted the Latin form of his family name. Dr Sylvius had long recognised the diuretic properties of the oil of the juniper berry. Using a distillation from rye, he rectified (re-distilled) it with the flavour of the juniper berry as he perfected his medicine in the laboratory of the famous University of Leyden in Holland. The apothecaries sold it as an infallible cure for ailments such as gout, kidney trouble and rheumatism. The medicine was first sold under the name *Genièvre*, the French word for juniper. Later it was called *Genever* and then *Geneva*.

English soldiers fighting in the low countries saw other possibilities for the medicine. They would drink it before going into battle and dubbed it 'Dutch courage'. On returning home they brought their comforting elixir with them and Geneva became immediately popular. Soon the English contracted the word to gin. In 1689 when the Dutch William of Orange came to the English throne, he openly encouraged the distillation and consumption of gin to combat the imports of wine and brandy from a hostile France. From then onwards gin became known as England's national drink.

It was so lightly taxed, everyone could afford it. Some of the gins were foul and as there was no quality control at that time, many of the products were seriously dangerous to health. By 1729 it was estimated that one in every four houses in London was distilling gin. By 1743 a population of 6.5 million consumed a staggering 18 million gallons of the stuff. The poor, especially, in attempting to forget their appalling social conditions, sought its solace and secumbed to the seductions of 'royal poverty' and 'mother's ruin'. Hogarth's celebrated morality painting *Gin Lane* is a clear condemnation of the depravity of the time, where drunken humanity portrays a scene of indolence, vice, misery and oblivion. The recklessness and abandon of the era was best demonstrated by a notorious notice displayed outside a 'strong water shop' in Southwark. It read 'Drunk for a penny, dead drunk for tuppence. Clean straw for nothing'. Such excess caused mental illness, ruination and often death. Several acts of parliament tried to curb and control the intake, but this only led to rioting, bootlegging and smuggling. Increased taxes resulted in the supression of the better gins. The 'brain damage' variety was readily obtainable from street hawkers who peddled their coloured mixtures from every street corner. Chemists sold it in medicine bottles disguised as colic water and gripe water. Brand names also appeared such as the Last Shift, Cuckold's Comfort and Old Tom. The latter was sold by a former government spy, Captain Dudley Broadstreet. He rented a house in London and nailed the sign of a cat to the ground floor window and put a leadpipe under its paw with a funnel attached inside. Passers-by would put money in the cat's mouth and call 'Puss, give me tuppence worth of gin'. The 'liquid madness' would then come pouring out to give a generous few mouthfuls. This could have been the first ever coin-in-the slot machine.

Eventually a combination of the temperance movement, more enlightened legislation, the growth in industrial prosperity and importantly, higher spirit prices, achieved the desired moderation in drinking. More professional distillers were encouraged to enter the business in the three centres of production, London, Bristol and Plymouth. As the business became more respectable, taverns became more comfortable. The early nineteenth century saw the emergence of the big, brassy, atmospheric gin palaces. An Act of 1871 sought to reduce their number by half but an outraged public saw to it that the Act was quickly withdrawn. In the 1880s, the Americans moved in with their gin-based mixed drinks. Forty years later saw the dawning of the cocktail era and the emergence of gin as a respectable drink. Many of the great, classic cocktails were gin based.

How gin is made

Gin is distilled from a fermented wash made from molasses or grain. It is always flavoured with juniper berries and some of the following 'botanicals' – cassia bark, coriander seed, angelica root, calamus, orris, fennel, liquorice, almonds, orange peel and cardamom.

The fermented wash is put in a patent still to produce an unrefined spirit. This is re-distilled (rectified) to eliminate the poisonous higher alcohols (fusel oils), congenerics and impurities. A high strength, colourless and flavourless spirit results. This is reduced in strength by the addition of distilled water and the botanical flavourings are added in one of three ways.

1   The traditional and best way involves the distillation of the pure spirit with the flavouring agents. This is done in a pot still and the flavour of the botanicals used – always a secret recipe – impregnates the final spirit.

2   The distillation of the botanicals can be added in concentrated form to the neutral alcohol.

3   Gin flavourings can be added to neutral spirit. This is by far the cheapest method.

Gin made by the first two methods may be described as London Dry Gin. If made by the third method that quality description may not be used.

Types of gin

London dry gin   Originally made in London, hence the name, this unsweetened, classic gin is now made elsewhere under licence and marketed under brand names such as Booths, Beefeaters, Burroughs, Gilbeys, Gordons, Seagrams and Tanqueray.

Plymouth gin   This pungent, aromatic gin is made by the Devonshire firm of Coates and Company in Plymouth. Because of its naval connections it is the standard gin used in the making of a Pink Gin (see page 282).

Old Tom gin   Now made in Scotland mainly for the export market, this is sweetened with additions of sugar syrup.

Dutch gin   Also known as Hollands, Genever or Schiedam, it is often sold in stone jars or crocks. The original spirit is not rectified so some of the basic grain flavours are retained. It is made from malted barley and rye and double distilled in a pot still with the flavouring agents being introduced on the second distillation. Its heavy, malt flavour makes it unsuitable for mixing. In Holland it is usually drunk out of tall, narrow, ice-cold glasses and then washed down by a lager chaser. This style of gin is principally made in Amsterdam and Schiedam by well-known producers like Bols and De Kuyper.

Steinhaeger   A German gin made in Westphalia, this has a distinct personality and is usually drunk as for schnapps, neat and ice cold.

Sloe gin   This is made by steeping sloes (fruit of the blackthorn) in basic gin and includes additions of sugar syrup and bitter almonds.

Fruit gins   These are usually artificially flavoured with orange, lemon or other appropriate essences.

VODKA

Vodka is a highly rectified spirit made from grain, potatoes or molasses. It is the national drink of Russia and Poland and it originated in one of these two countries in the twelfth century. The name vodka or wodka means 'little water' because the product looks like water, being odourless, colourless and usually tasteless. The latter factor has gained the drink a reputation for being a wife's deceiver. The finest quality vodkas are filtered through activated layers of charcoal or fine quartz sand. This ensures absolute purity. Although most vodkas are naturally flavourless, specially flavoured vodkas are also on the market. For example, the outstanding Polish vodka, Zubrówka, made with an infusion of Zubrówka grass – the grass on which the European bison or buffalo graze – is quite aromatic with a green tinge and slightly nutty flavour. A long blade of the grass floats inside each bottle.

Vodka came to prominence in the late 1940s, aided by such fashionable mixes as Bloody Mary (with tomato juice), Screwdriver (with fresh orange juice) and Moscow Mule (with ginger ale). Being flavourless, it is also an easy ingredient for cocktails and cups. On its own it is served straight from the fridge in glasses which have been in the freezer for a few minutes. No need to smash the glasses on the fireplace afterwards!

Popular brands

The most popular brands of vodka available are:

Wyborowa Zubrówka	} Poland	Muskovskaya Stolichnaya	} Russia
Saratof Nordoff	} Ireland	Cossak Smirnoff	} England
Steinhäger Schinkenhäger	} Germany	Absolut	Sweden

RUM

The Caribbean is the true home of rum, but the spirit can legally be made wherever the sugar cane grows freely. The principal centres of production are located in Jamaica, Barbados, Guyana, Trinidad, Martinique, the Virgin Isles, Hispaniola, Haiti, Cuba, Puerto Rico, the USA, Brazil, Bolivia, Mexico, South Africa, Australia and Venezuela.

The origin of the word rum is obscure. It could be a contraction of the Latin word *saccarum* meaning sugar or sweetness. The word may also have been coined from 'rumbustion', the name sailors, smugglers, pirates and adventurers gave to their favourite tot or tipple – or, as the Devon mariners used to call it, rumbullion, alias 'kill devil'. At first, rum was made solely from the juice of the sugar cane. Then as the sugar refineries demanded more and more cane, the distillers resorted to making the spirit from the by-product of sugar – molasses. However, some fine rums are still being made directly from cane juice.

How rum is made

The sugar cane is crushed and mangled between heavy roller mills to produce what is known as *bagasse*, a purée of cane and juice. This is crushed again to express all the juice which is then concentrated into a syrup by boiling. The syrup is put into centrifugal machines which crystallise the sugar. This is separated and taken elsewhere to be purified into sugar for domestic and other use. What remains is a by-product of sugar, a dark solution called molasses. It is from this murky mass that rums are fermented and distilled. Before fermentation, the thick molasses will be diluted with water and clarified for ease of control. The yeasts used in fermentation will be either natural or a secret strain of cultured yeast.

FERMENTATION
There are two methods of fermentation used – quick or slow. The one chosen will relate to the style of rum the distiller wants to produce.

Quick fermentation   This lasts no longer than two days but is frequently shorter. It is associated with the production of white and light-flavoured rums.

Slow fermentation   This may last for up to 12 days and is associated with the production of dark, heavy-flavoured rums. Dunder, the residue left in the still from a previous distillation, may be added to promote or reinforce the fermentation and impart an extra dimension of flavour. After fermentation, the liquid or wash now known as 'final molasses' will have an alcoholic strength of about 7 per cent by volume.

DISTILLATION

The fermented wash destined to produce light rums is distilled in patent stills to a strength of 91% alcohol by volume. The resulting spirit will be white or clear-coloured and have only a little flavour. If the spirit is matured in uncharred oak casks for a year, it will be later sold as white rum. Should it be matured in charred oak casks for three years and have a little caramel added, it will be known as gold rum.

The wash destined for dark rum production will be distilled in a pot still to a strength of 86% alcohol. The spirit will be rich in congeners – flavour and aroma agents. These will become more prominent as the spirit matures in cask. Some colour will be obtained from the oak cask. More colour will be added through a solution of caramel which is, of course, also made from sugar. Before bottling, rums are reduced to a potable strength of around 40% by the addition of demineralised water. Since 1917, rum may not be sold in Britain until it is three years old. Some rums are transported to Britain to spend their maturing years in cellars belonging to the United Rum Manufacturers in Dundee, Scotland. Here the climate ensures a much slower and economical rate of evaporation than, for example, the intense heat of the Caribbean would allow.

Styles of rum

White and light-flavoured rums   These are produced mainly in Puerto Rico, Cuba, the Virgin Isles, Barbados and Trinidad. They may be termed white, silver, gold or amber. They were once largely associated with Cuba where the brand Bacardi reigned supreme. Since the Castro revolution in the 1960s, the style is made in Puerto Rico and elsewhere under different names, one being Ron Rico.

White or silver describe clear-coloured and more neutral-flavoured rums. Gold or amber rums are deeper coloured, older, sweeter and more flavoursome. They are all at their best served as long cooling drinks with mixers such as cola, lemonade and fruit juices or as prime ingredients for cocktails.

Dark rums   These heavy, pungent, flavoursome rums have a pronounced personality and aroma. The finest are produced in Jamaica, Demerara (Guyana), Martinique, Haiti and Barbados. These are the style of rums that used to be issued to the Royal Navy to combat scurvy and act as a stimulant, anaesthetic and general purpose disinfectant. Stimulation is one thing, over stimulation is another and in 1740 Admiral Sir Edward Vernon commanded that the rum ration would henceforward be diluted with water. The Admiral was known throughout the Navy as 'Old Grog' because of the shabby coat he wore. It was made of grogram, a gum-stiffened, course fabric made from silk and wool. His 'three water rum' was very unpopular and was instantly dubbed grog   a name still used to describe a spirit served with an addition of water. The regular issue of rum to the Royal Navy was discontinued in 1970. Dark rums are more commonly referred to in naval terms as Nelson's blood. They are usually drunk neat or with added water (grog) or used as a base for cocktails, cups and punches. Some of these drinks may be extravagantly decorated with lime, coconut, pineapple, orange and cherries. Rum is also popular in the kitchen to flavour cakes, Babas, trifles, egg flips, and flambé dishes such as omelettes and bananas.

POPULAR BRANDS

The most popular brands of rum available are

Dark rums
Barbancourt
Myers
Captain Morgan
Lambs Navy
Appleton
Mount Gay
Woods
Hansen

White rums
Barilla
Bacardi
Ron Rico
Rhum St James
Dry Cane

TEQUILA

This Mexican spirit can be made anywhere in the state of Jalisco and in strictly defined areas of four other states.

Technically, true tequila is made from the Weber blue agave, a relative of the yucca and amaryllis. It must be bottled in the same region as the agave fields from which the spirit is distilled. The agave is not harvested before it is 12 years old and the sour juice after fermentation is known as pulque. This is distilled in pot stills and produces a raw, rough and fiery drink called mezcal. A second distillation refines the product which is then aged in cask or wax-lined vats for varying periods before being bottled for sale.

Tequila is available in the following styles:

- **White or Silver**: aged in wax-lined vats to retain its white colour.
- **Gold or Anejo**: aged in oak casks which impart colour and mellowness.

Tequila is accompanied by salt and a wedge of lime when drunk. First, you lick the salt, then swallow the drink quickly and immediately bite into the slice of lime.

Special brands include José Cuervo, Montezuma, Olmeca and Sauza.

OTHER SPIRITS

Aquavit, akvavit and schnapps

Aquavit is a spirit native to Scandinavian countries. It is distilled from grain or potatoes and flavoured with caraway, cumin, dill, fennel and bitter oranges. In Germany it is known as schnapps, in Denmark schnaps, and in Norway and Sweden snaps – the word means gasp or snatch. Aquavit is served well chilled in a small glass taken straight from the freezer and is drunk in one gulp which will certainly make you gasp as the spirit sends searchlights through your body. It is normally followed by a beer chaser to cool you down. Traditionally, aquavit or schnapps is served to accompany the Scandinavian smörgasbord as it cuts through the oiliness of the fish dishes on the presentation. Popular brands are Aalborg (Denmark), Linie (Norway), O.P. Anderson (Sweden) and Bommerlünder (Germany). In Germany, hardened drinkers always take schnapps before settling into a session of beer drinking. They claim it warms the stomach for the cold beer which follows.

Korn

Korn, or *kornbranntwein*, is another variety of schnapps, and is a low strength brandy-style spirit, but made from grain.

Doppelkorn

Doppelkorn is a much stronger version of korn, often flavoured with juniper berries and sold under such well-known labels as Fürst Bismarck and Doornkaat. It makes a great aperitif and goes very well with hors-d'oeuvre fish dishes such as smoked salmon, sardines, roll mops and *matjesfilet*.

Arrack

Arrack is a raw spirit, a distillate of fermented palm tree sap to which rice and molasses is sometimes added. It is often also made from dates, rice, grape juice, sugar cane and milk. The original Arabic for such concoctions and their varients meant 'sweat'. Not an inadequate description.

Tiquira

Tiquira is a rectified spirit which is distilled from tapioca roots. It is very popular in Brazil, its place of origin.

Eau-de-vie des fruits

The name means water of life made from fruit.

These are spirits which have been distilled from fermented fruit juice or made from an infusion of fruit and neutral spirit. When the result is white, as most of these spirits are, they are known collectively as *alcool blanc*.

The best examples come from France (especially Alsace), Germany (especially the Black Forest) and Eastern Europe.

Table 5.1   *Different sorts of eau-de-vie*

NAME	FRUIT	COUNTRY
Alisier	Rowanberry	France
Barack Palinka	Apricot	Hungary
Brombeergeist	Blackberry	Germany
Coing	Quince	France
Fraise	Strawberry	France
Himbeergeist	Raspberry	Germany
Houx	Holly Berry	France
Kirschwasser	Cherry	Germany
Mesclou	Greengage	France
Mirabelle	Yellow Plum	France
Mûre Sauvage	Wild Blackberry	France
Myrtille	Bilberry	France
Poire Williams	William Pear	France
Prunelle Sauvage	Wild Sloe	France
Quetsch	Blue Plum	France
Slivovitz	Blue Plum	Serbia and Bosnia
Tuica	Blue Plum	Romania

Absinthe and pastis

Absinthe was invented in the eighteenth century by Dr Ordinaire, a French physician and pharmacist who had taken up residence in Couvet, Switzerland. His drink had a base of brandy and flavourings of herbs, anise and wormwood (*Artemisia absinthium*). It was a very potent drink, being usually bottled for sale at 68% alcohol by volume. Drunk neat, the combination of strong alcohol and wormwood was lethal and had a devastating effect on mental health. So much so, it was banned in Switzerland in 1907, in the USA in 1912 and in France in 1915. Other countries followed suit. However, it is still made legally and comercially in Tarragona, Spain by the Pernod family who acquired the recipe in 1797.

Pastis is the generic name for aniseed or licorice-flavoured aperitifs made in the style of absinth but without the high alcohol content or the wormwood flavouring. Most of these drinks are colourless, but they go opalescent or milky when water is added through the precipitation of the volatile oils. In other words the water brings the oils out of solution into suspension. The amount of water added depends on personal preference but is usually between three and five parts of water to one of pastis. These drinks are particularly popular in countries bordering the Mediterranean. In France, they are known as Pastis de Marseilles, with Ricard and Pernod being the most favoured brands. Other countries make their own styles – Spain makes Ojen, Greece makes Ouzo and Mastikha, Turkey Raki and Italy Anesone. The non-alcoholic brands are Blancard and Pacific made by Pernod.

Poteen

Poteen, pronounced 'potcheen', (little pot) is a crude stab at making Irish whiskey without paying duty. It is made usually from potatoes along the Irish sea coast in mobile miniature pot stills. These are sometimes taken out onto the ocean to dissipate the odour emanating from the stills. Some of the stuff is really fine – white, smooth, wonderful – the only problem being that the drink is illegal. Poteen is the Irish equivalent of the American moonshine.

6

OTHER DRINKS

—

———

COCKTAILS AND MIXED DRINKS

Cocktails

The base of a cocktail is usually a spirit – gin, whisky, vodka, rum, brandy, tequila or calvados. The more common flavour contributors are liqueurs, fruit juices, syrups, flavoured fortified wines, eggs, cream, angostura, orange and peach bitters.

There are three basic styles of cocktail: those that require shaking, those that require stirring, and those that require layering or floating:

Shaken   These are cocktails which contain thick or cloudy ingredients such as eggs, cream, syrup and fruit juices.

Stirred   These contain ingredients which are mostly thin and clear.

Layered   The ingredients are poured over the back of a spoon into a glass to form layers according to the specific gravity of the ingredients. Pousse Café (Rainbow cocktail) is a good example of such a cocktail.

Floated   One of the ingredients is poured over the back of a spoon onto the top of the cocktail. For example, a layer of Galliano is floated on top in the making of a Harvey Wallbanger cocktail.

An introduction to and listing of cocktails and mixed drinks, their types and recipes is given at the end of the book (see page 280).

Types of cocktails and mixed drinks

Blended drinks	Using a liquidiser
Champagne cocktails	Such as 'Bucks Fizz' which has the addition of orange juice
Cobblers	Wine and spirit based, served with straws and decorated with fruit
Collins	Hot weather drinks, spirit-based, served with plenty of ice
Coolers	Almost identical to the Collins but usually containing the peel of the fruit cut into a spiral; spirit or wine based
Crustas	May be made with any spirit, the most popular being brandy; edge of glass decorated with powdered sugar; crushed ice placed in glass
Cups	Hot weather, wine-based drinks
Daisies	Made with any spirit; usually served in tankards or wine glasses filled with crushed ice
Egg noggs	Traditional Christmas drink; rum or brandy and milk based; served in tumblers
Fixes	Short drink made by pouring any spirit over crushed ice; decorated with fruit and served with short straws
Fizzes	Similar to a Collins; always shaken and then topped with soda; must be drunk immediately
Flips	Similar to egg noggs, containing egg yolk but never milk; spirit, wine or sherry based
Frappés	Served on crushed ice
Highball	'American', simple drink that is quickly prepared; spirit with 'mixer'
Juleps	'American', containing mint with claret, Madeira or bourbon whiskey base

Pick-me-ups	To aid digestion. Also known as *correctifs*
Pousse-café	Specific densities; layered
Smashes	Smaller version of a Julep
Sours	Always made with fresh juices to sharpen the flavour of the drink
Swizzles	Take their name from the stick used to stir the drink; 'swizzling' creates a frost on the outside of the glass
Toddies	Refreshers that may be served hot or cold; contain lemon, cinnamon, nutmeg

BITTERS

Once known as elixirs, bitters are spirits flavoured with herbs, bark roots and fruits resulting from both the infusion and distillation process. They have one thing in common – bitterness – and supposedly they all have stomachic qualities, which is why they can be drunk as an *apéritif*, *digestif* or *correctif*. The following list covers some well known bitters.

Amer Picon   Invented in 1835 by a distiller doing service with the French army in Algeria, it is pink-red in colour and flavoured with quinine, herbs and orange peel. It has a wine and brandy base and is usually served with ice and water.

Angostura   First made in 1825 by a Dr Siegert when he settled in Angostura (now Ciudad Bolivar), Venezuela, it was made to be sold as a medicine and used to stimulate Bolivar's troops in a hot and humid climate. Today it is made in Trinidad from a rum base and flavoured with gentian and vegetable spices. Known as the Worcestershire sauce of the cocktail bar business, it is an essential ingredient in the making of Pink Gin and Champagne Cocktails.

Byrrh   Pronounced beer, this style of bitters was first made in 1866 by a French shepherd of the Pyrenees, Simon Violet. It has a base of red wine and brandy and is flavoured with quinine and a variety of herbs.

Campari   One of the most favoured bitters and an excellent apéritif, it is usually served with ice and soda water. Stir the drink or the ingredients will stay separate. When combined with sweet red vermouth it forms the refreshing Americano cocktail. Campari, a rich red drink, was first made in Milan in 1867 by Gaspere Campari. Its secret recipe contains herbs and spirit and the result is oak aged.

Fernet Branca   This popular 'pick-me-up' was first evolved in Milan in 1845 by Fratelli Branca. It is now made, under licence, in other countries from ingredients which include ginger and Chinese rhubarb which are macerated in white wine and brandy. It has a reputation for dispersing hangovers, but in Italy it is drunk as an apéritif, either neat or with soda water.

Underberg   A German herb-flavoured bitter with a brandy base, the choice aromatic herbs come from 43 countries. It has been popular as an *apéritif* or *digestif* for well over a century and some regard it as an infallible cure for even the most desperate of hangovers. It is marketed in single nip portions which are meant to be swallowed in one gulp. For a more relaxing drink, soda water may be added.

There are many other well-known brands of bitters available. They are mostly considered as 'morning after the night before' drinks and are generally made more palatable by a minor addition of crème de cassis or Grenadine. Here are some examples.

- Abbots, Peychaud – USA
- Amora Montenegro, China Martini, Radis and Unicum – Italy
- Boonekamp and Welling – Holland

Orange bitters, peach bitters and Angostura bitters are essential ingredients for some cocktails and mixed drinks.

FORTIFIED WINES

Fortified wines such as sherry, port, Madeira, Marsala and Málaga are wines which have been strengthened by the addition of alcohol, usually a grape spirit. These are known within the EU as liqueur wines or *vins de liqueur*. Alcoholic strength may be between 15% and 22% by volume.

- Sherry (from Spain) 16–21%
- Port (from Portugal) 18–22%
- Madeira 18% – made on the Portuguese island of Madeira
- Marsala 18% – a dark, sweet wine from Sicily
- Málaga 18% – a sweet, dark, nutty aromatic wine from southern Spain

Other examples are Muscat and Muscatel, which are made from the Muscat grape. Most are sweet and raisin-like with a strong bouquet. One of the best known is Muscat de Beaumes-de-Venise, named after a village in the Côtes du Rhône where it is made. The wine is fortified with spirit before fermentation is complete so that some of the natural sugar remains in the wine. It is drunk young.

Sherry

Sherry has many imitators but real sherry comes only from Spain, more precisely from the demarcated area of Jerez de la Frontera in Andalucia, south-west Spain. Jerez (pronounced Hereth, from which the word sherry evolved) is the centre of production, along with Sanlúcar de Barrameda and Puerto de Santa Maria.

Grapes   The grapes used are the Listan Palomino, the Pedro Ximénez and the Moscatel. The Palomino accounts for 85% of the yield and provides the base wine from which all sherries are produced.

Soil   Three types of soil accommodate the vine. Albariza is white, chalky and the best. Barro is next best and is of heavy, mud clay. Arena is sandy soil which is gradually being used for crops other than the grape.

Climate   The climate is uneven and when the rains come torrenting down in late October and early November they have to be conserved. This is done by digging a square metre of soil down towards the roots of each vine. The excess soil is formed into a rim along the square or *serpia*. The rains lodge within the rim and later seep through to the roots to keep the vine healthy and productive in the torrid summer heat.

MAKING SHERRY

The grapes are gathered in September and laid out on esparato grass mats to dry. They are then taken to modern *bodegas* (cellars) where they are mechanically crushed. Fermentation takes place in oak casks or stainless steel vats. At first the fermentation is tumultuous – bubbling, seething, foaming as if a pot was boiling. Later it simmers and then slumbers gently to a completion. The new wine, with an alcoholic strength of 12.5%, is put into a group of small casks called *criaderas*. In this nursery or cradle, the wine's progress is monitored. By springtime a yeast-like fungus up to 10 mm (½ in) thick will form a crust on the surface of some wines. This development is

Copitas with and without flor

known as *flor* (flower) but technically it is a yeast strain called *Saccharomyces beticus*. *Flor* is a blessing; it seals the wine from harmful bacteria and prevents it from oxidising. It also contributes to the wine's individual taste and character. *Flor*, however, is unpredictable. In casks side by side, some will develop *flor*, others will not. Those that do are destined to become *Finos*, the joy of the sherry-maker. Those that do not will become *Olorosos*. As these are the two basic styles of sherry, flor has a profound effect on style. The finos are now fortified up to 15.5% alcohol by the addition of high-strength local brandy. The Olorosos are strengthened to 18% by volume. Both styles will be strengthened or fortified again before being sold. Bottled sherries vary in strength between 16 and 21% – the sweeter varieties are more heavily fortified. Once their final classification is agreed, all sherries are put into an appropriate solera, holding wines of similar character.

The solera system

The word solera comes from the Italian word *suelo* meaning sole (as in shoe) but translated to mean casks touching the ground. In reality the solera comprises of a group of casks placed one on top of the other, four or more scales high. The oldest wines are always in the bottom casks with the youngest, *criadera* wines, forming the top row. The solera system was introduced in 1800 and its purpose is to provide a consistent product. It is a system of blending and maturing. The wine required for sale is partially drawn off from the bottom casks – no more than one-third of the volume is extracted each year. This is replaced by a similar amount of wine taken from casks in the scale immediately above. And so it continues through the scales or tiers with the older wines being continually refreshed and replenished by those from above. The younger wines inevitably take on the characteristics of the old. Before being bottled the wine is tested for strength, quality and clarity. Sweetness and colour may be added to suit the style and the market. That is where the Pedro Ximénez and Moscatel grapes contribute. Their juice will be boiled down to one-fifth by volume and this dark, sticky syrup will be carefully added to the blend.

Styles of sherry

Fino   This is the ultimate sherry – pale, dry, light and delicate. Being completely natural it stands on its own merits. It has a wonderful bouquet. It is a producer's dream because it can virtually be converted into any style if a producer so desires. Serve chilled.

Manzanilla   This sherry is made from grapes grown by the sea at Sanlúcar de Barrameda. It is a type of Fino, light and dry with an attractive salty tang obtained from its maturation by the sea. As it ages, it loses its flor and becomes Manzanilla Pasada. Serve chilled.

Amontillado   Given its name because it resembled wines from the nearby region of Montilla, Amontillado is an extension of a fino but more robust in style. Very often it is slightly sweetened and coloured to suit international markets. Many have the prefix

The solera system

'dry' in the name. This market ploy is meant to appeal to those who like to order 'dry' but drink 'sweet'.

Oloroso   The name means fragrant, and like all sherries it is naturally dry. Sweetness has to be added and Oloroso is very sweet indeed. It is promoted under such names as Milk, Cream, Golden, Brown and Amoroso. The colour can be deep golden or brown. Pale cream sherries are nothing more than sweetened finos but are popular nevertheless. Serve at room temperature.

Palo Cortado   This wine is difficult to find outside Spain. It is a bit of a maverick, having an affinity with both an Amontillado in its smell and a dry Oloroso in taste. At its best it is a wonderful style of sherry. Serve chilled or at room temperature.

Almacenista   A term for a stockholder, warehouse or bodega owner who produces sherry to be sold to a bigger concern. These sherries are dry, old, unblended and usually of exceptional quality. Some are sold under the Almacenista label but mostly they are used to improve more mundane blends.

SHERRY SHIPPERS
The best known sherry shippers (producers) are:

- Croft
- Duff Gordon
- Garvey
- Gonzalez Byas
- Harveys
- La Riva
- Osborne
- Pedro Domecq
- Sandeman
- Williams & Humbert

Port

Port is one of the great fortified wines. Traditionally it has always been associated with England and, in fact, English wine shippers invented the drink. The name comes from Porto, the city we call Oporto, and the wine itself is made from grapes grown in the Upper Douro valley in northern Portugal. The region of production was demarcated in 1756.

Because of friction between England and France in the late seventeenth and eighteenth centuries, a special trade relationship developed between England and Portugal. This culminated in the Methuen Treaty of 1703 which allowed Portuguese wines to be imported into England at one-third less duty than for French wines. In return, English woollen goods were traded in Portugal for the first time. English and Scottish merchants soon flocked to Portugal – most went into textiles but some started dealing in wine. At the time the wines of the Douro were predominately red and sweetish to taste. There was one big snag – they travelled badly on their voyage to England. Very often a second fermentation would occur with most unpleasant results. When the wine was distributed, it tasted foul, especially to palates weaned on French wines. The solution for the British merchants was to add sufficient brandy to keep the wine healthy and stop it refermenting on its journey to England. Real success came when they started adding the brandy early in the fermenting process. This ensured that some of the natural sweetness was retained. The new strong, sweet, smooth wine was immediately popular.

Grapes   Many grape varieties may be used to make port. The most favoured for red ports are Bastardo, Donzelinho Tinto, Tinta Roriz, Tinta Francisca, Touriga Francesa, Tinta Cão and Mourisco. For white port, Gouveio, Malvasia Fina, Malvasia Rei, Donzelinho and Rabigato are best.

Soil   Most vineyards are sited on hillside terraces overlooking the Douro river. The soil is made up of outcrops of granite and schistose stone. Schist is brown and slatey in appearance and rich in minerals. It is very important in port production and is so tough that picks, crowbars and sometimes explosives are used to break it up for planting. Because of the steepness of some vineyards, mechanisation is not possible, which makes the cultivation of the vine extremely labour-intensive and expensive.

Climate   The climatic conditions in the Douro valley are extreme: winters are very cold and summers are very hot. Winter provides almost all the rainfall, most falling in December. When the rains come, the terraces are very important as the water lodges in them and the moisture is conserved to keep the vines healthy throughout the long, hot summer.

MAKING PORT

The grapes are taken to a centrifugal crusher which removes the required amount of grape stalks and crushes the grapes without breaking the pips. Stalks and pips contribute tannic acid, but only a certain amount of tannin is required for port. The juice and skins are pumped into a special vat called an autovinificator. The juice, or *must*, starts to ferment and build up pressure. With the help of a propelled *must-moving* machine, the *must* is forced up into an open reservoir at the top of the vat where escape valves, working on the principle of a coffee percolator, release the carbon dioxide. Once this happens, the *must* courses back down through the cap, or manta, of grape skins, extracting maximum colour and goodness. The escape valves close automatically on top and the procedure is repeated again and again until the saccharometer shows the desired sugar content reading. When the sugar level is at 6° Baumé, the *must* will have an alcoholic strength of between 6% and 8%. Then the *must* is pumped into a vat in the *adega* (barn-like cellar). At the same time, and through the same pipe, a clear flavourless style of high strength (78% alcohol) local or other Portuguese brandy, called Aguardente, enters the vat and stops further fermentation. The proportion allowed is 100 litres (22 gallons) of Aguardente to every 450 litres (99 gallons) of wine. The mixture is thoroughly roused and integrated. We now have port, a fortified wine with its own natural sweetness and an alcohol content of 16.5%.

The wine is left over winter to fall bright. As the wine rests, the sediment falls to the bottom of the vat. After about three months, and certainly before June, the wine is transported from the Douro to the shipper's lodges at Vila Nova de Gaia. Lodge is a translation of the Portuguese *loja* meaning warehouse. The lodges, cellars above ground, are located on the left bank of the Douro. The new port will be fortified up to 21% alcohol and given time to settle before being classified and transferred to wooden tuns or pipes (a pipe holds 523 litres (115 gallons)) to mature. A pipe of port is calculated to produce 660 bottles.

STYLES OF PORT

Apéritif white port   The driest port on the market, this is made from white grapes fermented until almost completely dry and then fortified. It is matured in wood and bottled for sale.

White port   This is processed as for other ports, but made from white grapes. It is pale gold in colour with a soft, rich, honeyed taste. White port is matured in wood before bottling.

Ruby port   This is a fresh young port which has changed colour from purple to deep red or ruby as it matures in cask. The colour change is due to air penetration and the racking process. It is a port of different blended years and is ready to drink after about four years. When port and lemon was the popular drink, this was the port used.

Tawny port   A blended port of different years and aged in cask until it becomes tawny or russet brown in colour. Classic tawny is aged from eight to 20 years in cask. Colheitas are old tawny ports from a single vintage. They are wonderfully smooth and delicate, often maturing for 20 to 40 years in cask. Cheap tawny ports are blends of ruby and white ports.

Crusted port   This is a blend of several vintages and bottled young. As it ages in bottle it forms a crust (deposit or lees), hence the name. Smooth and usually good value, it requires decanting.

Vintage character port   A blend of different years, matured in cask for about four years. It is of good quality but not vintage quality so the name is confusing and misleading. Once bottled it is ready to drink.

Single quinta port   This is a port made from one estate, usually, though not always, in a year when the general standard was not good enough to be declared a vintage. It may be treated as for vintage port.

Late bottled vintage (LBV)   This is a wine of a single good year, but it is kept twice as long maturing in cask than for vintage. It is bottled between 1st July of the fourth year and 30th June of the sixth year. Once bottled it is ready for drinking and does not require decanting.

Vintage port   The product of a single outstanding year when all the elements have combined to produce the ultimate in quality. Shippers declare a vintage on average once every four years. The wine only receives a short maturing period in cask and is bottled without fining between 1st July in the second year and 30th June of the third year. Then it will spend the rest of its life slowly maturing in bottle. A white splash is put on the top side of the horizontal bottle to indicate to the handler that the crust or sediment is forming on the opposite side. Otherwise mishandling will disturb and suspend the sediment, making it more difficult to decant. The wine is usually matured for well over 20 years. Corks, because of their long contact with alcohol, go brittle and crumbly and are usually replaced every 15 years or so.

CLASSIFICATION
Port that has spent most of its life maturing in cask – white, ruby, tawny – is classified as wood port. Port matured in glass for most of its life is classified as bottle port.

SERVING PORT
Port is traditionally served in clear or crystal dock glasses. If these are not available, a tulip glass or small Paris goblet will do instead. At special dinners, port in a decanter is passed clockwise around the table.

PORT WINE SHIPPERS
Port wine shippers include Cálem, Churchill, Cockburn, Croft, Delaforce, Dow, Ferreira, Fonseca, Graham, Quinta do Noval, Sandeman, Taylor and Warre.

Madeira

The Portuguese Island of Madeira produces a classic and unique style of fortified wine. The island lies out in the Atlantic some 560 km (348 miles) from Lisbon. It was discovered in 1418 by João Gonçalves Zarco who was then a Captain in the fleet of Henry the Navigator. The island was covered in trees and he named it Madeira, meaning 'wood or timber', before setting the lot on fire. The trees burned for seven long years, enriching the volcanic soil with potash, making it very suitable for the cultivation of the vine and other crops such as sugar cane. Helped by a sub-tropical climate, the vine flourished and by the end of the fifteenth century, the wines of Madeira were being exported to England and other European countries including France.

The grapes are grown near the coast on the steep terraced slopes, where irrigation is necessary to keep the vines healthy. In the more precarious locations the grapes are mainly trodden by foot and the juice is transported down the precipitous hillsides in goatskin containers to the central wineries at Funchal. There are four main vines in cultivation: Sercial, Verdelho, Bual (Portuguese Boal) and Malmsey, all producing white grapes. Each style of Madeira is based on one of these grapes. Another grape, the Tinta Negramole, is sometimes used to make a cheaper version of these famous brands. Most vines are trained on pergolas which gives the grapes some protection from the fierce sun rays. The grapes grown at sea level – Bual and Verdelho – are picked first, then the Malmsey and lastly the Sercial grapes which are cultivated on the higher, cooler terraces.

MAKING MADEIRA

Fermentation   The drier Madeiras – Sercial and Verdelho – are vinified as for sherry, that is to say, they are fermented to completion. The sweet Madeiras, Bual and Malmsey, are made in the fashion of port. Their fermentation is arrested by an addition of grape spirit (brandy) or by a rectified, flavourless spirit made from sugar cane (rum). This means that some of the grape sugar remains unfermented and a natural sweetness is preserved.

The estufa system   It was noticed in the sixteenth century that casks of Madeira when used as ballast on ships going to and from the East Indies had improved considerably in flavour on their return. It seems that crossing the equator twice, on the long sea journey going in and out the tropics, imparted an attractive 'cooked' flavour to the wine. When this practice was no longer commercially viable, a simulated version, known as *estufagem*, was introduced in 1800. An estufa is a heated chamber or room. It contains tanks which have a capacity of 40,000 litres (8,800 gallons). When filled with wine, the tanks are slowly heated, never increasing by more than 5° per day. As the temperature increases the wine is baked, over a month, up to a temperature of 45–50°C (113–122°F). It is held at this heat for a minimum of three months. Some shippers gauge their maximum temperature lower and keep the wine in the estufa longer – up to six months – as they feel lower and slower gives better results. Another month is then taken to turn the heat down in the same slow, gradual manner. A thermometer, with a governmental seal, is attached to each estufa. If the

An estufa in Madeira

estufa is heated beyond a certain permitted temperature the seal will break and the wine cannot be sold as Madeira. The wine is given a light fortification before going into the estufa and a more substantial one when it comes out. Madeira is eventually bottled at an alcoholic strength of 21%. Before that it will be matured through the solera system and rested before sale.

STYLES OF MADEIRA

Sercial   Comparatively dry with an amber brightness, Sercial has a nutty flavour and a crisp, piquant aftertaste. Served chilled as an apéritif, it really refreshes the palate.

Verdelho   Those who like Madeira love Verdelho. It is a beautiful, golden, versatile wine, medium sweet to taste but with a dry finish. It can be drunk as an apéritif, with soup or cake, or enjoyed supremely on its own.

Bual   Richer, stronger, deeper and sweeter than Verdelho, Bual has a slightly honeyed flavour that is never cloying. It is ideal as a dessert wine.

Malmsey   This is the most renowned of all Madeiras. The Duke of Clarence liked it so much he was drowned in a butt of it according to Shakespeare's play, *Richard III*. It is a deep-brown, luscious, fat, dessert wine. Although it is gloriously sweet it has a lovely, contrasting 'dry goodbye' on the palate.

Rainwater   A blend of the lighter Madeiras – Sercial and Verdelho – rainwater is popular in America and in some parts of England. It gets its name from the time when casks of Madeira were accidentally diluted with rainwater. The purchaser apparently liked the taste and ordered more.

Vintage Madeiras   These are very rare but solera-dated Madeiras are readily available. These are not vintage Madeiras. The date on the label indicates when the solera was first established.

SERVING MADEIRA
Madeira is served in a dock glass or in a copita or tulip glass.

MADEIRA SHIPPERS
Madeira shippers include Blandy, Cossart Gordon, Leacock, Lomelino, Rutherford and Miles.

Marsala

In the eighteenth century, war and trade embargoes curtailed the supply of French wine to Britain. John Woodhouse, a Liverpool merchant, recognised the potential of Marsala and he set up business in Sicily in 1773. When Nelson's fleet helped the Bourbon King of Naples escape in HMS *Vanguard* to Sicily, they were lavished with Marsala and soon the fortified wine became very popular, especially in Britain.

Marsala is made from local grapes: Catarratto, Grillo and Inzolia. The grapes are partly oxidised before being harvested. Then a sweet wine is made from the semi-dried grapes and mixed with local brandy. The combination is called *sifone*. To this, *vino cotto*, a cooked, caramelised reduction of unfermented grape juice, is added. Some Marsalas are matured in cask for only four months, but the better varieties are kept there for two to five years, often blended and matured by the solera system. There is no vintage Marsala. The style Marsala Vergine is dry and gets its name because it is a pure wine without the addition of *vino cotto* or *sifone*. Beware of varieties flavoured with chocolate, bananas, almonds, coffee and even egg yolks.

Quality Marsala is a delicious, deep golden-brown dessert wine – luscious, but with a bitter edge. It is also versatile in the kitchen, being used to flavour some veal dishes, and it is an essential ingredient for sweet dishes, such as zabaglione and tiramisu. It received DOC status (see page 209) in 1969.

Málaga

Once known in Elizabethan times as Malligo Sack and later as Mountain, this is Spain's most characteristic sweet liqueur wine. It is made principally from two grapes: Moscatel and Pedro Ximénez. According to location the grapes are picked from the middle of August to early September. Initially the grapes may be laid out in the sun to shrivel and concentrate the sugar content. For the drier Málagas the juice is extracted immediately after picking.

Classic Málaga is made by allowing the grapes to self press and to release their juices by the pressure of their own weight. This free-run juice, known as *Lagrimas* (tears), is the most prized and after processing is sold as Málaga Lagrima, a wine of great finesse. The juice is fermented in large oak or resin-lined cement vats and then matured and blended through the solera system. Although 'typical' Málaga is sweet (*dolce*), other styles are indicated as dry (*seco*) and medium sweet (*semi-dolce*).

AROMATISED WINES

Vermouth

Vermouth is an aromatised wine which has been fortified. The name originated in Germany where, in the sixteenth century, it was common practice to flavour some local wines with wormwood. These concoctions were used medicinally in the belief that the combination of wormwood and wine had therapeutic and digestive properties. The Italians and French saw other possibilities for the drink and the production of vermouth settled in Turin and Marseilles. In 1786 Benedetto Carpano of Turin was the first to offer vermouth for sale as a social drink. The French made a much drier product and opened elaborations in Marseilles and Chambéry. At that time there was a definite demarcation of styles. Italian vermouth was sweet and red and the French version was dry and white. Today, both styles are made in both countries.

INGREDIENTS

There are up to 50 ingredients used. The recipe is secret and closely guarded but consists of flavouring agents, wine, sweetener and spirit.

Flavouring agents   The main flavour comes from the flowers of the wormwood shrub. Other flavours include spices, hyssop, coriander, cloves, camomile, quinine and juniper.

Wine   A placid, two- or three-year-old, high-strength wine is used. For Italian Vermouth the wine can come from any part of the country, but the French tend to rely on the wines of the Midi.

Sweetener   This is either sugar syrup or *mistelle* (grape juice muted with brandy).

Spirit   The spirit is usually neutral brandy.

MAKING VERMOUTH

The flavouring agents are steeped or infused in the spirit. The flavoured spirit is added to the sweetened wine. The liquid is fined to free it from any haze-forming substances. It is refrigerated so that any remaining tartrates crystallise and drop to the bottom of the vat. Finally, it is pasteurised to stabilise and sterilise the wine and to keep it healthy and bright. Vermouth gets a short resting period and ideally a short shelf-life as the wine is meant and made to be drunk young.

STYLES OF VERMOUTH

Dry vermouth   Often called French Vermouth or simply French, this has a base of dry white wine and is light yellow with green tinges in colour. Served with ice and lemon and sometimes with a splash of soda, it is also a prime ingredient for the famous Dry Martini cocktail. It is often used in the kitchen to flavour fish dishes.

Sweet vermouth or bianco   This is made from a dry white wine which is flavoured, fortified and sweetened with *mistelle*.

Rosé vermouth   This, again, has a white wine base. A little of the sweetener is added to the wine and it is flavoured and fortified and then coloured pink with the addition of caramel.

Red vermouth   Often called Italian Vermouth, Italian or simply It (as in 'Gin and It'), it is made from a white wine base which is well sweetened, flavoured and fortified. The reddish brown colour comes from a generous addition of caramel.

Chambéry   A light and very delicate vermouth made in the vicinity of the Savoie mountains, this is flavoured with Alpine herbs and is the only vermouth produced in France with an AOC (see page 160) status.

Chambéryzette   A vermouth flavoured with wild Alpine strawberries.

Punt e Mes   Made by Carpano in Turin, the name originated in 1876. A broker from the stock exchange came into Carpano's shop-cum-wine-bar and asked for his vemouth to have a point and a half of bitterness added. Apparently, some precious stocks had fallen by a point and a half on that particular day. The name stuck. The drink itself is an acquired taste. It is heavily flavoured with quinine and has very pronounced contrasts of bitterness and sweetness. It has the colour of iodine.

POPULAR BRANDS OF VERMOUTH

- **Dry**: Chambéry, Cinzano, Martini, Noilly Prat, Torella
- **Bitter-Sweet**: Punt e Mes
- **Sweet**: Cinzano Bianco, Cinzano Red, Martini Bianco, Martini Rosé, Martini Rosso and Noilly Prat Red

Other aromatised wines

DUBONNET
Made at Thuir in south-west France, Dubonnet was invented by Joseph Dubonnet, who created the drink in 1846 to be used as a tonic. Modern versions have a wine base flavoured with quinine and bitter herbs with additions of *mistelle* and spirit. This popular apéritif may be blonde (white) or rouge (red).

ST RAPHAËL
This bitter-sweet drink from France is flavoured with herbs and quinine. It may be red and sweet or white and less sweet, or there is also an extra dry style. St Raphaël is a type of Ratafia, the 'good will' drink formerly offered when a legal document or contract was agreed, signed and ratified.

LILLET
A great favourite in France, Lillet is made from white Bordeaux wine, herbs and fruit peel and fortified with Armagnac brandy.

SUZE
Suze is a bright yellow French apéritif flavoured with gentian and herbs. It is bitter in flavour with supposedly digestive properties.

PINEAU DES CHARENTES
This is an increasingly popular sweet apéritif from the Cognac area. Pineau is a heady mixture of Cognac and grape juice. It was first produced over 400 years ago – the result of a mistake when a wine farmer put grape juice into a cask containing Cognac. It may be white or rosé in colour. If white, the following grapes may be used: Ugni

Blanc, Colombard, Sémillon and Montils; if rosé, Cabernet Sauvignon, Cabernet Franc, Merlot and Malbec grapes are used. The grapes are lightly pressed and left in vats for a day to remove the extract from the skins. The grape juice is then removed and mixed with aged Cognac which has a minimum strength of 60%. The proportion of grape juice to Cognac is three to one. No additives are used. Both the grape juice and the Cognac have to be produced in the same vineyard, so every producer distils his own Cognac and all producers have to submit their Pineau before bottling to the tasting committee at the Maison du Pineau. Pineau is aged in oak casks for a minimum of one year – more usually two. After the ageing process, it should have an alcohol strength of between 16 and 22% and a residual sugar content of 125–40 g per litre.

It can be drunk neat or with ice and is also adaptable for mixing with orange juice, white wine or tonic water. It can be drunk during, before or after a meal. Floc de Gascogne is a similar fortified grape juice but made in the Armagnac region. The Champagne version is Ratafia and in the Jura they make Macvin, but they spice this drink with cinnamon and other ingredients.

NON-ALCOHOLIC DRINKS

Non-alcoholic drinks may be classified into six main groups:

1   Aerated waters
2   Natural spring waters and mineral waters
3   Squashes
4   Juices
5   Syrups
6   Cordials

Aerated waters

These are charged or aerated with carbonic gas. Artificial aerated waters are by far the most common. The charging with carbonic gas imparts the pleasant, effervescent characteristic of all these beverages. The flavourings found in different aerated waters are imparted from various essences.

Some examples of these aerated waters, often called 'minerals', are as follows:

- **Soda water**: colourless and tasteless
- **Tonic water**: colourless and quinine-flavoured
- **Dry ginger**: golden straw-coloured with a ginger flavour
- **Bitter lemon**: pale cloudy-coloured with a sharp lemon flavour

Other flavoured waters which come under this heading are fizzy lemonades, orange, ginger beer and cola.

Natural spring waters and mineral waters

There has been an enormous increase in the consumption of mineral water in recent years. Whether this is because people no longer trust the tap (due to the well-publicised deterioration in the quality of our water) or whether they are concerned about their diet and general state of health, or simply because they enjoy the taste of a favourite brand is hard to tell. However, mineral waters are now very much in vogue.

In Britain, sparkling waters account for about 65% of mineral water sales. Many traditional still water producers, like Malvern, have now launched a sparkling variety on the market and many firms, at present, produce both the still and sparkling varieties. The sparkle is either natural or induced – when natural this will be clear on the label.

The EU has divided water into two main types: mineral water and spring water. Mineral water has a mineral content (which is strictly controlled), while spring water has fewer regulations, apart from those concerning hygiene. Water can be either still, naturally sparkling or it can be carbonated during bottling by the addition of carbon dioxide.

Table 6.1   *Mineral waters*

NAME	TYPE	COUNTRY
Appollinaris	Naturally sparkling	Germany
Contrex	Still	France
Perrier	Naturally sparkling or in fruit flavours	France
Royal Farris	Naturally sparkling	Norway
San Pellegrino	Carbonated	Italy
Spa	Still, naturally sparkling or in fruit flavours	Belgium
Spa Monopole	Still or sparkling	Belgium
Vichy Celestines	Naturally sparkling	France
Vittel	Naturally sparkling	France
Volvic	Still	France

Bottle sizes for mineral and spring waters vary considerably from 1.5 litres (2.6 pints) down to 190 ml (⅓ pint). Some brand names sell in both plastic and glass bottles whilst other brands prefer either plastic or glass bottles, depending on the market and the size of container preferred by that market.

Table 6.2   *Spring waters*

NAME	TYPE	COUNTRY
Ashboure	Still or carbonated	England
Badoit	Slightly sparkling	France
Buxton	Still or carbonated	England
Evian	Still	France
Highland Spring	Still or carbonated	Scotland
Malvern	Still or carbonated	England
Ballygowan	Still or carbonated	Ireland

Squashes

Squashes may be served on their own, mixed with spirits or cocktails, or used as the base for such drinks as fruit cups. They are indispensable in the bar and an adequate stock should always be held. Examples are orange, lemon and grapefruit.

Juices

Juices are sold bottled or canned. The main types of juices held in stock in the bar are:

- orange juice
- pineapple juice
- grapefruit juice
- tomato juice

These are normally purchased in small bottles termed 'babies' which contain 113.6 ml (4 fl oz). They may also be obtained canned.

It is often necessary to keep a small stock of fresh fruit juices (e.g. orange, grapefruit and lemon), made from fresh fruits. They would be used for cocktails and for mixing with spirits.

Syrups

The main use of these concentrated, sweet fruit flavourings is as a base for cocktails, fruit cups or mixed with soda water as a long drink. The most common ones used are:

- grenadine (pomegranate)
- cassis (blackcurrant)
- citronelle (lemon)
- gomme (white sugar syrup)

- framboise (raspberry)
- cerise (cherry)
- orgeat (almond)

Syrups are also used as flavouring agents in cold milk drinks such as milk shakes.

Cordials

Cordials are either alcoholic or non-alcoholic. Lime juice cordial and blackcurrant cordial are the best known non-alcoholic ones. Alcoholic cordials are usually added to spirits, for example, rum and peppermint, or used in cocktail recipes. Examples of others are:

Aniseed (5% vol)   The aniseed flavouring comes from the seeds of the anise plant.

Cassis rubis (15% vol)   Alcoholic version of blackcurrant cordial.

Ginger wine (13.5% vol)   Made from raisins, cowslip, cinnamon, cloves, elderflower, oranges, lemons and ginger, matured in oak vats for three years. Usually added to spirits, e.g. Whisky Mac.

Grenadine (8% vol)   This is a red-coloured alcoholic version of the pomegranate syrup and is used in cocktail recipes and fruit cups.

Lovage (8% vol)   Flavoured with celery, herbs and spices.

Peppermint (green or white) (5% vol)   Mint is used to flavour these cordials. They can be drunk neat and are considered to be good for upset stomachs.

Shrub (6% vol)   Flavoured with a blend of herbs and spices.

LIQUEURS

Liqueurs are flavoured, sometimes sweetened, often coloured, spirits. They were first made as curative herbal drinks by alchemists in France and Italy. The name comes from the Latin *liquefacere* which means to dissolve or melt – this is the manner by which a number of liqueurs acquire their flavours. Some liqueurs are centuries old, many have monastic connections and in medieval times it was common practice for monks tending those suffering from colds and fevers to make their medicines from a base spirit and an infusion of herbs and spices. Some of the early liqueurs were also made to disguise poor quality spirits – sugar and other flavourings were added to cover a multitude of sins.

By the fifteenth century, liqueur-making had progressed into the public domain and specialist liqueur elaborations were in production throughout Italy and in some parts of France. By the sixteenth and seventeenth centuries, a myriad of attractive and palatable drinks were marketed under the names liqueurs, digestifs and cordials. The base spirit used was either brandy, whisky, rum, eau-de-vie or neutral spirit. The flavouring agents were divided into three categories:

- fruit
- seeds and plants
- herbs and spices

Within these main categories there is an endless permutation of ingredients and flavours. Some liqueurs are only lightly flavoured whilst others, like Chartreuse, have up to 135 different ingredients in their composition. The more popular flavours are almonds, angelica, aniseed, berries, apricots, bananas, bilberries, blackberries, caraway, cashews, cherries, chocolate, cinnamon, citrus fruit peel, cloves, coconut, coffee, coriander, cream, fennel, figs, flower petals, gentian roots, ginger, grapefruit, grapes, hazelnut, herbs, honey, juniper berries, kumquats, lavender, lemon, melon, mint, nutmeg, nuts, oatmeal, oranges, peaches, pears, peppermint, quinine, raspberries, sloes, strawberries, sugar syrup, tangerines, vanilla and the wormwood herb.

Making liqueurs

There are three basic methods used to extract flavour.

Infusion   Also known as steeping, soaking or maceration, the ingredients, usually soft fruits, are crushed and steeped in the base spirit, normally brandy, for six to nine months. The process can be speeded up if the brandy is heated but generally cold, slow maceration gives the best results. The spirit extracts aroma, colour and flavour from the fruit. It is kept in a maturing vat for another year then, after further filtering and perhaps colour adjustment, it is bottled for sale.

Percolation   This works on the principle of a coffee percolator. The apparatus has two levels; the base spirit is put into the bottom level and the flavouring agents – usually herbs, seeds, spices and plants – are placed in the top level. The hot or cold spirit is continually pumped upward to mingle and merge with the flavour agents, extracting aroma and flavour with each visit. This is repeated for weeks until all the flavours and essential oils have been extracted. The product will be filtered and rested in vats to mature for varying periods. It will be sweetened with sugar syrup or honey and perhaps artificially coloured with natural vegetable colouring matter before being bottled.

Distillation   The flavouring agents, often called botanicals – plants, seeds, roots, herbs – are soaked usually in brandy for up to 48 hours. Afterwards the mash, with a supplement of brandy, is put in a pot still. Heat is applied and the resultant flavoured distillate – always colourless – is sweetened and often artificially coloured.

Sometimes a method based on vaporisation is preferred. The spirit is heated and the alcoholic vapours rise to permeate through a basket of botanicals which is suspended in the upper half of the apparatus. The vapours become imbued with the flavours and are condensed into a colourless, highly, flavoured liquid. This is sweetened, filtered and usually artificially coloured.

Types of liqueur

There are thousands of liqueurs of every conceivable colour, aroma and taste on the market today. Here, in alphabetical order, are the most popular.

Abricotine   Made at Enghien les Bains near Paris, this is created from a maceration of brandy, apricots and apricot kernels.

Advocaat   Almost every household in the Netherlands makes their own style of advocaat. Essentially, the ingredients should include brandy, egg yolks, sugar and vanilla. The established commercial brands are made by the Dutch producers Bols, De Kuyper and Warninks. It usually has a low alcohol content of about 17%. It combines with lemonade to make the long drink known as Snowball.

Amaretto   Legend has it that this almond-flavoured liqueur was invented by a beautiful widow who in 1525 posed for the Italian painter Bernardino Luini. He used her as his model for the Madonna in his Fresco of the Nativity at Saronno. She thanked him for her immortality by making him a liqueur from her own recipe. She steeped fresh apricots and their kernels in local alcohol to create Amaretto di Saronno.

Anisette   A particularly good example of this aniseed-flavoured, colourless liqueur is produced by the famous French firm Marie Brizard.

Archers   A crisp, clean tasting combination of peaches and schnapps.

Atholl Brose   This Scottish speciality is a kind of liqueur but perhaps more of a porridge. It is made from fine oatmeal, whisky, honey and cream.

Bailey's Irish Cream   Launched in 1975 it is now one of the world's best selling liqueurs. Made from a combination of Irish whiskey, honey, cream and chocolate, it has a well balanced flavour and a relatively low alcohol content of 17%.

Bénédictine   This liquer was first created for medicinal purposes at the monastery at Fécamp in Normandy in 1510 by Dom Vincelli of the Bénédictine Order. Bénédictine was banned after the French Revolution and the recipe was lost – but not forever. It was rediscovered by Alexandre le Grand in 1863 who updated the recipe. Today Bénédictine is made from double-distilled brandy and 75 different herbs, including hyssop, angelica, balm, coriander, cloves, cinnamon, saffron and nutmeg. The initials DOM on the bottle is the Bénédictine motto '*Deo optimo maximo*', 'To God, most good, most great'. Many people prefer to drink it half and half with brandy. This combination is known as B and B.

Brontë   A Yorkshire liqueur named after the Brontë sisters, it is flavoured with oranges, herbs and spices and has a base of French brandy.

Chartreuse   The basic recipe was given to the Carthusian Order by Maracel d'Estrées in 1605. By 1764 it had been perfected by the monks in their monastery at Voiron near Grenoble in France. It is an extremely complicated recipe using up to 135 different ingredients with a base of brandy. During the French Revolution, the monks were banned from making the liqueur. Some monks moved to Tarragona in Spain and continued to make the liqueur there. In 1931 the French Government allowed the monks to resume making their liqueur in Grenoble. Two styles are made. Green, which is coloured with chlorophyll and is dry and powerful with an alcoholic strength of 55%, and yellow, which is honey-sweet, coloured with saffron and has a strength of 43%.

Cherry brandy   Cherry Heering and other notable brands, such as Rocher, Dolfi, De Kuyper and Garnier, are made by infusing cherries in brandy. It is sweetened with sugar syrup or glucose.

Coconut liqueurs   These have recently become very popular, especially Malibu which has a white rum base, Cocoribe, and the Brazilian star Batida de Coco.

Coffee liqueurs   These also sell well, especially Tia Maria made with five-year-old Jamaican rum and flavoured with Blue Mountain coffee. This is often served with cream floating on top. Other coffee-flavoured liqueurs are Kahlúa, originally from Mexico now also made in Denmark, and Bahia from Brazil.

Cointreau   Created by two confectioners, Edouard and Adolphe Cointreau in 1849, Cointreau is made in Angers, France, where it used to be known as Triple Sec (as did Curaçao). It was so widely imitated that the name was changed to the family name Cointreau. It is made from bitter West Indian orange peel, sweet Mediterranean oranges and white spirit.

Cordial Médoc   This is a real cocktail of drinks, being a blend of brandy, curaçao and claret with additional flavours of oranges, cherries and herbs. Americans sometime used the word cordial to describe a liqueur. The name comes from the Latin *cor*, 'of the heart', because cordials were once considered to be heart stimulants or revivers.

Crême liqueurs
Crême d'ananas: pineapple flavour
Crême de bananes: banana flavour
Crême de cacao: chocolate and vanilla flavour
Crême de cassis: blackurrant flavour
Crême de menthe: peppermint flavour
Crême de noyaux: almond flavour
Crême de vanille: flavour obtained from the finest Mexican vanilla beans
Crême de violette: flavour obtained from the essential oil of violets

Cuaranta Y Tres This is a golden-coloured liqueur from Cartagena in Spain. It is made from 43 different ingredients including the discernable flavours of bananas and vanilla.

Curaçao Made originally from bitter oranges grown in the island of Curaçao off the coast of Venezuela, it used to be known as Triple Sec (as did Cointreau), a curious name since the product is very sweet. Today it is made in many colours by many companies in many countries.

Danziger Goldwasser Originally made in Danzig, Poland, this is flavoured with caraway and herbs and contains also tiny specs of gold leaf. The combination was thought to speed recuperation and to aid digestion. A similar drink, but with silver flakes, is called Danziger Silberwasser.

Drambuie After his defeat at the Battle of Culloden in 1745, Bonnie Prince Charlie fled for his life to the Isle of Skye with the Mackinnon of Strathaird. Mackinnon managed to get the Prince onto a ship bound for France, and in gratitude the Prince gave Mackinnon his secret recipe for his own special drink, *an dram buidheach*, the drink that satisfies. Today it is still made by the Mackinnon family from aged malt whisky combined with a variety of herbs and heather honey.

Fior d'Alpi This liqueur is made from Italian Alpine flowers and herbs. It is pale yellow in colour and sold in tall, narrow bottles each sporting a sugar-encrusted twig reminiscent of a Christmas tree.

Forbidden Fruit An American liqueur made from an infusion of shaddock – a type of grapefruit – honey and oranges in brandy.

Frangelico This Italian liqueur is flavoured with hazel nuts and an infusion of berries and flowers.

Galliano Named after Major Guiseppe Galliano who, during the Italian-Abyssinian War 1895–6, held the fort of Edna Jesus for 44 days against overwhelming odds. Eventually he was ordered to surrender and as a tribute to his heroism, the liqueur bears his name and the fort appears on every label. This golden liqueur is made from over 30 herbs and a variety of berries, flowers and roots. It is sold in very tall, narrow-necked bottles and is especially associated with the cocktail Harvey Wallbanger. Harvey was a skilled surfer from California.

Glayva A liqueur made in Scotland from whisky, herbs, honey, oranges and spices.

Grand Marnier This was created in 1827 by the Lapostolle family in a small village located between Lyon and Grenoble. Today it is made partly in Cognac and partly in Paris from aged Cognac, aromatics, and the juice of wild Caribbean oranges. Although popular as a liqueur, it is also used in the kitchen as an important ingredient for such classical dishes as soufflé Grand Marnier, crêpes Suzette and canard à l'orange.

Irish Mist   Very similar to Drambuie, this is a little more spicy with a base of Irish whiskey.

Izarra   The name means 'star' and the liqueur comes from the Basque country of France. It is made from herbs grown in the Pyrenees which are distilled and blended with brandy. It has two styles: yellow with 43% alcohol and the more flavoursome green with 55% alcohol.

Jägermeister   This dark red herb liqueur from Germany has digestive and tonic attributes. It used to be the hunters' favourite tipple after a hard day in the field.

Kirsch   Made in Alsace and the Black Forest in southern Germany, where it is known as Kirschwasser. It is made from a distillation of cherries and their kernels and is water-white in appearance.

Kümmel   This originated in Eastern Europe but is now made elsewhere in Europe and as far afield as the USA. It has a neutral spirit base and is flavoured with caraway and cumin seed, which contribute to its undoubted digestive qualities.

Kumquat   Made from a small, oval-shaped citrus fruit of the same name, it is orange-flavoured and produced in Corfu, Greece.

Mandarine Napoléon   This liqueur was first made in Belgium in 1892. Fresh tangerine peels are steeped in Cognac and the mandarins' essential oils are distilled and mellowed to ensure a balanced tangerine flavour.

Maraschino   First made in Dalmatia (former Yugoslavia) in 1779, this is now made in Italy by firms such as Drioli, Dolfi, Luxardo and Stock. It is made from sour Marasca red cherries and their crushed kernels and also flavoured with almonds and sugar syrup.

Midori   Created by Suntory in 1978, this is made from the Japanese musk melon. It is green-coloured, sweet, sticky and almost crystalline, with melon and apple overtones. *Midori* is Japanese for green.

Parfait Amour   Perfect love is the name; aimed at romantics and coloured purple to infer passion. It is flavoured with spices, citrus fruits and violets.

Petite Liquorelle   Not strictly a liqueur, this is an effervescent blend of old Cognac and Champagne.

Sambuca   Another liqueur with romantic connotations, this is ideal for a tête-a-tête after dinner. It is flavoured with elderberry and liquorice. When poured into a glass, three – and only three – coffee beans are floated on top and the liqueur is set alight to extract flavour from the beans.

Southern Comfort   This popular American liqueur is flavoured with peaches and oranges from Georgia which have been macerated in American Whiskey.

Strega   Reputed to have been first made by witches who were disguised as beautiful maidens, the name actually means 'witch'. The recipe, which includes 70 different herbs and citrus fruits, is made at Benevento, Naples. Locals say that those who share this liqueur will forever remain good friends.

Van der Hum   A South African liqueur, pale yellow in colour, made from Cape brandy and flavoured with a type of tangerine called Naartjie and spiced with nutmeg and herbs. It was created when Dutch colonists of the Cape tried to recreate their homeland favourite Cointreau using local ingredients. Van der Hum, roughly translated from the Afrikaans, means 'what's its name'.

Vieille Cure   This herb liqueur has a Cognac and Armagnac brandy base. It was originally made as a medicine at the Abbaye de Cenon in the Gironde, Bordeaux.

TEA AND COFFEE

Traditionally the term 'beverages' on a menu referred to coffee, but it has become more common for it to encompass tea, tisanes, milk drinks such as hot chocolate, and other proprietary drinks such as Bovril and Horlicks.

Tea

Most of the tea in Britain comes from four main countries, each producing distinctive styles.

China   This is the oldest tea-growing country and is best known for its delicately perfumed teas, examples of which are Lapsang Souchong, Rose Pouchong, Orange Pekoe and Jasmine.

India   This country is the world's largest tea producer, the best known teas being Darjeeling and Assam.

Kenya   Kenya produces medium-flavoured teas.

Sri Lanka (Ceylon)   These teas have a delicate, light lemon flavour and are regarded as afternoon teas. They also lend themselves to being served iced.

Other teas include:

Earl Grey   This is a blend of Darjeeling and China tea and is flavoured with bergamot.

Tisanes   These are fruit-flavoured and herbal teas, examples of which include:

- **herbal teas**: camomile, peppermint, rosehip and mint
- **fruit flavoured teas**: cherry, lemon, blackcurrant and mandarin orange

Russian/lemon tea   This tea is generally made from Indian or Ceylon tea and served with slices of lemon, often in special tea glasses.

Iced tea   This is a strong tea which has been cooled and then chilled in the refrigerator. It is served with lemon and sugar is offered.

BUYING TEA

Tea may be purchased in a variety of forms. The caterer's exact requirements will be determined by a number of factors such as type of establishment and clientele, the occasion, method of service, storage facilities available and cost.

The different means of purchasing are:

Bulk (leaf)   This allows for the traditional method of serving.

Tea bags   Tea bags are heat sealed and contain either standard or speciality teas. These tea bags come in one cup, two cup, pot for one or bulk brew form. The bulk brew may be 1.1, 2.2 or 4.5 litres (2, 4 or 8 pints).

String and tag   This comes as a one cup tea bag with string attached and a tag that remains outside the cup or teapot for easy and quick identification of the tea by the customer.

Envelopes   This is again a string-and-tag style but in an envelope for hygienic handling. It is regarded as ideal for trays in a room service operation.

Coffee

Coffee beans are grown in many countries in the tropical and sub-tropical belt of South America, Africa and Asia. Brazil is the world's largest producer, with Columbia second.

The beans are roasted to varying degrees to bring out the coffee flavour, the most common degrees of roasting being:

- **Light or pale**: suitable for mild beans, this preserves their delicate aroma.
- **Medium**: this gives a stronger flavour and well-defined character.
- **Full**: popular in many Latin countries, this often produces a bitter taste.
- **High**: this accentuates much of the strong and bitter aspects of the coffee and can destroy much of the original flavour.

METHODS OF MAKING COFFEE AND GRINDS

Instant   This is real coffee which has been made and then dehydrated. It is reconstituted by adding boiling water.

Filter or drip   This uses a fine to medium grind coffee. This method involves pouring boiling water into a container which holds coffee inside a filter paper or mesh. The coffee then drips through to a lower container. This system may be used for a single cup of coffee or multiple cups. Machines are available and the method is widely used.

Jug   Using a medium to coarse grind, the ground coffee is placed into a jug and boiling water added. After a time the grains will float to the surface. If a spoon is drawn over the surface, the grains will sink to the bottom, but it is still advisable to use a strainer when serving.

Cafetière   Using a medium grind, this is similar to the jug method but is made in a custom-designed jug which has a plunger to act as a filter.

Vacuum infusion   Using a medium grind, this method is characterised by the double pot or glass bowl and filter which many people know by the trade name 'Cona' – the company who make the glass equipment.

Espresso   Using a fine grind, this uses a process of forcing steam through a fine filter containing coffee. It is usually very strong.

Cappuccino   Using a fine grind, this is espresso coffee to which milk heated by steam has been added. In the UK, powdered chocolate is often sprinkled on the top of the frothing milk just before serving, and in America, cinammon is added in the same way. In Italy, the home of the drink, neither 'extra' is tolerated.

Percolator   Using a medium grind, this is a method of making coffee where the ground beans are contained in a filter which stands in the pot. This method has become less popular because the process boils the coffee as it is being made.

Turkish/Egyptian   Using powdered coffee, this is made from dark roasted coffee in special copper pots. The pots are filled with water which is then boiled and sugar is added. The powdered coffee is then added to produce a very strong beverage. Vanilla pods are sometimes included as additional flavouring.

Iced coffee   This is made from conventionally produced coffee which has been allowed to cool, often with the addition of milk. It is then chilled in the refrigerator. Whipped cream is sometimes served on top.

Speciality coffees
These are coffees made in the conventional way to which spirits or liqueurs are added and then double cream floated on top. Sugar is necessary both for taste and to ensure that the cream will float. The main varieties of speciality coffee are given on pages 274–5.

7

WINE AND DRINKS LISTS

—

COMPILING A WINE AND DRINKS LIST

The wine and drinks lists of an establishment are primarily selling aids. The lists identify for the customer what is on offer, the price of each item and information on things such as the measures in which each item is to be sold.

Wine and drinks lists come in a variety of different styles, usually reflecting the type of establishment. For bars it is common for the basic drinks list to be displayed on a wall. However, even in bars separate lists may be found for cocktails, wines, liqueur coffees or other special promotions

In compiling a wine and drinks list for a particular establishment there are a number of factors to be taken into account. These may be brought together under three main headings:

- attractiveness
- legibility
- layout

Attractiveness

Points to consider include:

1 **Overall presentation and design**: is it in keeping with the style of the operation?

2   **Size of the list**: is it easy for the guest to handle and for him/her to locate what is required?

3   **Shape**: again, this should relate to the style of operation and may be traditional or original. Remember the shape relates to size and ease of handling as well as being linked to the style of presentation. Should the list be in book form or just have the minimum number of pages? Should it be a single or folded sheet?

4   **Colour scheme**: this is important and should perhaps relate in part to the menu as well as to the colour theme within the operation. Should the cover and pages of the list be the same colour or different? Should the list be colour-coded and this indicated in the contents as a guide to the customer?

5   **Illustrations**: should the wine list be illustrated? Should the pictures be of general interest or related to specific drinks, of wine regions or, perhaps, wine labels? How much of this is of use to the customer and staff? Are illustrations an aid and therefore beneficial to the customer? Perhaps most important of all, what is the cost factor involved? What budget is there to work within?

6   **Durability**: this is a key consideration. How long will the list last and remain presentable once put into use? Cost is an obvious factor which will determine the quality of paper or card used and whether it can be laminated. Lamination ensures a longer life of the list as it introduces the wipeability factor, but is, of course, expensive.

7   **Flexibility of design and format**: this allows for alteration of prices, changing vintages, use in other areas, and insertions such as bin ends for special promotions and the like.

Legibility

Depending on the style of operation, the list may be:

- handwritten on cards, posters, blackboards, glass;
- typed and duplicated either in-house or by suppliers;
- printed professionally, with thought being given to the type of print, spacing, clarity, headings, layout, accuracy etc.

Layout

The considerations here are:

1   Should informative maps and/or photos be included?

2   How easy is it for the customer to find his/her way around the list?

3   How will the drinks be ordered? There are no specific rules here and it is a matter of personal preference linked to the customer's needs.

4   What general information is required? For example, how much of the following information would you include about the wines?

- bin number
- name and origin of wine
- quality indication, e.g. AOC, QmP, etc
- shipper

- château/estate bottled
- descriptive comments as appropriate
- vintage if applicable
- price per ½ bottle/bottle/magnum/carafe
- % alcohol by volume

Which of the following information would you include about other drinks?

- brand name
- style (e.g. sweet, dry etc.)
- description, e.g. cocktails
- alcohol content
- still or not

5   Does the list take into account legal requirements (see chapter 1, page 9)?

6   Is the wine taste guide to be used?

The Wine Taste Guide was developed by the Wine Development Board and is accepted as standard within the industry. It provides a quick and easy method of telling at a glance whether a white wine is bone dry or lusciously sweet. Very dry wines like the Chablis are graded as 1, Moscatel is at the other extreme and is graded 9. The Wine Taste Guide also clarifies the degrees of sweetness in between.

Red and white wine guide (courtesy of Grierson's Wine Merchants)

Dry to Sweet White Wine Guide

Number 1 signifies very dry white wines. Number 9 indicates maximum sweetness. The numbers in between span the remaining dryness-to-sweetness spectrum.

 Muscadet
Champagne
Chablis
Dry White
Bordeaux
Manzanilla Sherry
Tavel Rosé

 Soave
White Burgundy
Fino Sherry
Sercial Madeira
Rioja
Penedes

Brut Sparkling Wine
Gewürztraminer d'Alsace
Dry Amontillado Sherry
Medium Dry Montilla
Dry White Vermouth
Anjou Rosé
Medium Dry English

 Vinho Verde
Mosel Kabinett
Rhein Kabinett
Laski and
Hungarian Olasz
Riesling,
Medium Dry
Portuguese Rosé

 Vouvray
Demi-Sec
Liebfraumilch
Medium
British Sherry
Verdelho
Madeira

 Demi-Sec
Champagne
Spanish
Medium
Sherry
All Golden
Sherry types

 Asti Spumante
Rhein Auslesen
Premières Côtes
de Bordeaux
Tokay Aszu
Pale Cream
Sherry
Montilla Cream
Bual Madeira
Rosso, Rosé and
Bianco
Vermouths

 Austrian
Beerenauslesen
Spanish Sweet
Wine
Sauternes
Barsac
Cream and
Rich Cream
Sherry types

 Malmsey
Maderia
Muscat de
Beaumes
de Venise
Marsala

The Red Wine Guide

The five categories marked A to E identify styles of red wines in terms of light styles to big, full-bodied heavy wines.

Bardolino
Beaujolais
Valdepeñas

Côtes du Roussillon
Merlot
Navarra
Pinot Noir from all countries
Red Burgundy
Valencia
Valpolicella

Bordeaux Rouge/Claret
Côtes du Rhône
Rioja

Cabernet Sauvignon from Australia
Bulgaria, California, Chile, New Zealand,
Romania and South Africa
Châteauneuf du Pape
Chianti
Dão
Hungarian Red

Barolo
Crozes Hermitage
Cyprus Red
Greek Red
Shiraz from Australia and South Africa

The Red Wine Taste Guide works in a similar way but is based on fullness rather than sweetness or dryness. The biggest, richest reds rate at E while, at the other end of the scale, light summery reds are classified as A.

THE WINE LIST

The function of the wine list is similar to that of a menu, it is a selling aid. Careful thought must therefore be given to its planning, design, layout, colour and overall appearance for presentation purposes.

Briefly, the contents are traditionally listed in the order in which are likely to be consumed, namely:

- cocktails
- apéritifs
- cups
- wines
- liqueurs
- spirits
- beers, minerals and squashes
- cigars

Many lists also now include low calorie, low alcohol beverages, and those suitable for diabetics.

Wines are often listed area by area, with the white wines of one region first, followed by the red wines of that region. A more modern trend is to list all the white wines available area by area, followed by the red wines arranged in a similar way. This type of layout is often more useful to the customer. Sparkling wines, and therefore the champagnes, are often listed before all other wines available (see page 118–9).

Some establishments, in order to project the wine list image, may illustrate labels to present a more colourful and attractive list.

Wines featured on a wine list should complement the menu both in style and price and should encourage the more adventurous to experiment with wines that may not be readily available in other commercial outlets. Customers rarely purchase wine to accompany a meal when the price of the wine exceeds the price of the meal itself. Fair mark-ups, which become proportionately smaller as the wine gets more expensive, will encourage people to experiment and buy good wine.

A wine list should also take into account those who dine alone or the couple with different preferences – one who likes white wine and the other red. Good wine, other than house wine, should be available by the glass and there should be some choice in half bottles. People on diets, organic wine lovers, those with illnesses such as diabetes, the ever increasing number who strive to lead healthy lifestyles and, of course, car drivers should all be catered for: low or de-alcoholised wines are a must nowadays on every drinks list.

A wine list does not have to be extensive to be good, but it should show a well-balanced selection of wines, not only in terms of the country of origin but also of the grape used. Above all, it should be informative, giving the bin number, the name of the wine (sometimes with descriptive comments if appropriate), the vintage year if applicable, the producer's, bottler's or shipper's name, whether the wine is bottled at source (estate or château bottled), and the price per magnum, bottle or half bottle.

A wine list is a signpost for profitable sales. It makes a statement about the establishment, presenting the character and image the owners want to project.

TYPES OF WINE AND DRINKS LISTS

Bar and cocktail lists

These may range from a basic standard list offering the common everyday apéritifs, a selection of spirits with mixers, beers and soft drinks together with a limited range of cocktails, to a very comprehensive list offering a wide choice in all areas. The actual format and content would be determined by the style of operation and clientele you wish to attract. Dependent on this, the emphasis may be in certain areas such as:

- cocktails: traditional or trendy
- malt whiskies
- beers
- New World wines
- non-alcoholic drinks.

Popular cocktails and their recipes may be found on pages 281–291.

Champagne and sparkling wine

MOET ET CHANDON BRUT IMPERIAL NV 12%
Crisp, dry, bouquet, full and round palate.

BLANQUETTE DE LIMOUX CHRISTOPHERS CUVÉE 12%
Light, clean, dry and well balanced. Méthode Traditionnelle.

ANGAS BRUT ROSÉ, AUSTRALIA (BOTTLE FERMENTED) 11.5%
Full bodied creamy dry wine showing some class.

White wine

SPAIN: TORRES VINA SOL, PENEDÈS 1992 11%
A fresh, lively white made from Parellada grapes grown at high altitude.

PORTUGAL: VINHO VERDE, GAZELA 10%
Spritzy exciting and refreshing, packed with young fruit.

ALSACE: GEWÜRZTRAMINER, DOMAINE JUX 1993 12%
A strong rich full-flavoured wine, packed with spicy fruit.

LOIRE: DOMAINE DE LA JOUSSELINIERE 1993 12%
Muscadet de Sevre et Maine Sur Lie Refreshingly dry and light.

BORDEAUX: CHEVALIER VEDRINES SAUVIGNON BLANC 1993 12%
Crisp dry white with hints of gooseberries.

BURGUNDY: CHABLIS, PAUL DELOUX 1993 12%
Bone dry with flinty fruit and a long finish.

GERMANY: PIESPORTER MICHELSBERG QBA 1993 12%, SCHOENENBERG
Light, refreshing and fruity.

NIERSTEINER GUTES DOMTHAL 1993 9% SCHOENENBERG
A soft well balanced hock from the Rheinhessen

ITALY: PINOT GRIGIO ARMENTI COLLAVINI 1993 12%
A wonderfully fresh wine, dry with a lemony spritz.

AUSTRALIA: YALUMBA OXFORD LANDING CHARDONNAY 1994 12%
A full flavoured but fresh white wine, matured in oak barrels.

ENGLAND: LAMBERHURST SOVEREIGN, KENT 12%
Soft and light with scented nose.

NEW ZEALAND: DELEGAT'S SAUVIGNON, HAWKES BAY 1994 11%
A fragrant fruity nose with a crisp, dry finish.

CALIFORNIA: DRY CREEK FUMÉ BLANC, SONOMA 1992 12%
A fresh, fruity wine with intense honey & oak character.

Rosé wine

LOIRE: ANJOU ROSÉ, LA FONTAINE 1993 11%
A smooth fruity medium sweet rosé.

Red wine

FRANCE: CABERNET SAUVIGNON, VIN DE PAYS D'OC 1991/92 12%
Earthy yet fruity wine, firm structure and pleasant finish.

BORDEAUX: CHRISTOPHERS CLARET 11.5%
Full, firm and smooth

Sample wine list (courtesy of Thames Valley University)

BORDEAUX: CHATEAU DU SEUIL, GRAVES 1990 12.5%
Very classy, elegant and rounded with intensely ripe fruit.

BURGUNDY: CHATEAU DES CORREAUX BEAUJOLAIS VILLAGES 1992 12.5%
Deliciously ripe and soft, reminiscent of crushed raspberries.

HAUTES CÔTES DE BEAUNE, LES CAVES DES HAUTES CÔTES 1991 12%
A fruity wine made in the soft Beaune style.

RHONE: CÔTES DU RHÔNE, LES RIGAUDES 1992 13%
A strong full wine with generous flavour.

SPAIN: GRAN FEUDO CRIANZA, CHIVITE 1991 12.5%
From Navarra, near Rioja, comes this typical warm oaky wine.

ITALY: REMOLE CHIANTI RUFINA, FRESCOBALDI 1992 12%
Light and mellow from a famous producer.

BULGARIA: STAMBOLOVO MERLOT 1987 12%
A rich smooth beautifully mellow wine.

AUSTRALIA: OXFORD LANDING CABERNET SHIRAZ 1992 12%
Rich bold and full bodied.

SOUTH AFRICA: DROSTY-HOF PINOTAGE 1989/90 12%
Dry, well structured wine with a long finish.

CHILE: COUSINO MACUL CABERNET SAUVIGNON 1988 12%, ANTIGUAS RESERVAS
A fine full hearty South American wine.

Dessert wine

MUSCAT DE RIVESALTES ARNAUD DE VILLENEUVE 15%
Sweet dessert wine. Delicious raisiny flavour

House wine

ARNAUD DE VILLENEUVE BLANC 1993, COTES DU ROUSSILLON 12.5%
A fresh and fruity dry wine. Easy drinking.

ARNAUD DE VILLENEUVE ROUGE 1992, COTES DU ROUSSILLON 12.5%
Soft and well balanced, with a generous flavour.

Connoisseur's selection

MEURSAULT, REINE PEDAUQUE 1992 12.5%
A classic example of a ripe Chardonnay, elegant and stylish with a dry oaky edge.

SANCERRE, CHATEAU DE SANCERRE 1991 12%
A full bodied dry white wine with an aroma of gooseberries.

CHATEAU DESTIEUX, GRAND CRU, ST. EMILION 1986 12%
A smooth, rich wine with a predominant Merlot flavour.

FETZER BARREL SELECT CABERNET SAUVIGNON CALIFORNIA 1989 13%
Great depth of flavour, combining oak and blackcurrant fruit.

VOSNE ROMANEE 1985, THOMAS BASSOT 12%
A beautifully mature classic Pinot Noir wine.

CHATEAUNEUF DU PAPE CHATEAU DE BEAUCASTEL 1986 13%
A wonderfully deep coloured, deliciously fruity red wine.

SPAIN; DON JACOBO RESERVA, BODEGAS CORRAL 1985 12%
Smooth and mellow with traditional oak flavour.

Restaurant wine lists

These may take one of the following formats:

1   A full and very comprehensive list of wines from all countries, but emphasis on the classic areas such as Bordeaux/Burgundy plus a fine wine/prestige selection.

2   A middle-of-the-road, traditional selection, including some French, German and Italian wines together with some New World wines.

3   A small selection for well-known or branded wines; a prestige list.

4   Predominantly wines of one specific country.

After meal drinks lists (digestifs)

After meal drinks are often combined with the wine list, although they are occasionally presented as a separate liqueur list. The list should offer a full range of liqueurs, together with possibly a specialist range of brandies and/or a specialist range of malt whiskies. Vintage and LBV port may also be offered here. A range of speciality liqueur/spirit coffees might also be included.

Banqueting wine lists

The length of the banqueting wine list varies according to size and style of operation. In most instances there is a selection of popular wine names/styles on offer. There would be a range of prices from house wines to some fine wines to suit all customer preferences. In some instances the banqueting wine list is the same as the restaurant wine list.

Room service drinks list

There may be a mini-bar or choice from a standard bar list or they may offer a limited range of wines. The price range varies according to establishment.

PRICING

Essentially there are three basic methods of pricing used in the hotel and catering industry. These are:

Cost Plus   This method determines the selling price of an item by adding a specific percentage of the cost price to the cost of the item in order to achieve a predetermined percentage gross profit. (Gross profit = sales, less the cost of sales.) In practice, percentages are varied to achieve standard pricing for similar groups of products, for example all spirits or all minerals.

Rate of return   This method determines the total costs of the business for a given business level and then determines the percentage of the cost price required to be added to the cost price in order to ensure that the business will be viable.

Market orientated   This method determines selling prices by considering both what the customer is likely to pay as well as what others in similar local operations are charging.

Generally a combination of methods is used.

For drinks other than wine, it is usual to find that similar products will have the same prices. This makes it easier for staff to remember prices and avoids each item having a different price. In addition, the percentage that is added will vary in order to achieve a balance of selling prices between various items. This is to ensure that the selling prices are in line with what the customer is likely to expect. Thus lower cost items, such as minerals, tend to have a higher gross profit percentage whereas higher cost items, such as spirits, have a lower gross profit percentage.

As well as the simple cost plus approach, there are various formula approaches for determining the selling prices of wines. Double the cost plus, is one method. This takes the cost price of the wine, doubles it and then adds a fixed amount. The difficulty with both the cost plus and formula approaches is that the more expensive wines will tend to have a disproportionately higher selling price on the wine list, which does not encourage sales.

Another method for pricing wines is based on the recognition that a sale of a bottle of wine produces a potential profit irrespective of the cost price of the wine. Prices in this method are determined by adding a fixed amount to the cost price. In this case the higher priced wines look more attractive to the customer and this encourages sales.

In all cases, though, the most profitable wine is the one which produces the highest gross profit cash contribution. This is determined by multiplying the number sold by the individual gross profit cash contribution that it provides.

8

PURCHASING, STORAGE AND CONTROL

—

PURCHASING

The objective of good purchasing is to achieve the right amount of stock, at the right quality, at the right level and at the right price.

Unlike food, beverages generally have longer shelf-lives, with the exception of cask and keg beers. However, all items do have a limited life although in the case of good wines this could be several decades. Although longer shelf-lives will mean that greater stocks can be held, the cost of storage both in fuel and space costs has to be taken into account. In addition the holding of stock ties up capital that could be used for other purposes.

The costs of purchasing

There are three areas of cost associated with purchasing:

1 **Costs of acquisition**
   - Preliminary costs, such as preparation of specifications, supplier selection, negotiation.
   - Placement costs, such as order preparation, stationery, postage, telephone, etc.
   - Post placement costs, such as progressing, receipt of goods, inspection of goods, payment of invoices, and other clerical controls.

2 **Holding costs**
   - Financial costs, such as interest on capital tied up in inventory cost of insurance, losses through deterioration, pilferage.
   - Storage costs, such as space, handling and inspection, stores lighting, heating and refrigeration.
   - Clerical costs, such as stores records and documentation.

3 **Cost of stockouts**
   - Cost of alternatives, such as buying at enhanced prices, using more expensive substitutes.

Determining stock levels

Stock levels may be determined by using past sales data. A formula which can also be useful is:

$$M = W (T + L) + S$$

where

M = Maximum stock
W = Average usage rate
T = Review period
L = Lead time
S = Safety stock (buffer or minimum)

An example of using this formula could be:

W = 24 bottles per week
T = 4 weeks
L = 1 week
S = 1 week's usage, i.e. 24 bottles
M = 24 (4 + 1) + 24 = 144 bottles

Minimum stock (buffer or safety stock) may be calculated as follows:

$$L \times W = 1 \times 24 = 24 \text{ bottles}$$

ROL (Re-order level) may be calculated as follows:

$$(W \times L) + S = (24 \times 1) + 24 = 48 \text{ bottles}$$

Purchasing sources

For tied-house premises, where the establishment is linked to a particular brewer, the sources for purchasing beverages are determined by the brewer. It is common for brewers to own or have links or associations with specific suppliers of spirits, minerals and other drinks. In these cases the opportunities for selective purchasing are limited.

For free-house premises the establishment can determine who they wish to buy from. Some considerations are:

Using one main supplier   This has the advantage of having a simple, single source of supply. Deliveries will be regular and will cover all items. There are also additional benefits from the support that can be had from suppliers in producing wine and drink lists and menu covers, and from discounts that are available depending on amounts purchased. On the other hand, the range of beverages may be limited in some way thus reducing the potential range of beverages on offer in a particular establishment. In addition, using one main supplier can make the establishment overly dependent on that source.

Using a variety of suppliers   This has the advantage for the establishment of being able to buy a wider range of beverages and reduces dependency on any one particular source. It also means that advantage can be taken of special promotions or discounts at particular times and from differing sources. Potential disadvantages are that this approach increases the number of separate deliveries, increases paperwork and can lead to inconsistencies in the range of beverages on offer.

Generally establishments use a combination of the two approaches: mainly using one main supplier, but with additional purchases coming from other sources.

The buying of wines needs careful consideration depending on the particular policy of the establishment. Buying for laying down and service at some future time can build up a good stock of fine wines which can, when sold, produce good profits. However, the downside is the storage and initial capital costs together with the risks that could be associated with this approach.

STORAGE AND EQUIPMENT

Beer storage and equipment

Casks   Casks in use (on ullage) are supported on stillions or thrawls. A stillion, or stillaging, is the wooden rack or brick platform on which the casks are placed for service. Keg pressurised beer containers are usually situated together in one area of the cellar along with the necessary carbon dioxide gas cylinders strapped or bracketed to the wall. Casks will be properly settled if they are tapped 24 hours before they are needed.

Beer taps   Used for the dispensing of cask-conditioned beers direct from the cask, these are usually made from brass. They must be brushed through and sterilised immediately after use and stored.

In-line coolers   These may be provided for the cooling of keg beer. The beer pipes go through the coolers, which are adjusted to the correct temperature for each beer.

Beer engines   These are pumps which are operated by hand using a handle in the bar. They must be cleaned weekly when the pipe-lines are cleaned and should be stripped down and inspected on a regular basis. Some engines work by carbon dioxide top pressure, which applies a force downwards onto the beer in the cask and drives a measured amount up into the bar when a button is pressed.

Electrically impelled pumps   These are situated in the cellar and dispense an accurate amount of beer into the glass in the bar when the bartender presses the button.

Pipe-cleaning bottles   These are used to clean pressurised container pipe-lines. With the gas turned off, the assembly head should be taken from the keg and locked onto the nine-litre (two-gallon) cleaning bottle containing cleaning fluid. The carbon dioxide should be turned on and the pipes filled with the fluid. After about one hour the process should be repeated using clean water. Automatic beer-line cleaning equipment is also now available.

Dipsticks   These are used to determine how much beer is left in the cask. The dipstick is placed into the cask through the shive; when withdrawn it indicates how much beer remains unsold.

Scotches   These are triangular blocks of wood which are used to prevent a beer cask rolling from side to side.

Shives   These are round pieces of hard wood which are placed in the bung-hole of the beer cask just before it is sent out from the brewery after filling. The shive has a small hole in the centre which does not go completely through the wood. When the cask is vented, the hole is completed by punching out the thin centre section with a wooden mallet. The hole will permit gas to escape from the cask.

Spiles   These are used to bung the hole to allow or prevent the carbon dioxide gas from escaping. They are small pegs made of two different types of wood. The hardwood spile, when placed in the shive, does not allow any gas to escape. Instead, pressure builds up in the cask and the beer regains its condition (frothy head). The softer spile is made from bamboo and, when placed in the shive, it allows the gas to escape and so prevents the beer from being too gassy and difficult to serve.

Filters   These are used in the cellar to return sound beer to the cask. This could be beer which has been drawn out of the pipes before pipe cleaning started. Filters should be kept clean and used with clean filter papers. To filter beer is not in itself illegal, but to return to cask any overspill slops is an offence. Also to mix or dilute beer in the cask, or to adulterate any produce for sale, is also an offence.

Good cellar management

The following factors and practices contribute to good cellar management

- The cellar should be clean and well ventilated.
- Even temperatures of 13–15°C (55–58°F) should be maintained; strong draughts and wide ranges of temperatures should be avoided.
- On delivery all casks should be placed immediately upon the stillions; casks remaining on the floor should have the bung uppermost to withstand the pressure better.
- Spiling should take place to reduce any excess pressure in the cask.
- Tappings should be carried out 24 hours before a cask is required.
- Pipes and engines should be cleaned at regular intervals.
- Beer left in pipes after closing time should be drawn off.
- Returned beer should be filtered back into the cask from which it came.
- Care should be taken that the cellar is not overstocked.
- All spiles removed during service should be replaced after closing time.
- All cellar equipment should be kept scrupulously clean.
- Any ullage should be returned to the brewery as soon as possible.
- All beer-lines should be cleaned weekly with a diluted pipe-cleaning fluid and the cellar floor washed down weekly with a weak solution of chloride of lime (mild bleach).

Wine storage

It is important to locate wine away from excessive heat: hot water pipes, a heating plant or any hot unit such as a freezer! Heat does far more damage to wine than the cold. Attractive humidity and temperature controlled cabinets are available, but they are expensive.

Ideally, wine should be stored in an underground cellar which has a northerly aspect and is free from vibrations, excessive dampness, draughts and unwanted odours. The cellar should be absolutely clean, well ventilated, with only subdued lighting and a constant cool temperature of 12.5°C (55°F) to help the wine develop gradually. Higher temperatures bring wines to maturity more quickly, but this is not preferable.

Table wines should be stored on their sides in bins so that the wine remains in contact with the cork. This keeps the cork expanded and prevents air from entering the wine – a disaster which would quickly turn wine to vinegar. White, sparkling and rosé wines are kept in the coolest part of the cellar and in bins nearest the ground (because warm air rises). Red wines are best stored in the upper bins. Commercial establishments usually have special refrigerators or cooling cabinets for keeping their sparkling, white and rosé wines at serving temperature. These may be stationed in the dispense bar – a bar located between the cellar and the restaurant – to facilitate prompt service.

Storage of other drinks

Spirits, liqueurs, beers, squashes, juices and mineral waters are stored upright in their containers, as are fortified wines. The exceptions are port-style wines which are destined for laying down.

Re-ordering should be carried out on one set day every week after checking the bottle stocks of beers, wines, minerals, etc. Strict rotation of stock must be exercised, with new crates placed at the rear and old stock pulled to the front for first issue.

STOCK CONTROL

Administration

GOODS RECEIVED BOOK

All deliveries should be recorded in full detail in the goods received book. Each delivery entry should show basically, the following:

- name and address of supplier;
- delivery note/invoice number;
- order number;
- list of items delivered;
- item price;
- quantity;
- unit;
- total price;
- date of delivery;
- discounts if applicable.

The amount and deposit cost of all containers such as kegs, casks and the number of carbon dioxide cylinders delivered can also be recorded in this book or in a separate returnable containers book.

ULLAGE, ALLOWANCE, OFF-SALES BOOK

Each sales point should have a suitable book for recording the amount of beer wasted in cleaning the pipes, broken bottles, measures spilt, or anything that needs a credit.

The number of bottles, whether beer or spirits, at off-sales prices and the difference in price must be recorded in the same book or in a separate one, the off-sales book. This difference will be allowed against the gross profit.

TRANSFER BOOK

This book is used in multi-bar units to record movement of stock between bars.

CELLAR STOCK LEDGER

The cellar stock ledger may be used as either an extension of, or in place of, the goods received book. It shows movement of all stock into the establishment and issues out to the bars or dispensing points. All movement of stock in and out of the cellar is normally shown at cost price.

BIN CARDS

Stock item		Bin No.	
Date	Received	Balance	Issued

Figure 8.1 *Bin card*

Bin cards are used to show the physical stock of each item held in the cellar. The movement of all stock in and out of the cellar is recorded on each appropriate bin card. The bin cards are also often used to show the maximum stock and minimum stock.

The minimum stock determines the re-ordering level, leaving sufficient stock in hand to carry over until the new delivery arrives. The maximum stock indicates how much to re-order and is determined by such considerations as storage space available, turnover of a particular item, and to some extent by the amount of cash available within one's budget.

REQUISITION

Each unit dispensing alcoholic beverages should use some form of requisition to draw items from the cellar. These requisitions may be controlled either by colour or serial number, and are normally in duplicate or triplicate. The copies are sent as follows:

- top copy to the cellar;
- duplicate to the beverage control department;
- triplicate would be used by each unit to check its goods received from the cellar.

Information listed on the requisition would be:

- name of dispensing unit;
- date;
- list of items required;
- quantity and unit of each item required;
- signature of authorised person to both order and receive the goods.

The purpose of the requisition is to control the movement of items from the cellar into the dispensing unit and to avoid too much stock being taken at one time, thus overstocking the bar. The level of stock held in the bar is known as par stock. The amount ordered on the requisition, each day, should bring your stock back up to par. The amount to re-order is determined simply by taking account of the following equation: opening stock plus additions (requisition), less closing stock equals consumption (the amount to re-order, each item to the nearest whole unit).

Cellar control procedures

The cellar is a focal point for the storage of alcoholic and non-alcoholic liquor in an establishment. All the service points for such liquor, such as the lounge, lounge bar, cocktail bar, saloon bar, buttery, dispense bars and floor service should draw their stock on a daily or weekly basis from the cellar, this being determined largely by the amount of storage space available and the turnover of sales. All the bars within an establishment hold a set stock of liquor which is sufficient for a period of one day or one week. At the end of this period they requisition for the amount of drink consumed in that one day or week, thus bringing their total stock up to the set stock required. This is known as a par stock, bringing one's stock up to a particular set level, which is determined by turnover.

In the cellar where bin cards are used, every time stock is received or issued it must be entered on the appropriate bin card and the remaining total balance shown. Thus the bin cards should show, at any given time, the total amount of each particular wine held in stock. They also show, where applicable, a maximum and minimum stock as a guide to the cellarman when ordering. This is dependent on the storage space available.

In the bar, as all drink is checked before issue, a daily consumption sheet is completed each day after the service by copying down the sales shown on the top copy of the wine checks. The consumption sheet will list the complete stock held in the dispense bar.

Bin cards may also be completed for checking the wines. At the end of the week the consumption sheets (figure 8.3) may be totalled up, thereby showing the total sales for that period. These totals may then be transferred onto a bar stock book (figure 8.4) for costing purposes. Where drink consumed is not checked in any way, then either a daily or weekly stock is taken so that the amount to be requisitioned from the cellar may be noted. This then brings the bar stock back up to its required level, which is the par stock. The daily or weekly consumption (sales) would then be costed and the cash total for sales arrived at would be related to the daily or weekly income.

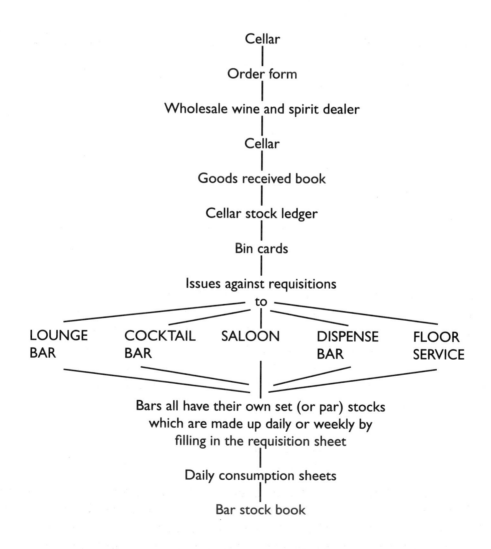

Figure 8.2 *Summary of the basic steps in bar and cellar control*

Name of drink	Bin No.	Mon	Tues	Wed	Thurs	Fri	Sat	Sun	Total

Figure 8.3 *Daily consumption sheet*

Name of drink	Bin No	Opening stock	Received	Total	Closing stock	Consumption	Price per unit	£

Figure 8.4 *Stock book*

GOODS ORDERED, RECEIVED AND ISSUED FROM THE CELLAR

When any alcoholic or non-alcoholic drinks need to be purchased for an establishment to keep up the level of stock, this is done by the cellarman. The cellarman's order should be written in duplicate on an official order form. The top copy is then sent to the supplier and the duplicate remains in the order book for control purposes when the goods are delivered. In some instances there may be three copies of the order sheet. If so they are distributed as follows:

- top copy to the supplier;
- duplicate copy to control and accounts department;
- third copy remains in the order book.

When the goods are delivered to an establishment they should be accompanied by either a delivery note or an invoice. Whichever document it may be, the information contained in it should be exactly the same, with one exception: invoices show the price of all goods delivered whereas delivery notes do not. The goods delivered must first of all be counted and checked against the delivery note to ensure that all the goods listed have been delivered. An extra check may be carried out by the cellarman by checking the delivery note against the copy of the order remaining in the order book. This is to ensure that the items ordered have been sent in the correct quantities and that extra or substitute items have not been sent which were not listed on the order sheet. At this stage all information concerning the goods delivered must be entered in the necessary books for control purposes.

No drinks should be issued by the cellarman unless he receives an official requisition form, correctly filled in, dated and signed by a responsible person from the department concerned. The cellarman should have a list of such signatures and ought not to issue anything unless the requisition sheet is signed by the appropriate person on the list. In order to aid the cellarman, all requisitions should be given to him at a set time each day, when all issues will be made. In certain instances, however, depending on the organisation of an establishment, it may be necessary to issue twice a day, once before opening time in the morning and again before opening time in the evening. All requisition sheets are written in duplicate. The top copy going to the cellar for the items required to be issued, and the duplicate to remain in the requisition book for the bar staff to check the drink on receipt from the cellar.

REVENUE CONTROL

A revenue control system essentially monitors areas where selling takes place.

1 There must be efficient control of all items issued from the various departments.

2 The system should reduce to a minimum any pilfering and wastage.

3 Management should be provided with any information they require for costing purposes, so that they may estimate accurately for the coming financial period.

4 The system should show a breakdown of sales and income received in order that adjustments and improvements may be made.

The main control methods in use in catering establishments are:

- sales analysis (see page 136);
- operational statistics (see pages 134–39, performance measures).

Methods of payment

CASH
The amount of cash received by the operator should always be checked in front of the customer and when change is given it should be counted back to the client. Any notes received by the operator should always be checked to ensure they are not forgeries.

CHEQUE

Payment by cheque should always be accompanied by a cheque card. The operator receiving the cheque should check the following points:

- the date is correct;
- it has been made payable to the correct firm or company;
- the correct amount in words and figures has been filled in;
- it has been signed by the person indicated on the cheque;
- the signature is the same as that on the cheque card;
- the bank code is the same as on the cheque card.

CREDIT CARDS

On receipt of a credit card the operator should check that it is still valid. A voucher is then made out and the appropriate details filled in. The customer is then requested to sign the voucher after which the operator should check the signature with that on the credit card. The customer receives a copy of the voucher as a receipt. In certain instances, the validity of the credit card is checked by passing it through an electronic machine, after which the details of the transaction are printed in the form of an itemised bill which the customer then signs. A copy of this itemised bill is then given as a receipt.

SWITCH-TYPE CARDS

These are not credit cards. They fulfil the same facilities as a cheque in that the amount is taken from the customer's bank account. They are processed in the same way as credit cards.

Electronic point of sale control (EPOS)

Electronic cash registers (ECR) can provide a more efficient service at the point of sale, as well as improving the flow and quality of information to management for control purposes. The advantages will vary from one system to another, but may include some or all of the following points.

1 There are fewer errors in entering sales information. In all but the simplest of ECRs, mistakes in the sequence of entries required for a particular transaction are not permitted. Where an automatic price check or pre-set key is used, this avoids the possibility of error by the assistant in keying in the price and other details.

2 Transactions may be processed faster. This may be achieved by:

- the automatic reading of price tags using a hand-held wand;
- single key entry of prices;
- eliminating any manual calculation or handwriting by the assistant.

3 Training time may be reduced from days on the conventional register to hours on the ECR. This is because many ECRs have a sequencing feature which takes the user through each transaction step by step. This is often achieved by lighting up the instruction for the next entry on a panel display.

4 More detailed information may be provided for management. ECRs provide more information directly in a computer-readable form. This can improve both the detail and quality of computerised stock control and accounting systems, and make them more economic for relatively small establishments.

5 Most ECR systems have additional security features. These include such things as:

- locks which permit the ECR to be operated only by authorised personnel, and totals, etc. to be altered and reset only by supervisors and managers;
- not disclosing at the end of the day the amount of money that should be in the cash drawer until the assistant has entered the amount actually in it.

6 Advanced calculating facilities. Most ECRs can be programmed to calculate the total price when a number of items of the same price are purchased, when there are a number of items at various prices, or if Value Added Tax (VAT) has to be added.

7 The ECR gives improved printout.

- The quality and the amount of information contained on the customer's receipt may be improved quite considerably.
- Receipts may be overprinted with Sales and Value Added Tax.
- Both alphabetic and numeric information can be presented in one or two colours.
- The receipt can contain an alphabetic record of the goods purchased as well as, or instead of, a simple reference number.

Most ECRs have storage facilities that record information on all items purchased, cash taken in different categories and so on, all for subsequent processing. For larger establishments there are units available which work on their own in separate food and beverage outlets, but which transmit all the information entered over a link to a central billing area. More sophisticated systems are those in which all the cash registers within the establishment work with, and are controlled by, a central computer.

PERFORMANCE MEASURES

Overage and shortage

An analysis of alcoholic beverage sales and stock held allows one to gain two important pieces of information: firstly the gross profit, and secondly the overage or shortage of the estimated monetary revenue and stock in hand. The gross profit is determined by finding the difference between revenue and the cost of the alcoholic beverage consumed.

To determine the overage or shortage it is necessary to estimate how much money should have been taken during a given period of time, based on the consumption at selling price. The consumption must be priced out bottle by bottle, keg by keg. For example, a bar has sold 12 bottles of whisky (which sells at £1.70 per 25 ml tot), six bottles of sherry (at £1.50 per 50 ml tot) and five kegs (40 litres (9 gallons) each, selling at £2.00 per pint):

Whisky	$12 \times 30 \times £1.70 = £612.00$
Sherry	$6 \times 15 \times £1.50 = £135.00$
Kegs	$5 \times 72 \times £2.00 = £720.00$

Note: 9 gallons $\times$ 8 pints = 72 pints

Estimated takings	£1467.00
Actual cash takings	£1476.00
Surplus	£9.00

£9.00 is 0.61% of estimated takings

Gross profit

Gross profit is determined by deducting the beverage cost from the sales. The proportion of beer to spirits consumed will sometimes help explain why a certain month's gross profit is low (a lot of beer sold) or high (more spirits have been sold). There are, however, other reasons for a larger or smaller gross profit. A number of points to look out for may be as follows:

1   Under-ringing and keeping the difference, for example by ringing perhaps 0.50 instead of £1.50, whereby the bar loses a £1. The cash register should be sited so that the customer can check visually the amount which has been rung up.

2   Too many 'No Sales' on the till roll may give a clue to shortages. The till roll should be examined each time it is removed. An excessive use of the 'No Sale' key should be queried at the time.

3   The till roll itself can be very revealing. It can be found, for instance, that there are a lot of very small sales recorded, or that the average sale is lower than usual, or lower with one operator than with another.

4   Working with the drawer open, if the till is not set on 'closed drawer'; giving change without ringing the amount up.

5   Never let bar staff cash up as this can throw suspicion on them if there is cause for concern.

6   All off-sales should be kept apart from the bar where measures are sold, and a

separate stock used. All off-sales should be entered into a separate book. The difference between tot prices and off-sales prices will be needed by the stocktaker.

7   Lounge sales or sales at a table away from the bar may also be vulnerable. The till ticket provides one simple method of control. If each waiter is provided with a float and has to pay for drinks at the time of collecting, then he or she can have a ticket to present to the customer.

The other advantage is that, unless there is collusion, the bar staff will not overcharge the waiter or under-ring the transaction. Even though this is a simple method of control, it is still open to abuse. Staff have been known to use the same chit twice, but only if they are able to get drinks without paying for them.

It is usual to count the money first and then read the till rather than read the till first and then check the money. In busy bars it is good practice to collect most of the cash before the end of a session, leaving a temporary receipt in the drawer.

Sales mix

The total sales of an establishment are usually summarised for a specific period. This could be per hour, per service period or per day. The total sales are often categorised according to the type of sales. This is known as the sales mix. This could be as simple as showing the totals for liquor sold with lunches, dinners or snacks as in table 8.1.

Table 8.1

SERVICE PERIOD	LIQUOR SALES	
	£	%
Lunch	220	29
Dinner	420	55
Snacks	125	16
Daily Total	765	100

This report shows the total of cash taken in liquor or beverage sales for the lunch and dinner service periods and also shows the amount sold with snacks. The report also indicates that 55% of the total sales were taken during the dinner service period.

Sales data may also be broken down further to indicate the type of beverages that were sold. This breakdown could include for instance:

- beers
- wines

- spirits
- mixers
- fortified and aromatised wines
- non-alcoholic drinks

This breakdown could therefore be used to indicate the amount and the percentage of sales according to the type of drink being sold.

Additionally, the sales under a specific heading could be broken down even further to show the sales of each individual item. The purpose of analysing the sales mix data in this way is to assist in:

- identifying popular and unpopular items in the wine and drinks lists;
- providing records for stock control purposes;
- predicting future demand for particular items or groups of items;
- identifying changes in customers' buying patterns over a period;
- providing for the reconciliation of sales of items with different gross profits;
- identifying where profits and losses are being made.

Elements of cost

In catering there are three elements of cost:

- labour, for example wages, salaries, staff feeding, uniforms;
- food or beverage costs often called cost of sales;
- overheads, for example rent, rates, advertising, fuel, etc

Sales in catering are always equal to 100%. The relationship between costs and profits in catering operations may be seen in the table 8.2.

Table 8.2   *Elements of cost*

Beverage costs	Cost of sales
Labour costs Overhead costs } Net profit	Gross profit
Sales	Revenue 100%

Costs such as wages may be classified in relation to sales. Thus all costs can be attributed to a return in revenue.

$$\text{Percentage of total wages cost} = \frac{\text{Department wage cost} \times 100}{\text{Total wage cost}}$$

$$\text{Percentage of sales} = \frac{\text{Wage cost} \times 100}{\text{Revenue}}$$

This may also be expressed as revenue per employee per department.

Table 8.3   *Cost percentages*

SALES	REVENUE £	DIRECT LABOUR COSTS £	PERCENTAGE OF TOTAL LABOUR COSTS %	PERCENTAGE OF DEPARTMENT SALES %
Food	125	35	78	17
Liquor	60	10	22	17
Total	175	45	100	26

Note: percentages have been rounded

Average check

Average check is also called spend per head. The calculation of the average spend assists in interpretation of sales figures. For example, if revenue goes up, is it due to higher selling prices or more customers being served? If, however, the revenue reduces, is it due to fewer customers being served or to customers spending less? Average check is calculated by dividing the total sales per department by the number of people or covers served.

An alternative is for bar operations to calculate the average order. This can be done by dividing the total sales in a given period by the number of individual till transactions.

Table 8.4   *Example of average check calculations*

SERVICE	DRINK TOTAL £	NO. OF COVERS	AVERAGE CHECK
Lunch	90	12	7.50
Dinner	80	10	8.00
Snack	15	7	2.14
Total	185	29	6.37

Stock turnover

The rate of stock turnover gives the number of times that the average level of stock has turned over in a given period. It is calculated as follows:

$$\text{Rate of stock turnover} = \frac{\text{Cost of food or beverage consumed in specific period}}{\text{Average stock value (food or beverage) at cost}}$$

The average stock holding is calculated by taking the opening stock value, adding the closing stock value and dividing by two.

Sales per seat available

Sales per seat available shows the sales value that can be earned by each seat in a restaurant, coffee shop, etc. and is used for comparison of different types of operation as well as a record of earnings per seat over a period of time. It is calculated by dividing the sales figure by the number of seats available in the dining area.

Sales per square metre

An alternative method of comparison is to calculate sales per square metre or foot. This is particularly useful in bar operations where earnings per seat cannot be calculated. It is calculated by dividing the sales by the square meterage of the service area.

9

WINE-PRODUCING COUNTRIES AND REGIONS

—

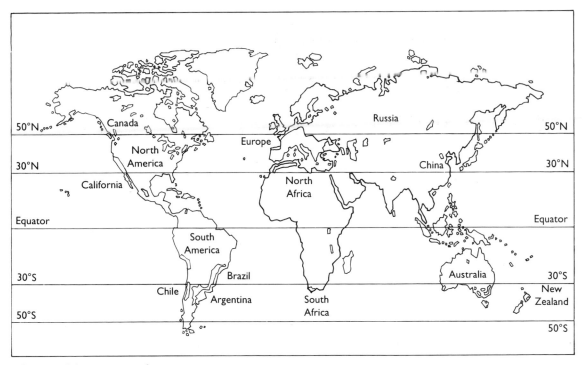

The world wine-producing regions

INTRODUCTION

The vine grows most successfully between the latitudes 30–50° north and 30–50° south of the equator. Some of the greatest wines, like champagne, come from the extremities of these wine belts where, because of the intense cold or extreme heat, the vine has a permanent struggle to survive. The vine usually produces good quality grapes when it is five years old and will continue to yield healthy grapes up to the age of 35 years.

The top ten wine-producing countries are:

1	Italy	6	Argentina
2	France	7	Germany
3	Spain	8	Portugal
4	CIS	9	South Africa
5	USA	10	Romania

The top ten wine-consuming countries (per capita consumption) are:

1	France	67.5 litres (14.8 gallons)
2	Portugal	66.5 litres (14.63 gallons)

3	Italy	62.0 litres (13.64 gallons)
4	Luxembourg	60.3 litres (13.27 gallons)
5	Argentina	45.8 litres (10 gallons)
6	Spain	45.5 litres (10 gallons)
7	Switzerland	44.5 litres (10 gallons)
8	Chile	41.0 litres (9 gallons)
9	Austria	39.2 litres (8.62 gallons)
10	Greece	31.8 litres (7 gallons)

As a contrast, the United Kingdom consumes 12.5 litres (2.75 gallons) per capita.

Although Britain is traditionally regarded as a nation of beer drinkers the consumption of the wine has now dramatically increased. One of the effects of the recent recession is that more and more people are dining at home rather than going out for a meal. For many people that means having a couple of glasses of wine when they eat. It is now estimated that home consumption of wine makes up 75% of the market. A greater interest in television and the obvious deterrent of the drink driving laws have also influenced this trend.

You can now get good quality wine at a reasonable price in supermarkets and other outlets. Wine has become socially acceptable and is perceived to be more healthy than other alcoholic drinks.

PRINCIPAL GRAPE VARIETIES

White grapes	**Favoured locations**
Aligoté	Burgundy
Bacchus	Mainly Germany but also grown in England
Blanc Fumé	*see* Sauvignon Blanc
Blanquette	*see* Colombard
Bual (Boal)	Madeira
Chardonnay	mainly Champagne, Burgundy, California, Eastern Europe, South America, Australia and New Zealand; sometimes referred to as Pinot Chardonnay
Chasselas	France, mainly the Loire (e.g. Pouilly-sur-Loire), Central Europe; known as Gutedel in Germany and Fendant in Switzerland
Chauché Gris	*see* Grey Riesling
Chenin Blanc	Loire (e.g. Vouvray, Saumur, Coteaux du Layon), California, South America, South Africa (known as Steen), Australia

Clairette	Mainly southern France
Colombard	France, especially in Cognac (also known as Blanquette elsewhere in France), California (known as French Colombard)
Fendant	*see* Chasselas
Folle Blanche	France, especially Cognac, Armagnac and the Loire, and California; also known as Picpoule
French Colombard	*see* Colombard
Furmint	Hungary (e.g. Tokay); also known as Sipon in Hungary
Gewürztraminer	France, in Alsace (also in the Jura where it is known as Savagnin), Germany, Austria, Australia, Northern Italy, California, New Zealand
Grey Riesling	France, California; real name Chauché Gris
Gutedel	*see* Chasselas
Johannisberg Riesling	Germany, mainly Rhine and Mosel, France in Alsace and the Jura, Central Europe, Australia, California; also called White Riesling
Listan Palomino	*see* Palomino
Malmsey	*see* Malvasia
Malvasia	California, Mediterranean, known as Malmsey in Madeira
Malvoisie	*see* Pinot Gris
Melon de Bourgogne	France, in Muscadet; also known as Muscadet
Müller-Thurgau	England, Germany, Austria, Central Europe
Muscadelle	Mainly in Australia, South Africa and some in France (in Bordeaux)
Muscadet	*see* Melon de Bourgogne
Muscat	France (e.g. Muscat de Beaumes-de-Venise), California, Spain, Italy (e.g. Asti Supmante), Mediterranean
Palomino	Spain for sherry; also known as Listan Palomino
Pedro Ximénez	Australia, California, South Africa, Spain for sherry
Picpoule	*see* Folle Blanche
Pinot Blanc	Burgundy, Alsace, Germany (where it is known as Weissburgunder), Italy, California
Pinot Chardonnay	*see* Chardonnay
Pinot Grigio	*see* Pinot Gris
Pinot Gris	France, mainly Alsace, Germany, Switzerland, northern Italy; known as Pinot Grigio in Italy, Ruländer in Germany, Tokay in Alsace and Malvoisie in Switzerland
Riesling	*see* Johannisberg Riesling and Sémillon
Ruländer	see Pinot Gris
Rabigato	Portugal, main white grape for port
Saint Émilion	*see* Ugni Blanc
Savagnin	*see* Johannisberg Riesling and Gewürztraminer

Sauvignon Blanc	France, mainly Loire Valley (e.g. Sancerre and Pouilly Fumé) and Bordeaux (e.g. Graves and Sauternes), Chile, Australia, California; also called Blanc Fumé
Sémillon	France, mainly Bordeaux (e.g. Graves and Sauternes), South America, South Africa, Australia, California; often called Riesling in Australia
Sercial	Madeira
Seyval Blanc	north American States, Canada, France, England
Silvaner	*see* Sylvaner
Sipon	*see* Furmint
Steen	*see* Chenin Blanc
Sylvaner	Central Europe, mainly Germany, France in Alsace, California; also known as Silvaner
Tokay	*see* Pinot Gris
Trebbiano	Italy (e.g. Soave, Orvieto, Frascati), France, California; also known as Ugni Blanc
Ugni Blanc	France, mainly Cognac and Armagnac where it is known as Saint Émilion; see also Trebbiano
Verdelho	Madeira
Verdicchio	Mainly central Italy
Viognier	France, mainly Rhône (e.g. Condrieu)
Welsch Riesling	Europe; no relation to Johannisberg Riesling
Weissburgunder	*see* Pinot Blanc
White Riesling	*see* Johannisberg Riesling

Red grapes	**Favoured locations**
Baco Noir	North American States, France
Barbera	Italy in Piedmont, South America, California
Bastardo	Portugal classic grape for port
Bouchet	*see* Cabernet Franc
Brunello	Italy in Tuscany (e.g. Brunello di Montalcino)
Cabernet Franc	France, mainly Loire (e.g. Cabernet d'Anjou, Chinon) and Bordeaux, Italy, California; also known as Bouchet in France
Cabernet Sauvignon	France, mainly Bordeaux and Provence, Chile, Bulgaria, California, Spain, Australia, almost everywhere
Carignan	France, mainly Rhône and Provence, California, Spain, North Africa
Chancellor Noir	North American States, southern France
Charbono	California
Cinsault	France, mainly Rhône, Languedoc Roussillon
de Chaunac	North American States, Canada
Dolcetto	Italy in Piedmont

Duriff	*see* Petit Sirah
Gamay	France, mainly Beaujolais but also Loire, Switzerland, California
Grenache	France, mainly south and southern Rhone (e.g. Châteauneuf-du-Pape, with other grapes, and for Tavel Rosé and Lirac), California, Spain
Lambrusco	Italy in Emilia-Romagna
Malbec	France in Bordeaux, Cahors, Argentina, California
Merlot	France, mainly Bordeaux, northern Italy, Switzerland, California, South America, South Africa
Meunier	France in Champagne; also called Pinot Meunier
Nebbiolo	Italy in Piedmont and Lombardy (e.g. Barolo, Babaresco), California
Petit Sirah	California; also called Duriff
Pinot Meunier	*see* Meunier
Pinot Noir	France, mainly Champagne and Burgundy, but also in the Loire, England, Switzerland, Germany (known as Spätburgunder), Eastern Europe, California, South America
Pinotage	Mainly South Africa (Pinot Noir/Cinsault cross)
Ruby Cabernet	California
Sangiovese	Italy in Tuscany and Emilia-Romagna (e.g. for Chianti, but blended with other grapes)
Shiraz	*see* Syrah
Spätburgunder	*see* Pinot Noir
Syrah	French, mainly northern Rhône (e.g. Hermitage, St Joseph, Cornas, also used in blend for Châteauneuf-du-Pape), Australia; also known as Shiraz
Tempranillo	Spain in Rioja, Argentina
Zinfandel	California, also used for blush and rosé wines

ALGERIA

It was once believed that anyone who had tasted French wine had tasted Algerian. The French colonised the country in 1830. Later they began using its mass-produced wines to give body and vigour to the light wines of the Midi and also, to a lesser degree, to stretch out other wines such as Burgundy. All that changed in 1962. Algeria gained her independence but lost her best customer. Stricter French regulations forbade the use of Algerian wines for blending. Consequently, the production of Algerian wines fell into a fast decline and the vineyard capacity was reduced almost by half. The best vineyards are now sited on hillsides in the departments of Alger and Oran.

The quality zones are:

Department of Alger

• Ain-Bessem-Bouïra	Red and white wines
• Côtes du Zaccar	Red and white wines
• Haut-Dahra	Red wines
• Médéa	Red and white wines

Department of Oran

• Coteaux de Mascara	Red (the best), white and rosé
• Coteaux de Tlemcen	Red and white wines
• Monts du Tessalah	Red, white and rosé wines.

The grapes used are:

Reds: Alicante-Bouschet, Carignan, Cinsault, Grenache, Mourvèdre and Syrah.
Whites: Clairette, Listan and Ugni Blanc.
Rosé: Cinsault and Grenache.

ARGENTINA

Argentina is the largest wine-producing country in South America and the sixth largest in the world. All styles are made and, before the Falklands conflict (1982), some of the reds, especially the claret-type Cabernet Sauvignon, were very popular in England. Today, not much wine is exported but there is a huge local consumption. Because of the very hot climate, Argentina has cleverly conserved the rains and snow of the Andes mountains which later can be distributed through a system of irrigation to keep the vines and other crops healthy. Mendoza is the best and largest producing region accounting for up to 70% of the national output. The other centres of wine production are San Juan, Rio Negra, La Rioja, Catamara and Salta.

The grapes used are of European stock, but the indigenous Criolla is widely used as well for white wines. The main white grapes are Chardonnay, Chenin Blanc, Riesling and Sémillon. For red wine, Cabernet Sauvignon, Malbec, Merlot, Lambrusco, Nebbiola, Barbera and Tempranillo are used. The Palomino and Pedro Ximénez grapes are used to make sherry-style wines of which Tio Quinto is best known.

Peñaflor is by far the largest wine company and makes an excellent Cabernet Sauvignon under the Trapiche label. Other good reds are made by José Orfila, San Telmo and Bianchi. Crillon makes good whites and a sparkling wine which they call Monitor Champagne. Other sparklers are Proviar's Champania; M. Chandon and H. Piper have good local reputations.

AUSTRALIA

Australia has emerged as the modern pace-maker in the highly competitive field of wine-making. How times have changed. Some 30 years ago, wine drinking in Australia was looked on with a suspicious eye. The male ego was more tolerantly massaged by guzzling beer. Now, thanks to the efforts of the Australian Wine Board and the sheer technical skill and brilliance of the wine-makers, the image and performance of Australian wines has changed almost beyond recognition. The per capita consumption in Australia itself is a staggering 22 litres (38 pints), mostly drunk from the ubiquitous bag-in-the-box or bladder packs which accounts for nearly 60% of the business. The exported wines have also done remarkably well, especially in Britain.

The technical development of the wine industry over the last few years has enabled wine-makers to limit the effects of any climatic excesses which some regions were prone to. In balancing technological control with nature, Australia has successfully put flavour and affordable quality into their vinous products.

The vine was first introduced to Australia by an English naval captain, Arthur Phillip, in 1788. He collected vine cuttings in Rio de Janeiro and had them planted, albeit with little success, at Farm Cove, now the site of Sydney's botanical gardens. Three years later, he moved to the Parramatta area of Sydney and established a 1.2 hectare (three-acre) vineyard which was more successful. In 1816, Gregory Blaxland, the explorer, chose the banks of the Parramatta River as his vineyard site. Six years later he shipped 136 litres (30 gallons) of red wine to England. By 1827 John Macarthur's vineyard near Penrith, Sydney, was producing over 90,000 litres (20,000 gallons) of wine annually. In 1832, the British Government sent a young Scott, James Busby, to the vineyards of Europe. He returned with 20,000 vine cuttings and planted them in a prime site in the Hunter Valley, New South Wales. The vines flourished and by 1852, there were 186 hectares (461 acres) under the vine, producing 280,000 litres (60,000 gallons) of wine and 4,500 litres (1,000 gallons) of brandy annually.

Today wine is successfully made in Victoria (Great Western, Yarra Valley, Geelong, Milawa, Rutherglen, Goulburn Valley), in South Australia (Clare Valley, Murray River Valley, Barossa Valley, Coonawarra, McLaren Vale, Langhorne's Creek, Southern Vales, Padthaway, and around Adelaide), in Western Australia (Mount Barker, Margaret river, Coastal Plain and the Swan River Valley), in Queensland (Granite Belt and Roma) in New South Wales (Upper and Lower Hunter Valley, Mudgee, the Murrumbidgee Irrigation Area and Cowra) and in Tasmania (Pipers Brook and Launceston).

GRAPE VARIETIES

Over 60 grape varieties are cultivated, some for experimental purposes, but all originate from the classic European family *Vitis vinifera*.

Principal grapes for white wine   Chardonnay (star performer), Rhine Riesling, Sémillon, Sauvignon Blanc, Gewürztraminer, Colombard, Marsanne, Muscat and Muscadelle (Tokay).

Principal grapes for red wines   The Cabernet Sauvignon is the star closely followed by the Shiraz, also known as Hermitage and originally called by its French name Syrah. Other red grapes used are Pinot Noir, Merlot, Malbec, Cabernet Franc and Petit Verdot.

WINE LABELS

In 1990 a Label Integrity Programme, aimed at controlling claims on label information, came into legislation. Blended wines, a large and very successful part of the industry, must list the grape varieties used in descending order of importance – for example, Aldridge's Estate Sémillon Chardonnay will have a higher proportion of Sémillon than Chardonnay in the blend. Eighty per cent of the wine bottled must be of the grape and region indicated. If the label shows a vintage year, the bottle must contain at least 95% of that year's wine.

   Australian wine labels are very informative, detailing product description which might include, when appropriate, terms such as oak matured, late harvested, botrytis affected. Bin numbers and vat numbers are often used to distinguish different styles or class of wine. They are, in effect, brand styles usually of excellent quality. When competition awards and gold medals are referred to, one can expect the wine to be of an exceptional standard. Because of consistent climatic conditions, vintage years are of no great importance, but they do help in revealing the age of the wine. Many wines are marketed under their grape name, but do not expect them to match exactly their European counterparts. Some show a good resemblance, for example:

* Chardonnay has an affinity to white Burgundy;
* Rhine Riesling to Alsace and some German Riesling;
* Cabernet Sauvignon to red Bordeaux;
* Shiraz to red wines from the Rhône.

Others like Gewürztraminer are not even remotely like the classic Alsace style. The Australians are not great imitators. Their wines are very individual and all the better for it.

SOME NOTABLE WINES

Note: The following abbreviations are used for the Australian states.

Victoria	VIC
South Australia	SA
Western Australia	WA
Queensland	QLD
New South Wales	NSW
Tasmania	TAS

Sparkling wines

Angas Brut (SA)
Croser Blanc de Blancs (SA)
Hermskerk Jansz (TAS)
Seppelt's Great Western (VIC)

Château Rémy (VIC)
Domaine Chandon Green Point (VIC)
Seaview Edmond Mazure (SA)
Seppelt's Salinger (VIC)

White varietal wines

Chardonnay

Brokenwood (NSW)
Coldstream Hill Reserve (VIC)
Leeuwin Estate (WA)
Padthaway (SA)
Pipers Brook (TAS)
Rothbury Estate (NSW)
Tyrrell (NSW)

Leon Buring (SA)
Lake's Folly (NSW)
Orlando's Jacobs Creek (SA)
Petaluma (SA)
Rosemount (NSW)
Saxonvale (NSW)
Yeringberg (VIC)

Rhine Riesling

Cape Vale (WA)
Moorilla (TAS)
Penfolds (SA)
Quelltaler (SA)
Seville Estate Yarra (VIC)
Wynn's Coonawarra Estate (SA)

Hill-Smith's Peusey Vale (SA)
Orlando's Eden Vale (SA)
Pipers Brook (TAS)
Seppelts (SA)
Tisdall Wines (VIC)

Sémillon

Aldridge Estate (SA)
Henschke (SA)
Kaiser Stuhl (SA)
McWilliams (NSW)
Rothbury Estate (NSW)

Cape Mentelle (WA)
Houghton (WA)
Leasingham Domaine (SA)
Quelltaler (SA)

Other white grape varieties are mainly used in blends.

Red varietal wines

Cabernet Sauvignon

Balgownie (VIC)
Brown Brothers (VIC)
Evans and Tate (WA)
Hermskerk (TAS)
Lake's Folly (NSW)
Lindeman Rouge Homme (SA)
Penfolds Bin 707 (SA)
Wolf Blass Black Label (SA)
Yalumba Menzies (SA)

Bannockburn (VIC)
Cullens (WA)
Henschke (SA)
Houghton (WA)
Leeuwin Estate (WA)
Moss Wood (WA)
Vasse Felix (WA)
Wynn's 'John Riddock' (SA)

Shiraz (also known as Hermitage)

Bowen Estate (SA)

Château Tahbilk (VIC)

Mitchelton (VIC)

Penfold's Grange Hermitage (SA)

Yarra Yering (VIC)

Brown Brothers (VIC)

Hardy's Eileen Hardy (SA)

Plantagenet (WA)

Tyrrell's (NSW)

Pinot Noir

Coldstream Hill Reserve (VIC)

Peter Lehmann (SA)

Tyrrells (NSW)

Moorilla Estate (TAS)

Pipers Brook (TAS)

Yarra Yering (VIC)

Other red wine grapes are mainly used in blends.

Liqueur Muscats

Brown Brothers (VIC)

Campbells Old Rutherglen (VIC)

Baileys of Glenrowan (VIC)

Botrytised Sémillon (Sauternes-style)

De Bortoli (NSW)

Hill-Smith Estate (SA)

Sherry-style wines

Mildara George Dry (VIC)

Yalumba Chiquitta (SA)

Quelltaler Granfiesta Dry Pale (SA)

Port-style wines

Elsinore Vintage (QLD)

Kaiser Stuhl Jubilee (SA)

Seppelt's Para (SA)

Hardy's Vintage (SA)

Lindeman's Macquarie (NSW)

Yalumba Galway Pipe (SA)

AUSTRIA

Since the fraudulent use of the toxic anti-freeze ingredient (diethylene glycol) in 1985, Austrian wines have suffered greatly on international markets. A few rogue producers added diethylene to their wines to give them a perceived fuller and 'natural' smooth-sweet flavour. Since then, new legislation has involved stricter testing procedures, curbs on production levels, and the imposition of higher levels of ripeness for each category of wine. About 80% of the wine is white, made from the native grape Grüner Veltliner and others such as Rhine Riesling, Welschriesling, Weissburgunder, Gewürztraminer, Müller-Thurgau, Muskat-Ottonel, Rotgipfler and Spätrot. Red wines are made from Blauer Spätburgunder (Pinot Noir), Blaufränkisch, Portugieser and Saint Laurent grapes.

The wine regions are located in the eastern part of Austria in the vicinity of Vienna. Austria's most popular white wine, Gumpoldskirchner, is produced south of Vienna in the village of Baden. Further along is the village of Bad Vöslau which has a very good red wine, Vöslauer. To the west of Vienna, in and around the Wachau district, fine white wines such as Dürnsteiner Katzensprung, Dürnsteiner Flohaxen, Loiben, Kaizerwein, Riede Loibenberg, Kremser Kögl and Kremser Wachtberg are made. In Burgenland around the hot, humid Neusiedlersee, noble rot grapes (see page 169) make wonderfully sweet, rich wines known as Ausbruch. A particularly good example is called Rust. Other good white wines are also made here, notably Neuberger, Mörbischer, St Georgener, Welschriesling and the light and fruity Blaufränkischer.

In Steiermark, south Austria, they make a blush wine called Schilcher and in West Steiermark their speciality is Zwiebelschilcher, an onion skin coloured rosé. A famous name in Austrian wine lore is Dr Lenz Moser who devised the high and wide method of vine cultivation, enabling tractors to work beneath the vines. This system has now been adopted in many other countries. Austrian labels usually follow the German model – Spätlese, Auslese, and so on (see page 195–7).

SPECIAL TERMS

Bergwein   Wines made in mountain vineyards.

Heurigerwein   New wine which is released for sale on the 11th November each year. This is sold by the jugful in bars (*Heurigen*) around Vienna.

Perlwein   A spritzig or semi-sparkling wine.

Reidwein   The product of a single vineyard.

Schluckwein   Wine for everyday gulping; a thirst quencher.

Schoppenwein   A swilling wine to keep you happy.

BOLIVIA

Some light table wines are produced around La Paz and Sucre. Most wine is for home consumption or destined to be distilled into the local speciality, Pisco brandy.

BRAZIL

Brazil was once colonised by the wine-drinking Portuguese. Surprisingly, they did not establish a wine industry, but a colony of Italian settlers did so after the First World War. Today wine is still made in the Italian tradition, but so far it is not quite good enough to venture onto export markets. The hot, damp climate tends to suit the grapes native to North America, particularly Isabella (*Vitis labrusca*) better than it does the European classic *Vitis vinifera*. However, a more assiduous approach, aided by modern technical development and expertise, has now permitted the cultivation of some of the classic grapes like Merlot, Cabernet Sauvignon, Pinot Noir for reds and the Riesling, Sauvignon Blanc, Sémillon, St Emilion and Trebbiano for whites. Most styles of wine are made, and the sparkling wine which they optimistically call champagne is perhaps best of all. The two main centres of production are Rio Grande do Sul in the extreme south and São Paulo further north. The major wineries are Georges Aubert, Companhia Monaco Vinhedos, Campanhia Vinicola Riograndense, Heublein do Brazil, Palomas, Vinicola Armando Peterlongo, and Vinicola Garibaldi.

BULGARIA

Wine promotion and exportation of Bulgarian wines is controlled by the state agency Vinimpex. The wines are extremely good value, which is why the country is listed sixth in the top ten of wine exporters worldwide. Strict wine laws were adopted in 1978, ensuring that the wines are made according to the most stringent regulations. The wines are promoted under the following categories.

Country wine range   These basic country wines are fresh and fruity in character and are meant to be drunk when young.

Varietal range   These are made from single grape varieties such as Chardonnay or Cabernet Sauvignon and the region of production is specified.

Premium wines   These are the choicest wines of the varietal range.

Reserve wines   These are superior in quality to all those above. The white wines are aged in wood for two years and the reds are oak aged for at least three years.

Special reserve   These wines are the *crème de la crème* of the reserve category.

Controliran wines   This range was introduced in 1985. The wines are the equivalent of the French AOC standard (see page 160). They are of a superior vintage and their origin and producing vineyards are guaranteed. Methods of viticulture and vinification are carefully supervised and the maturing wines are closely monitored.

Within these categories or ranges, 80 different styles of wine are produced. Some are marked by the grape species or place of origin. Others, especially the blended wines, are generally sold under a brand name label.

GRAPE VARIETIES
Only grapes from the classic *Vitis vinifera* family are used.

Grapes for white wine   Aligoté, Chardonnay, Dimiat, Misket, Muscat Ottonel, Riesling, Rkatziteli, Sauvignon Blanc and Traminer.

Grapes for red wine   Cabernet Sauvignon, Gamza, Mavrud, Melnic, Merlot and Pamid.

THE WINES

Examples of good white wines include:

- Karlova Misket
- Khan Krum Chardonnay
- Novi Pazar Chardonnay
- Preslav Chardonnay
- Sungurlare Misket
- Valley of Roses Riesling
- Varna Chardonnay

Examples of good red wines include:

- Assenovgrad Mavrud
- Oryahovitsa Cabernet Sauvignon
- Oryahovitsa Merlot
- Pavlikeni Gamza
- Pleven Cabernet Sauvignon
- Suhindol Gamza
- Stambolovo Merlot
- Svishtov Cabernet Sauvignon
- Yantra Valley Cabernet Sauvignon

Some sparkling wines to note are Iskra, Lazour, Magoura and Simfonia.

UNDERSTANDING THE LABEL

Byalo vino	White wine
Cherveno vino	Red Wine
Estestveno penlivo vino	Sparkling Wine
Lozia	Vineyard
Sladko vino	Sweet Wine
Sort grozde	Grape Variety
Vinimpex	State Trading Company for wine and spirit import and export
Vinoproizvoditel	Winery, wine product

CANADA

Very gradually Canada is emerging as a wine-producing country. However, the Canadians still rely heavily on the ordinary *Vitis labrusca* vines such as Concord, Catawba and Niagara and on the lacklustre hybrids such as Maréchal Foch, Baco Noir, Vidal Blanc, Seyval Blanc and Seyve Villard to make most of their wines. Traditionally, their output has produced sparkling and port- and sherry-style wines.

Within these last few years there has been a move towards the cultivation of *Vitis vinifera* wines: Aligoté, Chardonnay, Riesling and Gewürztraminer for white wines and Gamay, Pinot Noir and Cabernet Sauvignon for red wines.

The two most important provinces for wine production are Ontario (centred around the Niagara peninsula) and British Columbia (Okanagan Valley). Alberta, Nova Scotia and Quebec also produce wine, but the true home of the vine is Ontario which accounts for 85% of the wine produced in Canada.

One of the specialities here is ice wine. Blessed with the kind of weather which makes ice wine a certainty every year, Canada is now the largest producer of ice wine in the world. Made from the Riesling, Vidal or Gewürztraminer grapes, the sweet bunches of grapes are left on the vine long after the normal vintage – usually until December or January or February or whenever the grapes are frozen solid. When the temperature drops to −7°C or under, the grapes are picked. Grapes normally contain about 75% water and, when pressed, the frozen water is driven off as shards or fragments of ice. What remains is grape syrup, terrifically sweet but balanced by a welcomed acidity. The syrup is allowed to settle for a few days before being clarified of any dust or debris. It now goes into stainless steel vats where cultured yeast is added to activate fermentation. Because of the high concentration of sugar, fermentation is very slow and takes months before reaching completion. Once bottled, at 10–11% alcohol, the amber nectar can continue to improve and a bottle age of 10 to 15 years is not unusual. Inniskillin Ice wine is a particularly good example of this Canadian speciality.

The range and quality of Canadian wines may be found under the following labels: Andres Wines, Barnes Wines, Brights Wines, Charal, Château des Charmes, Château-Gai Wines, Claremont, Colio Wines, Hillebrand Estate Wines, Inniskillin Wines, Jordan and Ste, Michelle Cellars, London Winery, Montravin Cellars, Reif Winery Inc, and Willowbank Estate. Some of these wines are already to be seen on supermarket shelves in Britain. Brights Wines have now merged with Cartier and Inniskillin Vinters.

CHILE

Spanish missionaries brought the vine to Chile in the sixteenth century. Although the country escaped the devastating phylloxera disease, the vineyards were uprooted in the nineteenth century and replanted with the classic *Vitis vinifera* vines. This, along with modern technical advancement, has resulted in a great improvement in the quality of wine produced.

Chile has a wonderful climate for viticulture but some regions get little rainfall. The conserved melted snow of the Andes is used in a sophisticated form of irrigation to keep the vines healthy.

The best wines are produced in the Maipo and Aconcagua valleys with the red wines nearly always superior to the whites. The red wine grapes are the Cabernet

Sauvignon, Cabernet Franc, Malbec, Merlot and Pinot Noir. For white wines the Sauvignon Blanc, Riesling, Chardonnay, Gewürztraminer and Sémillon are the main grapes. Of all the wines produced, the Cabernet Sauvignon has star quality, showing classic style under the labels of Concha y Toro, Viña Cousíno Macul, Viña Linderos, Viña Santa Rita and Miguel Torres. Torres of the famed Spanish wine dynasty also produces good sparkling wine using the classic *méthode traditionnelle*. He also makes refreshing Chardonnay and Riesling white table wines, and a really fine Sauvignon Blanc called Santa Digna.

Understanding the label

Envasada en Origen	Estate Bottled
Producido y Fraccionado por	Produced and bottled by the vineyard
Viñedos Propios	The winery, the vineyard
Viñas Courant	One year old
Viñas Special	Two years old
Viñas Reserva	Four years old
Viñas Reservado	Six years old
Vino Blanco	White wine
Vino Tinto	Red wine

CHINA

There are six wine-producing regions in China: Kiangsu to the north of Shanghai, Hebei north-west of Peking, Liaoning in Manchuria, Sheris near Sian on the Yellow River, Sinkiang and the Shantung Peninsula. Some indigenous grapes are used in wine-making, such as Dragon's Eye, Cow's Nipple, Cock's Heart and Beichun, as well as Cabernet Sauvignon, Cabernet Franc, Pinot Noir, Gamay, Gewürztraminer, Riesling and Muscat. Wine names are fairly predictable: Dynasty, Great Wall and Heavenly Palace. Other more interesting wines are the white Qingdao Riesling, the Red Cabernet d'Est and the sparkling Imperial Court.

COLOMBIA

Colombia makes quite a variety of wines using *Vitis vinifera* grapes, *Vitis labrusca* grapes especially Isabella, and a combination of grapes and other native fruits such as blackberries, bananas and oranges. From this jamboree comes 'wines' which are classified as light table wines (distincly sweet), sparkling wines, vermouth, port, Madeira and Moscatel. Centres of production are Cauce Valley, Sierra Nevada de Santa Marta and Ocaña.

CYPRUS

Cyprus is perhaps best known in Britain for its two sherry-style wines – Emva and Mosaic – but the island also produces a good selection of table wines and the renowned dessert wine Commandaria. Cyprus was one of the few countries to escape the dreaded vine disease phylloxera. The majority of vineyards are sited on the southern slopes of the Troodos Mountains. The indigenous vines, Xynisteri for white wine and Mavron and Opthalmo for red wine, are cultivated. *Vitis vinifera* vines Cabernet Sauvignon, Cabernet Franc, Carignan, Grenache and Syrah for red wine and Chardonnay, Riesling, Palomino, Sémillon, Muscat and Ugni Blanc for white wine, are also grown. Four wineries dominate the business: Keo, Sodap, Loel and Etko-Haggipavlu. They produce a variety of wines as follows:

Light dry white wine   Amathus, Arsinöe, Palomino

Medium white wine   Aphrodite, Thisbe, Bellapais (semi-sparkling)

Sweet white wine   Hirondelle, St Panteleimon, St Hilarion

Rosé wine   Kokkineli, Coeur de Lion, Amoroso

Red wine   Afames, Agravani, Kolossi, Kykko, Othelo, Olympus Salamis

Sparkling wine   Avra, Duc de Nicosie

Dessert wine   Commanderia; this unique wine got its name from the Knights Templar, a crusading order of knights, in the twelfth century. The luscious wine is made from the native grapes Xynisteri, Mavron and Ophthalmo in 11 villages north of Limassol. The grapes are laid out to dry by the roadside and on rooftops for 10 to 15 days to concentrate the sugar within each grape. When the wine is made it is kept in the villages until the springtime and then it goes to the wineries at Paphos and Limassol. Here it is flavoured with cloves, resin and scented wood and fortified with local brandy. Commanderie St John is a particularly good example of this amber-red, honey-sweet wine.

EGYPT

Although wine was made in Egypt in ancient times, the modern wine industry was started in 1903 by Nestor Gianaclis. He planted a vineyard at Mariout near Alexandria west of the Nile Delta. Twenty-eight years later, a band of French gourmets considered the white wine to be on a par with Rhine wines and those of Burgundy. Very few people would make that comparison now. Many consider the best thing about the wines are their attractive names – Reine Cléopâtre, Cru des Ptolemées, for white and the red Omar Khayyam. Native grapes Fayumi and Rumi, as well as Chardonnay, Chasselas, Pinot Blanc, Muscat Hamburg, Gamay and Pinot Noir, are cultivated.

ENGLAND

The Romans brought the vine and the art of wine-making to Britain some 2000 years ago. When the Romans departed in the early part of the fifth century, most of the vineyards fell into decline. Some were revived by the Saxons in the sixth century. After the Norman invasion in 1066, the wealthy Norman aristocracy planted more vineyards and, wherever possible, established monasteries on site so that the Bénédictine monks, well versed in wine-making, could operate them. The Domesday Book survey of 1086 recorded the existence of 45 vineyards spread over 14 English counties. The nobility and the church continued to expand their wine interests.

In 1152, Henry Plantagenet, Duke of Anjou, married Eleanor of Aquitaine. Two years later, he became Henry II, King of England. Eleanor got Gascony as part of her dowry. Bordeaux and its vineyards was part of that territory which remained 'English' for the following 300 years. The much superior Bordeaux wines flowed freely and cheaply onto the English market and the native wines suffered badly. The Black Death of 1348 added further to the decline and when Henry VIII, embroiled in matrimonial troubles, dissolved the monasteries in the 1530s, most of the vineyards were abandoned. By 1918 and for the next 30 years, no commercial vineyards existed in England.

The grand revival came after World War II when Sir Guy Salisbury-Jones started a 1.2-hectare (3-acre) vineyard in Hambledon, Hampshire in 1952. Other brave pioneers, like Jack Ward of Merrydown, Sussex and the Gore-Brownes of Beaulieu Abbey, Hampshire, followed. Today, there are some 347 vineyards in commercial production. Most of the wine is white and made from German vine strains which can withstand the rigours of the English weather. The extreme limit of cultivation is a rough line across the country from the Wash. Cold, wet summers are a major problem as they produce wines high in acidity but low in alcohol. However, when the summers are favourable, the English vineyards are capable of delivering top-quality white wines.

GRAPE VARIETIES

Grapes for white wine   The Müller-Thurgau is the most important, followed by the Reichensteiner, Schönburger, Seyval Blanc, Bacchus, Madeleine Angevine, Huxelrebe, Morio Muscat and Ortega.

Grapes for red and rosé wines   The Pinot Noir, Gamay and Zweigeltrebe are cultivated without ever reaching the aspired-to standard.

THE SEAL OF QUALITY
The EVA, The English Viticultural Association, was formed in 1965. In order to be able to display the EVA quality seal on a wine label, the vine grower has to declare the quantity of *must* (unfermented grape juice) that has been pressed from the grapes. The volume is strictly controlled. The grower has to present the wine for random

sampling and for chemical analysis. Finally, the wine must receive critical approval from a tasting panel comprising of Masters of Wine. In other words, the Quality Seal is a genuine guarantee of quality.

MAJOR ENGLISH VINEYARDS

Adgestone (Isle of Wight)
Ascot (Berkshire)
Barkham Manor (Sussex)
Barton Manor (Isle of Wight)
Beaulieu (Hampshire)
Biddendon (Kent)
Bothy (Oxfordshire)
Breaky Bottom (Sussex)
Bruisyard (Suffolk)
Carr Taylor (Sussex)
Cavendish Manor (Suffolk)
Chilford Hundred (Cambridgeshire)
Chilsdown (Sussex)
Denbies (Surrey)
Ditchling (Sussex)

Elms Cross (Wiltshire)
English Wine Centre (Sussex)
Felsted (Essex)
Hambledon (Hampshire)
Lamberhurst Priory (Kent)
Merrydown (Sussex)
Pilton Manor (Somerset)
Spots Farm (Kent)
Staple (Kent)
Stocks (Worcestershire)
Thames Valley (Berkshire)
Three Choirs (Gloucestershire)
Wellow (Hampshire)
Wootton (Somerset)
Wraxall (Somerset)

Some table wine is also made in Wales, Jersey and Ireland.

BRITISH WINE

This is a term used to describe wines made in Britain from grapes grown elsewhere. The concentrated grape juice is imported from Cyprus or some other source, reconstituted here, and made into light table wines or into fortified wines imitating sherry and port.

FRANCE

France vies with Italy as being the largest producer of wine, but France has no equal worldwide in terms of sheer quality and variety. France sets the standards to which others aspire. Wine is produced throughout the country, except for the part north of a line extending from Nantes through Paris to the Eastern frontier abutting Luxembourg.

Stringent wine laws control the productions and these regulations known as *Code du Vin*, together with the natural endowment of soil and climate, contribute to France's esteem and pre-eminence as wine producer. Nowadays, the making and labelling of French wines is controlled by EU wine laws under the following definitions.

FRANCE

VINS DE QUALITÉ PRODUITS DANS DES REGIONS DETERMINÉES (VQPRD)

These are quality wines produced from grapes grown in specific regions. They are subdivided into two categories:

Vins d'appellation d'origine contrôlée (AOC)
This labelling guarantees:

- area of production;
- grape varieties used;
- pruning and cultivation methods;
- maximum yield per hectare;
- minimum alcohol content;
- methods of vinification and preservation.

Vins délimités de qualité supérieure (VDQS)
These are wines of superior quality produced in delimited areas with the following conditions guaranteed:

- area of production;
- grape varieties used;
- minimum alcohol content;
- methods of viticulture and vinification.

Although the wines have to be good to merit the VDQS label, they are less fine than the AOC wines.

VINS DE TABLE
The second labelling category, Vins de table, is also divided into two:

Vins de pays (VP)
Local or country wine. Medium in quality, these wines must be made from recommended grapes grown in a certain area or village. They must have a minimum alcohol content, and come from the locality stated on the label.

Vins de consommation courante (VCC)
Wines for everyday consumption and sold by the glass, carafe or *pichet* in cafés and bars all over France. Often completely authentically French, these wines may also be blended with other EU wines of similar style. Non-EU wines may not be blended with French wines.

UNDERSTANDING THE LABEL
French wine labels will indicate which of the above categories the wine is classified under. Wine labels may also include some of the following terms:

Blanc	White
Cave	Underground cellar
Cépage	Vine variety
Chai	Overground cellar
Château	Castle or estate
Clos	Walled-in vineyard especially associated with Burgundy

Reading the label

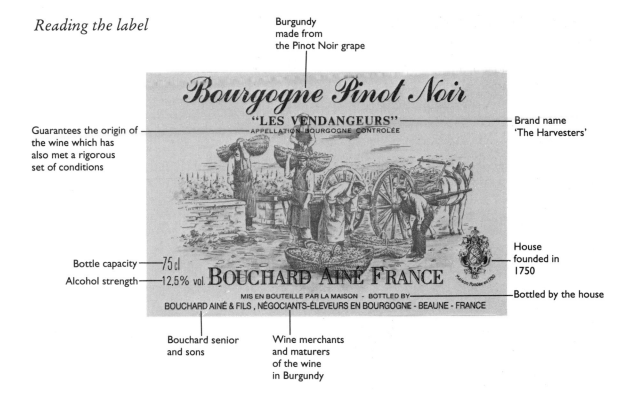

Burgundy made from the Pinot Noir grape

Guarantees the origin of the wine which has also met a rigorous set of conditions

Brand name 'The Harvesters'

Bottle capacity — 75 cl
Alcohol strength — 12.5% vol.

House founded in 1750

Bottled by the house

Bouchard senior and sons

Wine merchants and maturers of the wine in Burgundy

Côte	Hillside
Crémant	Creaming, foaming, sparkling
Cru	Growth, used to describe a vineyard of importance
Cuvée	Blend
Cuve close	Bulk method for making sparkling wine in a closed tank
Demi sec	Medium dry
Domaine	Estate
Doux	Sweet
Eau-de-vie	Water of life, spirit
Grand vin	Great wine
Manipulant	Grape grower and also the wine-maker
Méthode traditionnelle	Classic (champagne) method of making sparkling wine
Mise en bouteille au Château / Domaine	estate bottled
Négociant	Wine handler
Négociant-éleveur	Wine handler who also 'brings-up' or matures the wine in his own cellars
Propriétaire	Estate owner
Récolte	Harvested, followed by the year

Rosé	Pink
Rouge	Red
Sec	Dry
Sur lie	Wine left to mature on its lees or sediment before being bottled
Supérieur	Indicates a slightly higher alcohol content – perhaps an extra 1%
Vendange	Grape harvest
Vendange tardive	Wine made from late-harvested grapes, usually a sweeter wine
Vignoble	Vineyard

Regions and principal wines

Alsace

The Alsace region is one of the most picturesque in all France. The Vosges mountains dominate and the hills which project from the mountains provide a micro-climate which shelters the vineyards they embrace from severe winds and excessive rain. The soil varies even over a short distance and can be of granite, red sandstone or chalk. In 1962 the region was granted AOC status. In 1971 the sale of Alsace wines in litre bottles was prohibited and since 1972 all Alsace wines have to be bottled in the departments of Haut-Rhin and Bas-Rhin.

Some vineyards are more favourably sited than others. In 1985 and again in 1987 the outstanding vineyards, most of them in the Haut-Rhin, were classified as *grands crus* – great growths. For these wines, only four noble grapes are permitted: Gewürztraminer, Riesling, Muscat and Tokay (Pinot Gris). Other grapes, such as Sylvaner, Pinot Blanc and Chasselas may not be used. The Pinot Noir is used to make a little red wine and also a rosé known locally as Schillerwein or Clairet d'Alsace.

THE WINES
Most Alsatian wines are white and usually named after their grape variety, such as Alsace Riesling. Between 1817 and 1917 Alsace belonged to Germany and the influence has resulted in the wines having more of an affinity to Germany than to French wines. They are sold in the standard green flûte bottles of the same shape, but longer than the German bottles. Besides the grape-named wines there are some Alsace specialities.

Edelzwicker   (edel = noble, zwicker = mixture) This is a wine made from a blend of noble variety grapes.

Vendange tardive   This wine is produced when good harvesting conditions continue right through to mid-November. The desired combination of morning mists and warm weather causes the grapes to become susceptible to the noble rot fungus (*Botrytis cinerea*). The fungus attacks the grapes, feeds on the water and concentrates the juice and likewise the sugar. The producer then decides whether to vinify the sugar completely or to allow some residual sugar to remain. The wine produced can, confusingly, be either dry or sweet.

Selection des grains nobles   This term was invented by Hugel, one of the great Alsace wine-makers. It entails a much more rigorous selection of individual botrytis-affected grapes. The process is very time consuming, but worth the effort as the resulting wine is luscious and creamy. Frequent inspections ensure that quality levels are complied with at all times.

Crémant d'Alsace   This is a particularly good sparkling wine made from a combination of grapes and by the *méthode traditionnelle*.

Bordeaux

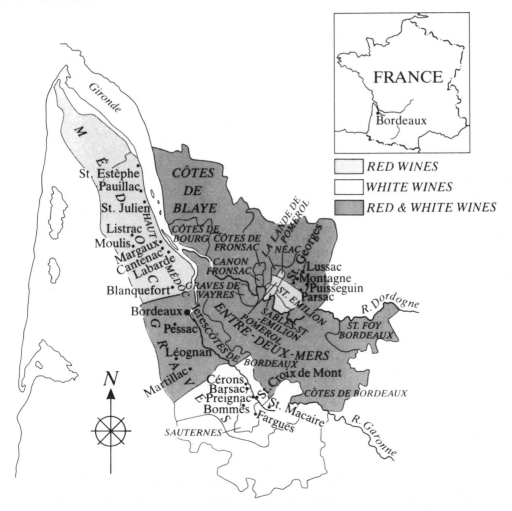

The vineyards of Bordeaux are located in the Gironde department of south-western France. Because of its strong links with England (Bordeaux, as part of Gascony, was under English rule for 300 years from 1154) Bordeaux wines have always been popular in Britain. In the old days, the Gascons called their bright, light-coloured red wines 'clairet' and later they became known as claret in England, as they still are. The trade base for the wines is the city of Bordeaux which lies on the left bank of the Garonne, a river sourced in the Pyrenees. The Garonne runs through the city before merging with the Dordogne, whose source is in the Massif Central. The confluence of the two rivers traces the shape of a swallow's tail before forming the River Gironde and flowing towards its estuary in the Bay of Biscay. It is on the banks of these rivers that most of the finest Bordeaux vineyards are located.

Soil   The predominant soil is gravel with clay or sand covering a sub-soil of lime.

Climate   The mild and humid climate is influenced by the rivers and the close proximity of the Atlantic. Spring frosts are a hazard.

Grapes for red wine   Cabernet Sauvignon, Cabernet Franc, Merlot, Malbec and Petit-Verdot.

Grapes for white wine   Sémillon, Sauvignon Blanc and Muscadelle.

THE WINES
The general appellation is Bordeaux, which means a wine so described can come from anywhere within the viticultural region of Bordeaux. Bordeaux Supérieur has a slightly higher alcohol content.

Médoc   This is the classic area of Bordeaux, producing only red wines usually of extraordinary quality. The area is divided into the Haut Médoc and Bas Médoc, with the real stars coming from the southern Haut Médoc communes or parishes of Pauillac, Margaux, Saint-Julien, Saint-Estephe, Moulis and Listrac. The individual wines were so outstanding that in 1855 an official committee classified 61 of the best red wines into five *crus* or growths known collectively as *crus classés*. The classification was based on quality assessment, on prestige and on the prices the wines were fetching. Since then, a few changes have occurred – some leading to improvements, some leading to deterioration. However, the basic classification still holds good. Only four wines merited the highest distinction of *premiers grand crus* and one of these, Château Haut Brion is, in fact, from Graves, a neighbouring district.

Table 9.1 *Grands crus classés of the Médoc: 1855 classification*

	VINEYARDS	COMMUNE
First growths (*Premiers crus*)	Ch. Lafite-Rothschild	Pauillac
	Ch. Latour	Pauillac
	Ch. Margaux	Margaux
	Ch. Mouton-Rothschild	Pauillac[1]
	Ch. Haut-Brion	Pessac[2]
Second growths (*Deuxièmes crus*)	Ch. Rausan-Ségla	Margaux
	Ch. Rauzan-Gassies	Margaux
	Ch. Léoville-Lascases	St Julien
	Ch. Léoville-Poyférré	St Julien
	Ch. Léoville-Barton	St Julien
	Ch. Dufort-Vivens	Margaux
	Ch. Gruaud-Larose	St Julien
	Ch. Lascombes	Margaux
	Ch. Brane-Cantenac	Cantenac
	Ch. Pichon-Longueville-Baron	Pauillac
	Ch. Pichon-Longueville-Lalande	Pauillac
	Ch. Ducru-Beaucaillou	St Julien
	Ch. Cos-d'Estournel	St Estèphe
	Ch. Montrose	St Estèphe
Third Growths (*Troisièmes crus*)	Ch. Kirwan	Cantenac
	Ch. d'Issan	Cantenac
	Ch. Lagrange	St Julien
	Ch. Langoa Barton	St Julien
	Ch. Giscours	Labarde
	Ch. Malescot-Saint-Exupéry	Margaux
	Ch. Boyd-Cantenac	Cantenac
	Ch. Palmer	Cantenac
	Ch. La Lagune	Ludon
	Ch. Desmirail	Margaux
	Ch. Cantenac-Brown	Cantenac
	Ch. Calon-Ségur	St Estèphe
	Ch. Ferrière	Margaux
	Ch. Marquis-d'Alesme-Becker	Margaux

[1] Upgraded from the second to the first growth in 1973
[2] Graves district

Table 9.1 *Continued*

	VINEYARDS	COMMUNE
Fourth growths (*Quatrièmes crus*)	Ch. Saint-Pierre-Sevaistre	St Julien
	Ch. Talbot	St Julien
	Ch. Branaire-Ducru	St Julien
	Ch. Duhart-Milon-Rothschild	Pauillac
	Ch. Pouget	Cantenac
	Ch. La Tour-Carnet	St Laurent
	Ch. Lafon-Rochet	St Estèphe
	Ch. Beychevelle	St Julien
	Ch. Prieuré-Lichine	Cantenac
	Ch. Marquis-de-Terme	Margaux
Fifth growths (*Cinquièmes crus*)	Ch. Pontet-Canet	Pauillac
	Ch. Batailley	Pauillac
	Ch. Haut-Batailley	Pauillac
	Ch. Grand-Puy-Lacoste	Pauillac
	Ch. Grand-Puy-Ducasse	Pauillac
	Ch. Lynch-Bages	Pauillac
	Ch. Lynch-Moussas	Pauillac
	Ch. Dauzac	Labarde
	Ch. Mouton Baronne Philippe	Pauillac
	Ch. le Tertre	Arsac
	Ch. Haut-Bages-Libéral	Pauillac
	Ch. Pédesclaux	Pauillac
	Ch. Belgrave	St Laurent
	Ch. Camensac	St Laurent
	Ch. Cos-Labory	St Estèphe
	Ch. Clerc-Milon-Rothschild	Pauillac
	Ch. Croizet-Bages	Pauillac
	Ch. Cantemerle	Macau

Graves   The appellation covers 40 communes producing red and white wines possessing true elegance of style. The aromatic reds are perhaps the more outstanding. The district is named after the gravel content of the soil and was classified in 1959 as follows.

Table 9.2   *Wine of the Graves: 1959 classification*

	VINEYARD	COMMUNE
Red wines (classified in 1953 and confirmed in 1959)	Ch. Bouscaut	Cadaujac
	Ch. Haut-Bailly	Léognan
	Ch. Carbonnieux	Léognan
	Domaine de Chevalier	Léognan
	Ch. Fieuzal	Léognan
	Ch. Olivier	Léognan
	Ch. Malartic-Lagravière	Léognan
	Ch. La Tour-Martillac	Martillac
	Ch. Smith-Haut-Lafitte	Martillac
	Ch. Haut-Brion	Pessac
	Ch. La Mission-Haut-Brion	Pessac
	Ch. Pape Clément	Pessac
	Ch. La Tour-Haut-Brion	Talence
White wines (classified in 1959)	Ch. Bouscaut	Cadaujac
	Ch. Carbonnieux	Léognan
	Domaine de Chevalier	Léognan
	Ch. Olivier	Léognan
	Ch. Malartic-Lagravière	Léognan
	Ch. La Tour-Martillac	Martillac
	Ch. Laville-Haut-Brion	Talence
	Ch. Couhins	Villenave d'Ornon

Cérons   Adjacent to Graves, produces dry and sweet white wines.

Entre-deux-Mers   These dry or medium dry white wines come from a triangle of land between the rivers Garonne and Dordogne. A little red wine is made for local consumption. The AOC status is for the dry whites only.

Premières Côtes de Bordeaux   Home of Cadillac, Loupiac and St-Croix-du-Mont, these are, in the main, sweet white wine zones producing full, creamy, luscious end-of-the-meal wines.

Côtes de Bourg, Blaye and Fronsac   produce light red and white wines of *cru bourgeois* quality (châteaux not included in officially classified lists). The wines are usually good value and ideal for lunch-time drinking.

St-Emilion   This region is famous for its generous full-bodied red wines, influenced by the Merlot grape. The wines classified in 1955 and revised in 1969 and 1985 are somewhere between classical Médoc and fine Burgundy in flavour.

Table 9.3   *St-Emilion wines: 1955 classification*

First great growths (premiers grands crus)

Ch. Ausone	} Grade A	Ch. Beauséjour-Duffau-Lagarrosse
Ch. Cheval-Blanc		Ch. Beauséjour-Bécot
		Ch. Bel-Air
		Ch. Canon
		Ch. Figeac
		Clos Fourtet
		Ch. La Gaffelière
		Ch. La Magdelaine
		Ch. Pavie
		Ch. Trottevieille

Grade B applies to the right-hand column (Ch. Beauséjour-Duffau-Lagarrosse through Ch. Trottevieille).

Pommerol   Again, the Merlot influence produces big, velvet-smooth red wines. One of them, the outstanding Château Pétrus is the most expensive red wine in the world. No official classification has ever been made but the following are high calibre wines.

Table 9.4   *Pommerol wines*

Cru exceptionnel	**Château Pétrus**
Other principal crus	Ch. Certan de May
	Ch. Certan-Giraud
	Ch. la Conseillante
	Ch. l'Eglise-Clinet
	Ch. l'Evangile
	Ch. la Fleur Pétrus
	Ch. la Grave-Trigant-de-Boisset
	Ch. Latour à Pomerol
	Ch. Petit-Village
	Ch. le Pin
	Ch. Trotanoy
	Clos de l'Eglise (Moreau)
	Vieux Ch. Certan
	Ch. Beauregard

Sauternes   These are classic dessert wines – luscious, unctuous in flavour, rich golden in colour with a generous, though concentrated, complex bouquet of spice and honeyed fruit. Made mainly from the Sémillon grape and a small blend of Sauvignon Blanc and Muscadelle, the wines enjoy a remarkable reputation for quality and finesse. When conditions are right – and these do not prevail every year – the grapes become affected by a fungus called *botrytis cinerea*. This fungus is induced when climatic conditions result in morning haze (even a modicum of rain is beneficial) followed by hot sunny afternoons. The fungus, also popularly known as *pourriture noble* or noble rot, causes spores to form on the outer skins and these feed on the water within the grapes, reducing the juice to a quarter of its volume. As the water diminishes, the sugar and glycerine content remains virtually untouched, becoming more and more concentrated as each day passes. As the grapes shrivel and take on a rotting appearance, the tartaric acids become decomposed and it is at this optimum ripeness that the grapes are gathered in late September through October. Because of the necessary careful selectivity, each sector of the vineyard has to be gone over again and again. Each visit is called a 'passage'. Wine made from grapes not harvested before the bad weather, or made from grapes not affected by *pourriture noble*, are usually sold as Bordeaux Blanc Moelleux.

The name Sauternes embraces wines from the villages of Bommes, Fargues, Preignac, Barsac as well as Sauternes, although Barsac is often sold under its own name.

Sauternes were also classified in 1855 and the extraordinary Château d'Yquem has still no serious rival for true greatness.

Noble rot grapes

Table 9.5 *Wines of the Sauternes and Barsac: 1855 classification*

	VINEYARD	COMMUNE
First great growth (*premier grand cru*)	Ch. d'Yquem	Sauternes
First growths (*Premiers crus*)	Ch. La Tour-Blanche	Bommes
	Ch. Lafaurie-Peyraguey	Bommes
	Clos Haut-Peyraguey	Bommes
	Ch. Rayne-Vigneau	Bommes
	Ch. Suduiraut	Preignac
	Ch. Coutet	Barsac
	Ch. Climens	Barsac
	Ch. Guiraud	Sauternes
	Ch. Rieussec	Fargues
	Ch. Rabaud-Promis	Bommes
	Ch. Sigalas-Rabaud	Bommes
Second growths (*Deuxièmes crus*)	Ch. de Myrat	Barsac*
	Ch. Doisy-Daëne	Barsac
	Ch. Doisy-Dubroca	Barsac
	Ch. Doisy-Védrines	Barsac
	Ch. d'Arche	Sauternes
	Ch. Filhot	Sauternes
	Ch. Broustet	Barsac
	Ch. Nairac	Barsac
	Ch. Caillou	Barsac
	Ch. Suau	Barsac
	Ch. de Malle	Preignac
	Ch. Romer	Fargues
	Ch. Lamothe	Sauternes

* No longer in production

Burgundy

Prior to the French Revolution of 1789, most of the Burgundy vineyards were owned by the church. When the vineyards were seized, they were split up into small plots or parcels and sold back to the locals. Today, most of the vineyards are cultivated by small growers and, standards being relative, it is more important to know the grower or producer rather than the name of the vineyard or its location. For example, Clos de Vougeot has some 80 different owners, each making a wine of slightly different quality and nuance to that of his neighbour, but each with the entitlement to sell their

BURGUNDY

Map key:
- CHABLIS
- CÔTE DE NUITS
- CÔTE DE BEAUNE
- CÔTE CHALONNAISE
- CÔTE MÂCONNAISE
- BEAUJOLAIS

wine under the vineyard name. Also, because of its northern location, the grapes do not ripen properly in poor years and sugar is added to the must (*chaptalisation*) to counteract high acidity and low alcohol. All of which combines to make the choice of Burgundy wines more haphazard.

Soil The soil in Burgundy varies between clay, limestone and granite. The climate is continental with very hot summers and very cold, hard winters.

The grapes for red wine The classic is the Pinot Noir and the secondary grape is Gamay. For white wine the classic is Chardonnay and the secondary grape is Aligoté. Burgundy can produce extremely fine red and white wines and sparkling wines of merit.

The Wines
The general appellations are as follows:

Bourgogne Grand Ordinaire   This basic wine can be red, white or rosé.

Bourgogne Aligoté   This is a good, standard white wine made from the Aligoté grape. It is the base wine traditionally used for the French apéritif, Kir.

Bourgogne Passe-tout-grains   This red (usually) or rosé wine is made from a combination of the Pinot Noir and Gamay grapes. One-third Pinot must be contained in the blend.

Chablis   There are four quality grades of Chablis, a dry fruity white wine, famous all over the world.

Petit Chablis   The basic wine, this is a lower quality wine, as the name suggests.

Chablis   This is of better quality and can be good in vintage years.

Chablis Premier Crus   Worth the extra money, but standards can vary.

Chablis Grand Crus   These are wines of great delicacy and incomparable refinement – a true product of the great Chardonnay grape. Only seven vineyards merit the distinction. These are Bougros, Les Preuses, Les Vaudésirs, Les Grenouilles, Valmur, Les Blanchots and Les Clos.

Bourgogne Irancy   A light, red wine made from the Pinot Noir grape in the commune of Irancy, near Chablis, south of Auxerre.

Table 9.6

COMMUNE	VINEYARD
Gevrey-Chambertin	Chambertin
	Clos de Bèze
Morey Saint-Denis	Clos de Tart
	Clos Saint-Denis
Chambolle Musigny	Musigny
	Les Bonnes-Mares
Vougeot	Clos de Vougeot
Flagey-Echézeaux	Echézeaux
	Grands Echézeaux
Vosne Romanée	La Romanée-Conti
	Le Richebourg La Romanée Saint-Vivant
Nuits-Saint-George	Les Saint-Georges
	Clos de la Maréchale

Côte de Nuits   A pedigree red wine region, producing highly distinctive wine from the Pinot Noir grape, they have exceptional class and style and a unique bouquet.

The names of the villages or communes and their principal wines are legendary and some are listed in table 9.6.

At one time the villages were known by their first name, such as Gevrey, Chambolle and so on, but as the renown of the vineyards spread, the vineyard name was added – thus we get Gevrey-Chambertin and Chambolle Musigny.

Côte de Beaune   This region, together with Côte de Nuits, makes up the famous Côte d'Or – the golden slopes – so called because of the wonderful golden colour of the vineyards in late autumn or, perhaps more realistically, because of the wealth the vineyards generate for their owners. Côte de Beaune makes red and white wine of great quality from the Pinot Noir and Chardonnay grapes respectively. Some of the best are given in table 9.7.

Table 9.7

COMMUNE	VINEYARD
Reds	
Pernand-Vergelesses	Les Vergelesses
Aloxe Corton	Le Corton
	Corton Clos du Roi
Savigny-les-Beaune	Les Lavières
Beaune	Les Marconnets
	Le Clos des Mouches
Pommard	Les Epinots
	Les Rugiens
Volnay	Les Caillerets
	Les Champans
Santenay	Les Gravières
	Le Clos de Tavannes
Chassagne-Montrachet	Clos Saint-Jean
Whites	
Meursault	Les Perrières-Dessous
	Les Charmes-Dessous
Puligny-Montrachet	Le Montrachet
Chassagne-Montrachet	Le Chavalier Montrachet
	Le Batard Montrachet (overlaps both communes)
Aloxe Corton	Le Corton-Charlemagne

Côte de Beaune can be a combination wine from the Beaune area. Côte de Beaune Villages comes from one or more villages which have a right to the appellation. Hospice de Beaune is a hospital home for old and unwell people. The hospice owns many vineyards, some the finest in the region. These have been bequeathed to the charity since its foundation by Nicholas Rolin in 1443. The wines are auctioned on the third Sunday in November in the Market Hall in Beaune. Money received is the main source of income for the hospital. Each lot of wine is put under the hammer *à la chandelle*. The candle is lit to start the bidding and doused when the bidding ends. The candle is relit to start the bidding for the next lot and so on. The prices realised are a good barometer for Burgundy prices for that year.

Côte Chalonnaise   Also known as Region-Mercurey, this produces good light-red and white Burgundies, as well as some good sparkling wine sold as Crémant de Bourgogne or Bourgogne Mousseux. There are five main producing villages: Bouzeron, Rully, Givry, Mercurey and Montagny.

Bouzeron   Best known for its sharp, dry white wine, Bourgogne Aligoté de Bouzeron.

Rully   This region produces red, white and sparkling wine; the white wine made from the Chardonnay grape is best.

Givry   This region produces predominantly light to big red wines using the Pinot Noir grape.

Mercurey   This region produces an abundance of good red wines made from the Pinot Noir. The five *premier cru* vineyards are Clos des Fourneaux, Clos Marcilly, Clos des Montaigns, Clos du Roi and Clos Voyen. Clos means a walled-in vineyard built high enough to keep out prying eyes.

Montagny   This region produces good, dry white wines from the Chardonnay grape. Should the wine reach a natural 11.5% alcohol, it can glory in the appellation *premier cru*.

Côtes Mâconnaise   Mâcon produces both red and white wine, with the white having much the better reputation. The red wine is made from the Gamay grape with a little Pinot Noir in the blend. It is usually sold as Mâcon Rouge or if it has 11% alcohol as Mâcon Supérieur. These wines have only a modest reputation. Mâcon Blanc or Mâcon Supérieur Blanc (11% alcohol) are ordinary white wines, but the real star is Pouilly Fuissé. This dry, soft, full-flavoured wine is made from the Chardonnay grape in the villages of Chaintré, Fuissé, Pouilly, Solutré and Vergisson. Two satellite villages, Pouilly-Vinzelles and Pouilly Loché make a similar style of wine. Under the appellation Mâcon-Villages, good refreshing whites are made, again from the Chardonnay grape and with the village name appended. Examples to seek out are Mâcon-Chardonnay (which could have given its name to the grape variety), Mâcon Clessé, Mâcon Lugny, Mâcon Prissé and Mâcon Viré. St-Véran is another stylish white wine first made in 1971 as an alternative to the more expensive Pouilly Fuissé wines. It is made using the Chardonnay grape in vineyards which overlap Mâcon and Beaujolais.

Beaujolais   This is the most southern and largest of the Burgundy wine areas. It takes its name from the village of Beaujeu. Red wines from the Gamay grape and white from the Chardonnay and Aligoté grapes are produced. The reds, especially the Beaujolais *crus* are much the best. The ten *crus*, all located in Haut Beaujolais, are Brouilly, Chénas, Chiroubles, Côte de Brouilly, Fleurie, Juliénas, Morgon, Moulin-à-vent, Régnié and Saint-Amour. Most red Beaujolais is light and fruity in flavour. It is served slighly chilled and meant to be drunk when it is young and vigorous. Beaujolais de l'année emphasises the point. It is made to be consumed within a year.

Beaujolais Nouveau   Half the production of Beaujolais is now sold as Nouveau. This light, vivid, fresh, fruity wine is made by the *macération carbonique* method. Whole bunches of unbroken grapes are put into a sealed vat full of carbon dioxide. Fermentation occurs within each grape before the grapes burst open, releasing their wine. Simultaneously, the grapes at the bottom are crushed by the weight of those above before undergoing a normal fermentation. Once bottled, the wine is ready for drinking. Traditionally it is released on the third Thursday in November. It is intended to be drunk before Christmas or Easter at the latest. Beaujolais Primeur is very much the same as Nouveau. The release date for this style ends on 10th December.

Champagne

Champagne is unquestionably the greatest and most famous sparkling wine in the world. It is produced 145 kilometres (90 miles) north-east of Paris in the following zones:

- the Mountains of Reims;
- the Valley of the Marne around Epernay;
- the Aube department;
- the Côtes des Blancs – so called because it is entirely planted with the white Chardonnay grape.

The total area permissable for the cultivation of the vine is 34,000 hectares (84,000 acres) of which 28,000 hectares (69,000 acres) are in actual production. The soil is generally chalk of belemnite which affords good drainage and is ideal for producing light, white wines. The climate is chilly and cool with an average annual temperature of 10°C (50°F) – just one degree above the extremity for the ripening of grapes.

The three grapes permitted are Pinot Noir (black), Pinot Meunier (black) and Chardonnay. The black grapes give richness, softness and predominance of flavour and the white Chardonnay adds elegance and balance to the blend. Most blends are two parts black to one part white, but sometimes champagne is made entirely from black grapes and labelled Blanc de Noirs. When made from the Chardonnay grape only it is sold as Blanc de Blancs. The vineyards are graded by the champagne governing body, the *Comité Interprofessionnel du Vin de Champagne* (CIVC), from 100% (*grands crus*) to 80% (*premiers crus*), with relative prices for the grapes per kilo at harvest time. The CIVC are responsible for ensuring that the traditionally high production standards are maintained. They also deal with the general marketing and promotion of the wine – including the protection of the name Champagne.

BACKGROUND

The wines of Champagne always had a tendency to sparkle. The cold weather of autumn would mute the fermentation process and the warmer weather of spring would rejuvenate the yeasts, causing a second fermentation to develop. At the age of 30, Dom Pérignon (1638–1715), a blind Bénédictine monk and head cellarer at the Abbey of Haut-Villers, recognised that this prickly wine had potential for improvement. He experimented with compensatory blending of grapes from different locations. He got bottle-makers to make stronger bottles so as to withstand the pressure better. He introduced the use of proper corks instead of the previously used oil-soaked hemp or rag stoppers. The combined initiatives were successful. Today, Champagne can be a blend from the products of as many as 40 different vineyards. The bottles are strong enough to withstand an internal pressure of 6 kg per cm^2, equivalent to the tyre pressure of a London Transport Bus. Corks, of the finest quality, are assiduous in their confinement of the sparkle to a life sentence in the bottle.

THE VINTAGE

The grapes are hand-picked in September – mechanical harvesting is forbidden as it might mangle the black grapes and cause discolouration of the juice. Only grapes in prime condition are gathered. This selectivity, so important for quality, is called *épluchage*. The premier producers use only the juice from the first pressing, known as *vin de cuvée*, to make their champagne. A subsequent pressing – *premier taille* – which gives a slightly darker juice, is often sold to co-operatives to make their champagne or sold to concerns who specialise in making BOB (buyer's own brand) champagne. In 1992 the authorities abolished the use of the *deuxieme taille* – third pressing of the grapes – to be used for making champagne. This is usually fermented and distilled into local brandy – Marc de Champagne.

FERMENTATION

When the pressed juice emerges it is allowed to settle for about 12 hours, so that any impurities and solid matter descend to the bottom of the vat. This practice is known as *débourage*. Fermentation follows in stainless steel vats at a temperature of 20°C (68°F). The resulting dry white wine will have an alcoholic strength of 11%. The new wine is rested until the following spring when the cuvée or blend is made. Once the blend has been agreed by the principals of a champagne house, the still wine is pumped into a large vat. A controlled proportion of *liqueur de tirage* – a mix of old champagne, sugar and yeast – is added. The wine is immediately bottled and crown caps are attached.

MÉTHODE CHAMPENOISE

A second fermentation, which can last up to three months, takes place within each bottle and as the carbon dioxide is unable to escape it becomes chemically bonded in the wine. This slow process, known as *prise de mousse* (capturing the froth) produces a continuous stream of minute bubbles – the smaller and more intense they are the better. It also raises the alcohol content from 11% to 12% and the internal pressure to a peak of about six atmospheres (one atmosphere = 15 pounds per square inch). The bottles lie horizontally, piled high, resting on wooden slat dividers – *sur lattes*.

The wine is now powerfully effervescent but it is not clear, as an opaque deposit of dead yeast, tannin and other matter has settled along the inside of the bottle.

REMUAGE

Remuage or riddling is the traditional method used to clear the wine. The bottles, still horizontal, are taken to a holed wooden frame called a *pupître*. This is made up of two rectangular boards hinged together to form an inverted V shape. The holes can accommodate the bottles (necks inwards) in any position from the horizontal to the vertical. The *remueur* (the removal person) manipulates the bottles, turning, oscillating and tilting each one gradually to encourage the sediment into the neck of the bottle. At the end of this skilful but labour-intensive operation, which takes up to three months, the bottles will be almost vertical and the sediment resting on the cap. Many firms have now replaced their *remueurs* with mechanical, computerised *gyropalettes* which can do the same job equally well in one week. The bottles may be rested – *sur pointes* – upside down (the neck of one in the punt of another) for some

Remuage

time. The minimum ageing for non-vintage and vintage champagne is one year and three years respectively. However, the maturing period is more likely to be three years for non-vintage and five years for vintage quality.

DÉGORGEMENT À LA GLACE

When required for sale the bottles, still upside down, are passed along an automated line and the necks are immersed in a freezing liquid of brine for seven minutes. The sediment is frozen into a pellet of ice which is removed by the process of *dégorgement* (disgorging). The *dégorgeur* (the discharger) removes the temporary crown cap and the pressure of carbon dioxide within the bottle expels the pellet of ice. What is left behind is brilliantly clear champagne with an internal pressure of about five to six atmospheres. The little champagne lost by the discharge is replaced by a dosage or solution of cane sugar and older champagne called *liqueur d'expédition*. The amount of sugar in the dosage will determine the style and relative sweetness of the champagne. This will be indicated on the label (see table 9.4).

The bottles are now sealed with best-quality corks from Portugal or Spain and wire cages are affixed to hold the corks in place. They may get a little more ageing before being dressed – neck foil and label – for sale.

Sediment in a champagne bottle

Disgorging of sediment

STYLES OF CHAMPAGNE

Cuvée de prestige   Luxury Cuvée. These fabulous and fabulously expensive flagship champagnes are made in the best years. They may be of a single vintage or a combination of different vintages (even sometimes having some non-vintage wine in the blend). But the final quality is deluxe. They are mostly marketed in elegant bottles which are sometimes stylishly decorated to mark a special occasion. Examples are Dom Pérignon, Roederer Cristal, Bollinger RD, Pol Roger Winston Churchill, Dom Ruinart and Tattinger Comtes de Champagne.

Table 9.8   *Terms describing the amount of sugar in champagnes*

TERM	SUGAR IN DOSAGE	DESCRIPTION
Extra brut	None	Bone dry
Brut zero		These rare styles are
Nature		becoming popular
Brut	up to 1%	Very dry
Extra sec, Extra dry	1–2%	Dry to medium dry
Sec	2–4%	Medium sweet
Demi-sec	4–6%	Sweet
Demi-doux	6–8%	Sweeter
Doux	8% upwards	Luscious

Vintage champagne   This wine is made from grapes of a single good year. The year will always appear on the label. These wines are well matured before being released for sale.

Non-vintage champagne   This is a blend of wines from different years. The finest will have some vintage quality wine in the blend.

Pink champagne   May be of vintage or non-vintage character. Classically made by leaving the black grape skins with the juice until it becomes pink in colour. It can also be made by adding red wine, such as Bouzy, to white wine, before bottling.

Crémant   This is a style of champagne which is semi-sparkling – having about 3½ atmospheres of pressure. It sometimes has a village name attached, for example Crémant de Cramant.

THE SMALL PRINT ON THE LABEL
Besides the more obvious descriptive information, the label will show in small letters at the bottom the type of producer, followed by a matriculation number which is coded to each wine-maker.

NM (Négociant-Manipulant)   The term means merchant-handler and is associated with the great champagne houses who buy grapes from other sources besides their own.

RM (Récoltant-Manipulant)   This harvest-handler makes their own wine from their own grapes and sells the product usually under their own name.

CM (Coopérative-Manipulant)   The co-operative handler makes the wine from grapes or base wine obtained from all kinds of sources.

MA (Marque Auxilaire)   A brand name which can be associated with the producer who sells their wine under a second label, either to facilitate a purchaser's requirement or to distinguish the wine from their own main brand.

Sometimes the letters RD appear on a label. They mean *récemment dégorgé* – recently disgorged. Those wines have been left upside down (*sur pointes*) in their bottles to mature, in contact with the yeasts deposits, for many years. This produces a fine, beautifully balanced wine, often of deluxe quality. They are usually released for sale after eight to ten years, sometimes longer. They are disgorged just prior to selling in order to maintain their vigorous brilliance.

Table 9.9

NAME	METRIC	IMPERIAL
Quarter-bottle	20.0 cl	6.0 fl oz
Half-bottle	37.5 cl	12.7 fl oz
Bottle	75.0 cl	25.4 fl oz
Magnum (2 bottles)	1.5 litres	50.7 fl oz
Jeroboam (double magnum) (4 bottles)	3.0 litres	101.4 fl oz
Rehoboam (6 bottles)	4.5 litres	152.1 fl oz
Methuselah (methusalem) (8 bottles)	6.0 litres	202.8 fl oz
Salmanazar (12 bottles)	9.0 litres	304.2 fl oz
Balthazar (16 bottles)	12.0 litres	405.6 fl oz
Nebuchadnezzar (20 bottles)	15.0 litres	507.1 fl oz

Corsica

The beautiful island of Corsica, where Napoleon was born, was once ravaged by the phylloxera vine disease. Many of the growers moved on to north Africa, but when Algeria became independent from France, some growers were repatriated and set about re-establishing Corsican viticulture. The appellation *Vin de Corse* covers the whole island and includes the areas Ajaccio, Calvi, Coteaux du Cap Corse, Figari, Patrimonio, Porto Vecchio and Sartène. Local grapes Sciacarello and Nielluccio are used to make much red and rosé wine and Malvasia, Muscat and Vermentino are the important white wine grapes. Much is expected of recent plantings of Chardonnay, Chinon Blanc and the red grapes Cabernet Sauvignon and Merlot. A feature of Corsican wines is their high alcohol content. Patrimonio is a big, strong red wine, with a minimum alcohol content of 12.5%. Porto Vecchio is a nice crisp and fruity white wine and the red, white and rosés from Figari, Sartène and Calvi are all pleasing. A sweet white wine is made in the Coteaux du Cap Corse and in Patrimonio. A local speciality is the wine-based, rusty red, medium sweet apéritif called Cap Corse. *Vin de Pays* quality wines are made all over the island and are sold as *Vin de Pays de l'Ile de Beauté*.

Jura

The Jura extends from south of Alsace to the Swiss border. The vineyards are located on the western slopes of the Jura mountains. The soil is a mixture of limestone and clay and the climate is continental – hot summers, cold winters with a reasonable supply of rain. There is a unique variety of wines produced: red, white, rosé or grey, straw, yellow and mad.

Arbois is the most prestigious regions not only for its variety of wine but also because it was here that Louis Pasteur was born and where he carried out most of his research on vinification.

For red wines, the main grapes used are Trousseau, Poulsard and Pinot Noir. For rosé wines, Poulsard grapes are used. For white wines, Chardonnay and Savagnin are favoured, often in combination.

THE WINES
The wines are made under four appellations:

- Arbois (red, white rosé and vin jaune)
- Château Chalon (vin jaune)
- Côtes du Jura (red, white, rosé and vin jaune)
- l'Etoile (white, vin jaune and sparkling)

The most unusual wines of the region are *vin jaune* (yellow wine) *vin de paille* (straw wine) *vin fou* (mad wine) and *Macvin*, a unique apéritif.

Vin jaune   A very distinctive wine, this is made from the savagnin grape in the normal fashion. The wine is put into small oak barrels and kept there, without being racked or topped up, for six years. As the wine very gradually loses some of its volume, a film of yeast known as *voile* develops on the surface of the wine. This is technically known as *Saccharomyces bayanus*, somewhat similar to the flor that develops on fino sherries. This slowly oxidises the wine, resulting in a colour change to yellow. At the same time, the wine also develops a lovely hazelnut flavour and a rich bouquet of almonds. It has a minimum alcohol strength of 11.5% – sometimes it can be as high as 15%. The wine is bottled in the traditional *clavelin* – a short, dumpy bottle, first developed in the sixteenth century. Château Chalon is the most distinguished style of vin jaune.

Vin de paille   This wine is made from a blend of red and white grapes. After harvesting, the grapes are spread out on straw or on plastic trays or suspended from rafters in rooms with good ventilation. They are kept like that for six months to concentrate the sugar and the flavour. Because of the high sugar content in the grapes when pressed, fermentation can lumber on for up to two years. The wine is then aged in small oak barrels for another three to four years. The wines are usually vinified to be very sweet and luscious and usually have an alcohol content of 15%.

Vin fou   Mad wine or crazy wine is, in fact, a sparkling wine made by the *méthode traditionnelle* in Arbois by Henri Maire. They are not classics – just meant to help you have a good time. Other sparkling wines are made in l'Etoile and in the Côtes du Jura.

Macvin   This local apéritif is similar to Pineau de Charente, but with spices such as cinnamon and coriander added. The name derives from Marc-Vin, as eau-de-vie de marc is used to mute the fermentation.

Loire

The Loire, the longest river in France, stretches from its source in the Cévennes mountains in central France to its estuary at Nantes on the Brittany coast. On its banks and low hillsides, and also along its tributories, the vine is cultivated amongst magnificent scenery and turreted châteaux. The range of wines produced is also splendid – dry, medium, sweet white wines, reds and rosés and some excellent sparkling wines.

For white wines the important grapes are Muscadet, Sauvignon Blanc and Chenin Blanc. For reds and rosés the main grape is the Cabernet Franc, and for sparkling wines the Chenin Blanc is favourite.

There are four main wine-producing regions. Starting at the Loire Atlantique these are:

- Pays Nantais
- Anjou-Saumur
- Touraine
- Central Vineyards

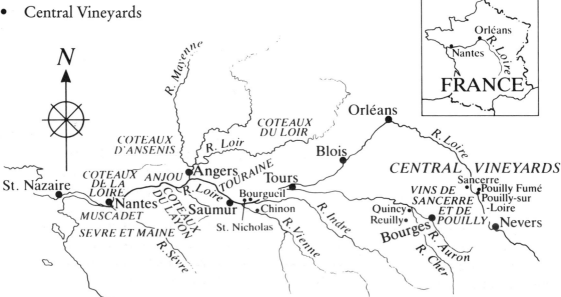

Pays Nantais   The home of Muscadet, one of the most popular of all French wines, made from a grape which originated in Burgundy and which was called Melon de Bourgogne because of its rounded leaves. In Nantes the grape is known as Muscadet. The best Muscadet is produced in Sèvre-et-Maine, a district south of Nantes. Its best style is Muscadet-sur-lie, which is traditionally bottled off its lees or sediment. The wine will have spent the winter 'on its lees' in barrel in order to obtain maximum freshness and flavour. At its best Muscadet is dry, crisp and light and is most refreshing when drunk young or, as they say locally, from two months to two years. It makes an excellent apéritif or an accompaniment to shellfish.

Gros Plant du Pays Nantais is another local wine, but made from the Folle Blanche grape, known here as Gros Plant. This wine, high in acidity, is not too popular elsewhere.

Anjou-Saumur   The reputation of Anjou rests chiefly with its very popular rosé wines, much of which is made from the Groslot or Gamay grape. However, the wine becomes more distinguished when made from the Cabernet France grape. Anjou also makes some white wine using the Chenin Blanc grape; the best style comes from the small appellation called Savennières. The Cabernet and Gamay grapes are used to make Anjou Rouge. Côteaux du Layon is renowned for its sweet white wines which are mostly made from botrytis-affected Chenin Blanc grapes. Quarts de Chaume and Bonnezeaux are the best appellations for these rich, perfumed, honeyed wines. Their richness is pleasingly balanced by a refreshing lemon acidity. Saumur makes red, white and rosé still wines as well as sparkling wines. The reds can be ordinary, as in Saumur Rouge, or they can be very fine as exemplified by Saumur Champigny, a product of the Cabernet France grape. The white wine – Saumur Blanc – is dry and sharp. Although it is made chiefly from the Chenin Blanc, other grapes such as Chardonnay and Sauvignon Blanc are often used in the blend. The Cabernet France grape makes the rosé wine Cabernet de Saumur. The sparkling wines are usually superb, especially those made by Ackerman-Laurence and by Gratien et Meyer. The Chenin Blanc is the main grape, but sometimes Chardonnay and Cabernet Franc grapes are added to give a softer, more stylish finish. The grapes are grown on tufa or limestone soil and the wines are made by the *mèthode traditionnelle*. These deservedly popular wines are marketed as Saumur Mousseux or Crémant de la Loire. A small amount of red and rosé sparkling wine is also made.

Touraine   This region makes an array of table wines with Vouvray the most famous appellation. Made from the Chenin Blanc grape, it can be a dry, medium sweet, or sweet white wine. It can also be semi-sparkling (*pétillant*) or wholly sparkling (*mousseux*). Opposite Vouvray on the left bank of the Loire is Montlouis, producing dry to sweet, still and sparkling white wine, again, from the Chenin grape. Lovely raspberry/redcurrant-scented red wines are made from the Cabernet France grape, under four classifications: Touraine Rouge, Bourgueil, St-Nicholas-de-Bourgueil and Chinon. They range from light to firm, with Touraine and Chinon being lightest. These benefit from being served slightly chilled.

Central vineyards   So called because they are located in the centre of France, in this region, the Sauvignon Blanc (locally called Fumé Blanc) is the major grape for white wines. The most famous wine of the region is Pouilly Fumé, or Pouilly Blanc Fumé as it is known here. This crisp, fruity, steely white wine should not be confused with the inferior Pouilly-sur-Loire made from the Chasselas grape or with the famous Mâcon white wine, Pouilly Fuissé. Sancerre is another very popular, dry, fragrant and flinty white wine with a distinctively pungent aroma of gooseberries. Sancerre red and rosé wines are also made using the Pinot Noir grape. West of Sancerre is the river Cher and it is along here that two good white wines, Quincy and Reuilly, are made. A similar style of wine, Menetou-Salon, is made nearby.

The Midi

This is the largest vineyard area in France. It is generally known as Languedoc and Roussillon and makes an enormous quantity of inexpensive wines. The area extends from the Cévennes in the north to the Pyrenees in the south and includes the departments of Gard, Hérault, Aude and Pyrénées-Orientales. The wines are greatly popular and in terms of output the area produces over 40% of the French harvest, which is why the Midi is known as 'the belly of France.'

LANGUEDOC WINES

Costières du Gard   This large arid area between Montpellier and Nîmes produces red, white and rosé wines. The reds made from Carignan, Cinsault and Mourvèdre grapes are considered best.

Clairette de Bellegarde   A dry, white wine produced within the appellation Costières du Gard.

Clairette du Languedoc   Made from Clairette grapes grown in Hérault, this is a full-bodied, dry white wine. The Rancio version is made from late-gathered grapes with good concentration of sugar. It is aged for many years until it fully develops a maderised flavour.

Minervois   This gets its name from the town of Minerve. The wines are principally red, light and delicate of flavour. The Carignan and Grenache are the grapes used.

Corbières   This mountainous region behind Norbonne makes good red wines from the Carignan, Syrah and Mourvèdre grapes. Fitou and La Clape are rich, distinctive red wines and are separate appellations within Corbières.

Coteaux du Languedoc   An embracing appellation covering the wines of 74 villages; two of these, Faugères and St Chinian, are now important appellations of the Hérault, having being granted AC status in 1982. They are fullsome red wines from the Grenache, Mourvèdre, Syrah and Carignan grapes.

Picpoul de Pinet   A dry, acidic wine made from the Picpoul grape (also known as Folle Blanche).

Vins Sables du Golfe de Lion   These red, white and rosé wines are produced around Montpellier. The vines are cultivated in the sand dunes and in the sandy marshes adjacent to the Camargue. The region is known to have the largest vineyard in all France, Domaines des Salins du Midi. The wine is generally marketed under the brand name Listel, of which the blush wine Gris de Gris is a prime example of Listel's style. The Grenache and Cinsault are the important grapes.

ROUSSILLON

This region is best known for its fortified wine, but good red table wines are also made and sold either as Collioure, Côtes du Roussillon or Roussillon-Villages. The best styles of all come from two villages, Caramany and Latour de France, in the valley of Agly.

The fortified wines give Roussillon its fame. They can be *vins doux naturels* (VDN) or *vins-de-liqueur* (VdL). Both styles have their fermentation muted by the addition of brandy. The distinguishing factors are the degrees of sugar in the *must* and the grape varieties allowed in the manufacture. The best appellations are the Red Banyuls, Banyuls Rancio and Banyuls Rancio Grand Cru. The latter is very strong and sweet and very expensive. Other good sweet fortified wines are Grand Roussillon, Muscat de Frontignan, Muscat de Lunel, Muscat de Rivesaltes, and Muscat de St Jean de Minervois.

Sparkling wines   One of the world's finest sparkling wines, Blanquette de Limoux, is made in the department of Aude. It is made by the *méthode traditionnelle* from the Mauzac, Chardonnay and Chenin grapes. It has a fine mousse and an elegant, distinguished flavour.

Provence

This sun-kissed region in the south of France stretches from south of Avignon through Marseille, past St Tropez and onwards to the Italian border.

It produces a variety of wines, red, white and rosé: the reds and rosés from the Grenache, Cinsault, Carignan, Mourvèdre, Syrah and Cabernet Sauvignon grapes; the whites from the Ugni Blanc, Rolle, Bourboulenc, Clairette, Sauvignon Blanc and Marsanne grapes. The most significant appellation is Côtes de Provence which produces good sound wines, but especially good rosés and reds. Although the co-operatives dominate the business, the best wines are usually made by private firms such as Domaine Ott.

Côteaux d'Aix-en-Provence   Red, white and rosé wines are made here. The reds are best and are produced over a large area of the Bouches-du-Rhône.

Côteaux des Baux   These red, white and rosé wines are made in a few parishes to the west of Alpilles. Again, the reds are the best buys and are of a good standard.

Cassis (Bouches-du-Rhône)   This is not to be confused with the blackcurrant liqueur, crème de cassis. White wines are the chief product here although some reds and rosés are also produced around this beautiful Mediterranean fishing port.

Bandol (Var)   The Reds, made entirely from the Mourvèdre grape, are really fine here and so are the rosés. Little white is produced.

Bellet (Alpes-Maritimes)   Red, white and rosé wines of nice fragrance and refined flavour are produced here. Most of the output is reserved for the restaurants and bars in the Nice area.

Palette (Bouches-du-Rhône)   Mostly red wines are produced, but some rosé and white wines are also made. The red is of good quality and it develops an attractive bouquet as it ages. Château Simone, a 20-hectare (50-acre) property, is the largest and most important producer.

Rhône

The Côtes du Rhône extends from Lyon in the north to Avignon in the south. In between there is a gap of 40 km (25 miles) where the vine is not cultivated.

The northern vineyards enjoy a continental climate of warm summers and fairly mild winters. The southern vineyards get hot, dry summers and cool winters. All the vineyards are subject to the mistral, the fierce wind which blows down the valley from the alps at the rate of up to 104 km (65 miles) per hour. Cypress trees are grown as windbreakers along its path.

NORTHERN RHONE

The grapes used are Viognier, Marsanne and Roussanne for white wines and Syrah for red wines.

Côte Rôtie   One of the finest Rhône red wines, this is made from a minimum of 80% Syrah and a maximum of 20% white Viognier grapes. The wine has a wonderful bouquet and tannic, heady flavour.

Condrieu   This light, golden wine, made from the Viognier grapes grown on steep terraces, has a distinctive fragrance and an intense flavour of apricots.

Château Grillet   This celebrated dry, white wine from the Viognier grape is the smallest appellation in all France. It comes from a tiny vineyard with less then three hectares (seven acres) of vines.

Hermitage   This is a dark, full-flavoured red wine made from Syrah grape. It needs ageing and can continue to improve in bottle for years. There is also a white Hermitage made from a combination of Marsanne and Roussanne grapes.

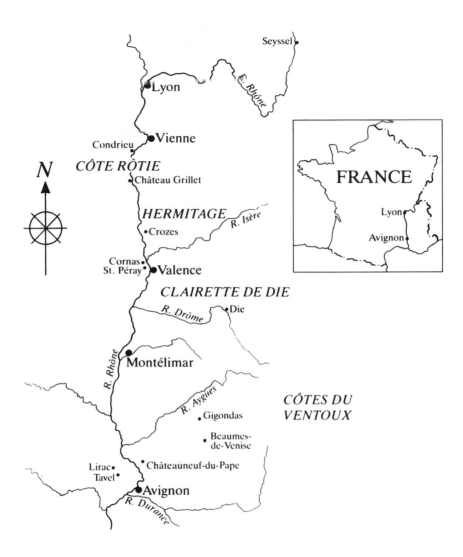

Crozes-Hermitage This is a less fine, more robust red wine than Hermitage. It is made from the Syrah grape and is usually cheaper and more easily obtainable than its famous neighbour. Some white wine is also made.

St Joseph This can be red or dry white. It is made on the west side of the Rhône across the river from Hermitage.

Cornas A deep, dark red wine from the Syrah grape; in youth it is highly tannic, but as it ages it develops a wonderful bouquet and mouth-filling flavours.

St Péray Dry, still or sparkling white wine made from Marsanne, Roussanne and Roussette grapes. St Péray Mousseux is bottle-fermented – *méthode traditionnelle*.

Clairette de Die A fine sparkling wine made by the *méthode traditionnelle*, using at least 75% Clairette grapes and some Muscat *à petits grains*.

Clairette de Die Tradition This is made by the local *méthode dioise*. This involves a lengthy continuation of the first fermentation which is slowed down by adding sulphur dioxide. The wine is bottled in January when the unresolved sugar provides the effervescence.

SOUTHERN RHONE

The main grape for white wine is the Muscat, but the Clairette and Roussanne are also used. For reds the Grenache predominates, together with the Syrah, Mourvèdre and Cinsault.

Rasteau This is a big, red wine which is becoming popular. A local speciality is Rasteau Vin Doux Naturel made from the Grenache grape.

Gigondas A generous, powerful, robust red wine, which always improves with additional ageing.

Muscat de Beaumes-de-Venise This classic, VDN, golden dessert wine from the Muscat grapes is extremely popular either as an apéritif or dessert wine. It is made by muting the fermentation with brandy to retain the sweetness. The muting occurs when an alcoholic strength of between 5% and 8% is reached.

Châteauneuf-du-Pape Thirteen different grapes may be used in the production of this rich, full-bodied red wine. Consistency is not its middle name, so it is best to know a producer whose style appeals to you. The wine has a minimum alcoholic strength of 12.5%

Lirac Produces red, white and rosé wine – the rosé being by far the best.

Tavel Made principally from the Grenache and Cinsault grapes, this rosé wine is considered to be France's finest. It is dry and slatey, almost austere on the palate.

Côtes du Ventoux Produces light, fruity, refreshing red and rosé wines principally from the Grenache, Syrah, Cinsault and Mourvèdre grapes.

Côtes du Lubéron Before having its own appellation, these wines were sold as Côtes du Rhône red, white and rosé. For the reds and rosé, the grapes are the same as used for Côtes du Ventoux. For white wine, the important grapes are Clairette, Bourboulenc and Ugni Blanc.

Côtes du Rhône These red, white and rosé wines can come from any part of any region and usually consist of blended wines.

Côtes du Rhône Villages A more distinguished blend of red, white or rosé wines from southern Rhône.

Savoie

The Savoie vineyards are located in the heart of the French Alps in the departments of Savoie and Haut Savoie. The vineyards in this ski resort lie on the lower slopes, but some, like Bugey, can be so steep that mechanical aid to assist the work is not always possible. The vines for white wines are Chasselas, Jacquère, Roussette (Altesse) and Bergeron. For red wines, Mondeuse, Gamay and Pinot Noir grapes are used.

Most wines produced are white or sparkling. The whites such as Apremont, Crépy, Roussette de Savoie, Roussette de Bugey and Seyssel are best enjoyed *in situ*, after an enjoyable time on the piste. The sparkling wines, Mousseux du Bugey, Mousseux de Savoie and especially Royal Seyssel are refreshingly good. There is also a *pétillant* wine made called Crépy Crepytant, very much an *après-ski* favourite. Of the red wines, Cruet and Montmélian are best.

South-west France

The following are the main wine producing regions: Bergerac, Cahors, Gaillac, Jurançon, Irouléguy, Madiran, Buzet and Duras.

Bergerac   The vineyards of Bergerac start east of Bordeaux and the grape varieties are much the same as in Bordeaux. Good red, white and rosés are made but the regional star is Monbazillac, a luscious, golden, creamy wine made from botrytis-affected grapes. The wine must have a natural alcohol strength of 14%, otherwise it is sold as Côtes de Bergerac Moelleux. The red wines, Merlot dominated, have an affinity with St Emilion wines, with the best examples coming from Pécharmant. Of the white wine produced, Montravel, made from the Sauvignon Blanc grape, is best.

Cahors   These exclusively red wines are made in the lovely valley of the Lot from the Malbec (Auxerrois), Tannat and Merlot grapes. The wines were once known as black wines, as their colour was so intense, but today they range from fruity and light to the more full, tannic varieties.

Gaillac   Gaillac wines come from some of the oldest vineyards in France. The vines are planted on both sides of the Tarn river. The Mausac grape is used together with L'en de L'el, Sauvignon and Sémillon to make choice white wines. Some of the best whites are *pétillant* or *perlé* (slightly sparkling). Other sparkling wines – Gaillac Mousseux – are made by the *méthode Gaillaçoise* (*méthode rurale*). This entails bottling the wine before the fermentation is terminated. The residual sugar enables the fermentation to continue inside the bottle. The Gamay, Duras and Cabernet Franc grapes are used to make the strong-flavoured, peppery reds. The rosés, which are popular locally, are made from the Gamay and Syrah grapes.

Jurançon   This region in the foothills of the Pyrenees, south and west of Pau, makes dry white wines and some good quality red wines. However, the area is best known for its sweet but expensive white wine, Jurançon Moelleux. This is made by a system called *passeillage*. The grapes are left on the vine until November, by which time their water content will have been reduced and their sugar content will be more concentrated.

Irouléguy   This small appellation comes from an area west of St Jean-Pied-de-Port in the Atlantic Pyrenees on the Spanish border. Big red, earthy wines and orange-pink rosés are the main products. These are made from the Tannat, Cabernet Franc and Cabernet Sauvignon grapes.

Madiran   The traditional Madiran is a tough, inky-red wine made from the local Tannat grape. The more modern wine uses Cabernet Sauvignon, Cabernet Franc as well as Tannat in the blend, which makes a wine with a softer edge. Adjoining Madiran is Côtes de St Mont, which make good, sturdy reds and nice, flavoursome white wines.

Côtes de Buzet   This small region uses Bordeaux grapes to make rich flavoursome red wines, so intensely coloured they virtually dye your teeth.

Côtes de Duras   Another small region which makes good but less aggressive claret-style wines and also some decent whites using the Sauvignon Blanc grape. In the brandy country of south-west France, two wines are noteworthy: Charentais, the crisp, dry, white table wine from Cognac, and Côtes de Gascogne, the Sauvignon Blanc-based tangy, flowery white wine from Armagnac.

Summary of French regions and wine styles

REGION	SOIL	GRAPES	WINE STYLE
Alsace	Granite, marl, limestone, gravel	Gewürztraminer, Riesling, Muscat, Tokay, Pinot Noir	Dry, crisp to full bodied and spicy whites. Good quality sparkling. Thinnish reds and rosés.
Bordeaux	Gravel, alluvial	Cabernet Sauvignon, Cabernet Franc, Merlot, Malbec, Petit-Verdot, Sémillon, Sauvignon Blanc, Muscadelle	Prestigious tannic reds, dry, medium and luscious whites.
Burgundy	Limestone, marl, quartz, calcareous clay	Pinot Noir, Gamay, Passe-Tout-Grains, Chardonnay, Aligoté	Powerful, silk-smooth reds, crisp reds, dry to soft, full-flavoured whites. Also red and white sparklers.
Champagne	Limestone, belemnite, chalk	Pinot Noir, Pinot Meunier, Chardonnay	World's finest sparkling wine. May be white or pink. Ranges from extremely dry to sweet. Some still red and white wines also made.
Corsica	Pebbles, clay, limestone, granite	Sciacarello, Nielluccio, Malvasia, Muscat, Vermentino	Big strong reds and rosés, crisp and fruity whites, medium sweet apéritif.
Jura	Limestone, clay, marl, gravel	Poulsard, Trousseau, Pinot Noir, Chardonnay, Savagnin	Red, white, Vin Jaune, Vin de Paille and sparkling wine. Also an apéritif called Macvin.

REGION	SOIL	GRAPES	WINE STYLE
Loire	Alluvial, clay, granite, quartz, limestone, tufa chalk	Cabernet Franc, Pinot Noir, Groslot, Cabernet Sauvignon, Chenin Blanc, Sauvignon Blanc, Muscadet	Light fruity reds, semi-sweet rosés, dry, medium, sweet whites and fine sparkling wines.
The Midi	Alluvial, sand, clay, gravel, schistose, limestone	Carignan, Cinsault, Mourvèdre, Grenache, Syrah, Cabernet Sauvignon, Clairette, Picpoul, Chenin Blanc, Chardonnay, Mauzac	Light to distinctive reds, tart to medium-dry whites, excellent sparkling wine, good *vins doux naturels*.
Provence	Granite, porphyry, calcareous	Grenache, Cinsault, Carignan, Mourvèdre, Syrah, Cabernet Sauvignon, Ugni Blanc, Rolle, Bourboulenc, Clairette, Marsanne, Sauvignon Blanc	Reds, whites and rosés of reasonable quality. Reds are usually the best buy.
Rhône	Alluvial, granite, schistose, pebbles	Syrah, Grenache, Mourvèdre, Cinsault, Viognier, Clairette, Roussane, Picpoul, Marsanne	Big, dark, full-flavoured red. Dry earthy rosés, some excellent whites and sparkling wines, classic *vins doux naturels*.
Savoie	Generally calcareous	Mondeuse, Gamay, Pinot Noir, Chasselas, Jacquère, Rousette, Chardonnay	Light reds and rosés, sharp dry whites and good sparkling and pétillant wines.
South-west France	Sand, silica, gravel, limestone, calcareous	Merlot, Malbec, Cabernet Franc, Tannat, Cabernet Sauvignon, Gamay, Syrah, Sémillon, Mauzac, Sauvignon Blanc, L'en de L'el	Fruity, light sometimes tannic reds, orange pink rosés, crisp dry to flowery whites, excellent luscious creamy whites, good sparkling and pétillant wines.

Note   Fortified wines are detailed in chaper 6

GERMANY

Germany produces a great diversity of wines with a wonderful range of flavours within each style. That Germany is so successful as a wine-producer is remarkable, considering the innumerable difficulties these dedicated wine-growers have to contend with. For a start, the vineyards lie at the northern extremity for ripening grapes. The constant struggle against the elements, the lack of sunshine, the real danger of springtime frosts all cause problems, especially for the growers in the most northerly regions. Many of the vineyards have to be sited on steep, precarious, south-facing terraces in order to catch the sun. The difficulty and awkwardness of such terrain makes grape growing hazardous, labour-intensive and inevitably expensive. Yet Germany produces an abundance of light, fruit-flavoured, low alcohol and low priced table wines which are greatly popular in Britain and in America. The country, of course, is also renowned for exquisite, expensive, sweet, honeyed, golden wines, the result of very sophisticated harvesting procedures as we shall see.

Reading the label

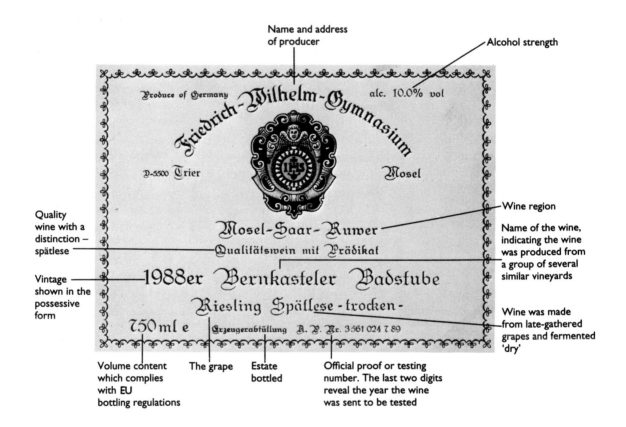

Name and address of producer

Alcohol strength

Quality wine with a distinction – spätlese

Vintage shown in the possessive form

Wine region

Name of the wine, indicating the wine was produced from a group of several similar vineyards

Wine was made from late-gathered grapes and fermented 'dry'

Volume content which complies with EU bottling regulations

The grape

Estate bottled

Official proof or testing number. The last two digits reveal the year the wine was sent to be tested

STRENGTH AND SWEETNESS

There are some 50 grape varieties in production, many of them hybrids cultivated especially to withstand erratic climatic conditions. In bad years even these do not ripen sufficiently and, left in their natural state, the resulting wines will be quite undrinkable. To redress the balance it is common practice to add beet or cane sugar to the *must* before fermentation. This enrichment, known as *anreicherung*, is similar to the French *chaptalisation*. Its purpose is to improve (*verbesserung*) the alcohol content, raising it to that of a similar wine produced in a good year. Sometimes also, *Süssreserve* (sweet reserve, unfermented must which has its yeasts removed by fine filtration) is judiciously added to the wine before bottling in order to give the wine a more agreeable mouth-feel and a more acceptable level of sweetness. Wines so treated can never be marketed in the highest range of German quality wines.

THE GRAPES

Germany has about 100,000 hectares (250,000 acres) of land under the vine. Some 87% of the vineyards grow only white grapes. The three noble grapes are the Riesling, Müller-Thurgau and Silvaner.

Riesling   This is the classic grape producing nearly all the really great white and sparkling German wines. It accounts for about 21% of the crop.

Müller-Thurgau   A cross from the Riesling and Silvaner, this was developed in Geisenheim in 1882 by Professor H. Müller from Thurgau, Switzerland. This sturdy vine is the most widely planted in Germany – 24% of the crop.

Silvaner   This accounts for 8% of the crop. An early ripener, it makes soft, gentle, flowery wines.

Some other varieties of white grapes cultivated are:

- Kerner (Riesling × the Black Trollinger)
- Scheurebe (Silvaner × Riesling)
- Ruländer (Pinot Gris or Grauburgunder)
- Bacchus (Silvaner × Riesling × Müller-Thurgau)
- Elbling (a Mosel-Saar-Ruwer favourite)
- Morio-Muskat (Silvaner × Weissburgunder)
- Gewürztraminer (Spicy Traminer)

The principal red wine grapes are:

- Spätburgunder (Pinot Noir)
- Trollinger (originally from the Tyrol)
- Portugieser (originated in Austria)
- Müllerrebe (Pinot Meunier)
- Dornfelder (a hybrid of complex parentage originating in Württemberg)

Types of wine produced

White Wine   Dry (*trocken*), medium dry (*halbtrocken*), medium sweet (*liebling*) and sweet (*süss*).

Red Wine   Made from black grapes only.

Weissherbst   Pink wine made from a specific black grape.

Rotling   Pink wine made from a combination of black and white grapes producing such specialities as Rotgold in Baden and Schillerwein in Württemberg.

Sekt   White sparkling wines produced from white grapes; especially fine when the Riesling grape is used.

Perlwein   Also known as Spritzig, this is a lightly sparkling white or red wine which may be artificially injected by carbon dioxide.

In 1971, German wine laws divided the wine into two major categories: *Tafelwein* (table wine) and *Qualitätswein* (quality wine).

Tafelwein (table wine)
This category can be subdivided into:

- Deutscher Tafelwein (German table wine)
- Deutscher Landwein (German country wine)

Deutscher Tafelwein   This is the basic table wine made from grapes grown in Germany. There is also a simple Tafelwein made – a Euroblend from a mixture of German and other EU grapes.

Deutscher Landwein   Similar to the French Vin de Pays, it is superior to the Deutscher Tafelwein and will have a slightly higher alcohol content. The wine is dry or semi-dry and can be produced in any one of 17 designated *landwein* areas.

Qualitätswein (quality wine)
This category can be subdivided into:

- *Qualitätswein bestimmter Anbaugebiete* (QbA).
- *Qualitätswein mit Prädikat* (QmP).

Qualitätswein bestimmter Anbaugebiete (QbA)   These are quality wines from 13 designated wine regions. The wines have to be made from authorised vine stocks. The *must* weight, expressed in oechsle degrees, has to reach a certain minimum level. This is gauged by using a hydrometer which has a graduated scale of measurement. This will reveal the potential alcohol content of a wine by comparing the specific gravity of the *must* to the specific gravity of water. QbA wines will also undergo a chemical and sensory evaluation (*amtliche prüfung*) and they must not be blended with wines from outside their own region. The wines are normally made from fully ripened grapes but, like Tafelwein and Landwein, these wines can be alcoholically 'improved' (*verbesserung*) by *chaptalisation*.

Qualitätswein mit Prädikat (QmP)   These are quality wines with an added distinction or embellishment. They are completely natural wines – no sugaring of the *must* is allowed.

The greatest wines produced in Germany fall into the following six categories of quality.

Kabinett   At one time it was customary for the wine-growers to keep some of the best wine for their own cupboard or cabinet – but now they let you have it instead – hence, the name. It is a completely genuine wine and the lightest in style and in alcohol of the Prädikat wines.

Spätlese   Wine made from late harvested grapes – picked not earlier than seven days after the start of the main harvest. These riper grapes make fuller and slightly sweeter wine.

Auslese   These are wines made from specially selected sugar-enriched bunches of grapes. They have more body and are usually on the sweet side and are long lasting on the palate.

Beerenauslese   These are rare and rich wines made from over-ripe single grapes which probably have been attacked by the fungus known in France as *Botrytis cinerea* (*pourriture noble*) but known here as *edelfäule* – meaning noble rot.

Eiswein grapes

Eiswein   Ice wines are made only when conditions are favourable. The sugar within the grape must reach at least Beerenauslese level. The farmers then wait for the snow or frost to come and freeze the water within the grapes into ice crystals. The harvest may take place late November, December, sometimes even in January. The grapes are gathered when the temperature reaches at least –8°C (17.6°F). Picking is usually done under floodlight and certainly before the light of day – when the temperature is coldest. The grapes are immediately taken to be pressed in their frozen state. Only the water within the grape freezes and this is driven off as fragmented ice and skimmed clear of the amber-coloured, rich, concentrated syrup which remains. The resulting wines are indeed luscious but never cloying as they are balanced by a good level of acidity. Eiswein was first introduced in 1842. Its manufacture is a risky business. Mild, damp weather is the scourge of the producer.

Trockenbeerenauslese   Wines made from shrivelled, botrytis-affected, over-ripe grapes. Because of the rich concentration of sugar, the juice does not ferment easily so a long, slow fermentation is the norm. These wonderful wines are the ultimate in quality and are enormously expensive.

SEKT

Sekt, made in all the German wine regions, is a short term for *Qualitätsschaumwein*, meaning quality sparkling wine. Schaumwein itself is basic, cheap and cheerful, and bubbly. *Deutscher Sekt* must now be made from grapes grown in Germany. Sekt BA is quality sparkling wine made from grapes grown in the region declared on the label. Most Sekt is produced by the charmat method, that means the second fermentation takes place in a sealed tank and the wine is then filtered and bottled under pressure. However, real star quality Sekt is made after the fashion of champagne.

UNDERSTANDING THE LABEL

German wine labels are very informative and easy to understand once you know the terminology. Wine regions are called *anbaugebiete*. Each region is divided into districts known as *bereiche* or into villages or communities (*gemeinde*). Every *bereich* will have a collection of vineyards (*grosslagen*) and each *grosslage* will have single vineyards (*einzellagen*). For example:

- Mosel-Saar-Ruwer is a region – *Gebiet*.
- Bernkastel is a district – *Bereich*.
- Bernkasteler Badstube is a collective site – *Grosslage*.
- Bernkasteler Doktor is a single vineyard – *Einzellage*.

The following terms, when applicable, may also appear on labels.

1   The wine category.

2   The vineyard name preceded by the district name carrying the suffix 'er', so *Bernkastel* becomes *Bernkasteler* – just as someone from London is a Londoner.

3   The vintage year, also in possessive form, such as 1994er.

4   Taste or style of the wine, e.g. *trocken* (dry), *diabetikerwein* (suitable for diabetics).

5   QbA – quality wine from a designated region.

6   QmP – quality level and distinction of the wine and manner of harvesting, such as *Spätlese*.

7   *Amtliche Prüfungsnummer* (AP number) – the official testing number which proves that the wine has passed official chemical and sensory tests. The last two digits indicate the year the wine was sent to be tested.

8   *Erzeugerabfüllung* – estate Bottled. Sometimes the Bottler's name (*abfüller*) will be given.

9   *Winzergenossenschaft* – co-operative.

Regions and principal wines

Ahr

This is a predominately red wine region and one of the smallest in Germany. The vineyards are sited on the steep hillsides that overlook the Ahr River as it journeys to meet the Rhine south of Bonn. The red wines made from the Spätburgunder (Pinot Noir) and Portugieser grapes range from velvet smooth to light and pleasant. The whites from the Riesling and Müller-Thurgau grapes are clean and refreshing and are mostly drunk locally.

VILLAGE	VINEYARD
Heimersheim	Heimersheimer Landskrone
Neuenahr	Neuenahrer Sonnenberg
Walporzheim	Walporzheimer Gärkammer

Mittelrhein

This beautiful wine region begins at Königswinter just below Bonn and extends for about 96 km (60 miles) upstream on both banks of the Rhine. The Riesling, Müller-Thurgau and Kerner vines are cultivated on terraced slopes and produce fresh, lively wines with a pronounced acidity. Bacharach is the principal wine village but most of the wine is consumed locally. The Riesling is used to make good quality Sekt.

VILLAGE	VINEYARD
Oberwesel	Oberweseler St Martinsberg
Boppard Hamm	Bopparder Hamm Ohlenberg
Kaub	Kauber Backofen
Bacharach	Bacharacher Posten

Mosel-Saar-Ruwer

The Mosel rises in the Vosges Mountains and some 500 km (310 miles) later decants itself into the Rhine at the Deutscher Eck, Koblenz. The Saar and Ruwer (pronounced Roover) are its tributaries. Many of these steep-terraced vineyards overlooking the river have been recently modernised, but the slatey soil, so essential to the steely character of these wines, remains the same. In such a cold climate, slate is also important as a heat reflector to ripen the grapes. These green-tinged, lively, fresh-tasting wines are usually light in alcohol – about 9% – and are made from the Riesling, Müller-Thurgau and Elbling grapes.

VILLAGE	VINEYARD
Bernkastel-Kues	Bernkasteler Doktor
	Bernkasteler Schlossberg
Enkirch	Enkircher Steffensberg
Erden	Erdener Prälat
	Erdener Treppchen
Graach	Graacher Himmelreich
	Graacher Josephshöfer
Kasel	Kaseler Hitzlay
	Kaseler Nieschen
Ockfen	Ockfener Bockstein
	Ockfener Herrenberg
Piesport	Piesporter Goldtröpfchen
	Piesporter Gunterslay
Wehlen	Wehlener Sonnenuhr
Zell	Zeller Domherrenberg

Rheingau

This classic wine region lies between Hochheim on the river Main and Lorch near the Mittelrhein. It has a river frontage of about 24 km (15 miles) and the vineyards on the banks of the Rhine are sheltered by the Taunus mountains. This protection from the northern winds, and the reflected heat from the river, is not only good for ripening the grapes, but sometimes brings the beneficial mists which encourage *edelfäule* (noble rot) to develop. The Riesling is the most important white grape, producing wines of elegance and fine balance. Around Assmannshausen, full, flavoursome red wines are made from the Spätburgunder grape.

VILLAGE	VINEYARD
Assmannshausen	Assmannshausener Höllenberg
Erbach	Erbacher Marcobrunn
	Erbacher Michelmark

VILLAGE	VINEYARD
Geisenheim	Geisenheimer Kläuserweg
	Geisenheimer Rothenberg
Hallgarten	Hallgartener Schönhell
Hattenheim	Hattenheimer Nussbrunnen
	Hattenheimer Wisselbrunnen
Hochheim	Hochheimer Domdechaney
	Hochheimer Kirchenstück
Johannisberg	Johannisberger Hölle
	Schloss Johannisberg
Oestrich	Oestricher Doosberg
	Schloss Reichhartshausen
Rauenthal	Rauenthaler Baiken
Rüdesheim	Rüdesheimer Berg Rottland
	Rüdesheimer Berg Schlossberg
Winkel	Schloss Vollrads

Hock is the English name for Rhine wines. It gets its name from the village of Hochheim where Queen Victoria visited in 1850. Because she thought these wines were so special, they renamed a vineyard – Hochheimer Königin Victoria Berg – as a tribute to her. With Royal patronage, these wines became immediately popular.

The Nahe

The vines are grown on the steep slopes along the Nahe and its tributaries, with the best vineyards located between Schlossböckelheim and Bad Kreuznach. The Riesling is planted on the most favoured sites, but the Müller-Thurgau and the Silvaner grapes are also cultivated. The wines are crisp, delicate and fresh tasting.

VILLAGE	VINEYARD
Bad Kreuznach	Kreuznacher Brückes
	Kreuznacher Narrenkappe
Munster	Munsterer Dautenpflänzer
	Munsterer Pittersberg
Niederhausen	Niederhausener Hermannsberg
Schlossböckelheim	Schlossböckelheimer Felsenberg
	Schlossböckelheimer Kupfergrube

The Pfalz

The most productive wine region in Germany, the Pfalz runs from Bockenheim to Schweigen near the French border, covering an area of some 80 km (50 miles). Most vineyards are located along the slopes of the Haardt mountains and enjoy a generally dry climate with plenty of summer sunshine. The principal grape is the Müller-Thurgau, but the Riesling, Silvaner, Morio-Muskat, Gewürztraminer and Kerner are also cultivated to produce soft, spicy, aromatic yet clean, fresh white wines. The reds are made principally from the Portugieser grape and are mild and mellow, though some incline towards spiciness. The largest wine festival in the world is held at Bad Dürkheim during the third week in September. It is traditional then to drink the wine from a *schoppen* – a wine glass holding 500 ml (¾ pint).

VILLAGE	VINEYARD
Bad Dürkheim	Dürkheimer Fuchsmantel
	Dürkheimer Spielberg
Deidesheim	Deidesheimer Hohenmorgen
	Deidesheimer Leinhöhle
Forst	Forster Jesuitengarten
	Forster Musenhang
Kallstadt	Kallstadter Annaberg
	Kallstadter Steinacker

Rheinhessan

This is the birthplace of Liebfraumilch, one of the most popular wines sold in Britain today. Originally, Liebfraumilch was made from grapes grown in vineyards, surrounding the church *Liebfrauenkirche* in Worms. Nowadays the wine can come from one of four regions: Rheinhessan, Nahe, Pfalz and Rheingau. In practice, 97% still comes from the Rheinhessan and Pfalz. The Rheinhessan is the largest wine region in Germany, stretching from Bingen to Worms and covering an area of 32 by 48 km (20 by 30 miles). In output, it is second only to the Pfalz, but some 70% of its wines are sold in bulk to be bottled elsewhere. Müller-Thurgau, Silvaner and Riesling are the main grapes. The Portugieser and Spätburgunder grapes make a relatively small quantity of red wine. In 1986 a special category of Rheinhessan Silvaner was initiated, introduced and marketed as RS. It must be pure Silvaner and must have passed two quality control tastings. The standard black and gold label must be used by all RS producers.

VILLAGE	VINEYARD
Bingen	Binger Scharlachberg
Oppenheim	Oppenheimer Kreuz
	Oppenheimer Sackträger
Nierstein	Niersteiner Orbel
	Niersteiner Hipping

Franken

Franken vineyards are located in northern Bavaria, with Würzburg the commercial centre. The vines are cultivated on both sides of the River Main and produce full-bodied, earthy white wines of classic quality. The wines were formerly called Steinwein after the famous Stein vineyard and also because of their stone dry character. They are mostly marketed in flat, flagon-shaped, green bottles known as *bocksbeutel*. The Müller-Thurgau, Silvaner and Bacchus are the principal grapes used.

VILLAGE	VINEYARD
Castell	Casteller Kirchberg
Iphofen	Iphofener Julius-Echter-Berg
	Iphofener Kalb
Würzburg	Würzburger Innere Leiste
	Würzburger Stein

Hessische Bergstrasse

These terraced vineyards are sited on the bank of the Rhine between Darmstadt and Heidelberg. They are fragrant, fruity, white wines made from the Riesling, Müller-Thurgau and Silvaner grapes, mostly produced by the *winzergenossenschaften* (co-operatives). They are nearly always consumed locally.

VILLAGE	VINEYARD
Bensheim	Bensheimer Streichling
Heppenheim	Heppenheimer Centgericht

Württemberg

Most of the vineyards are sited on both banks of the River Neckar, a tributory of the Rhine. Almost equal quantities of red and white wines are produced. The reds, light and tannic, are amongst the best in Germany and are made from the Trollinger, Spätburgunder, Portugieser, Dornfelder, Müllerrebe (Pinot Meunier) and Lemberger grapes. The whites from the Riesling, Müller-Thurgau, Silvaner and Kerner grapes have a fruity, earthy flavour. The regional speciality is the Schillerwein (*schiller* means to change colour). This is a light shimmering pink wine which is drunk, like all the other wines produced, in and around Stuttgart. Rotling is a pink wine made from a blend of red and white grapes.

VILLAGE	VINEYARD
Gundelsheim	Gundelsheimer Himmelreich
Maulbronn	Maulbronner Eilfingerberg
Weikersheim	Weikersheimer Schmecker

Baden

The most southern of all the German wine regions, Baden is also the warmest. This narrow strip of land stretches from near Heidelberg in the north to Lake Constance (*Bodensee*) in the south – real Black Forest country. The vineyards face those of Alsace which are located on the opposite side of the Rhine. Over 80% of the output is handled by co-operatives, but there are also some very fine private estates. The Müller-Thurgau is the main white grape but the Ruländer, Riesling, Gutadel, Gewürztraminer and Silvaner are also used. These make fresh, fragrant, sometimes spicy white wines, some of which can be slightly *spritzig*. The Spätburgunder, when grown on the volcanic soils of Kaiserstuhl, can produce fiery yet full-bodied red wines. The same grape also makes the popular rosé wine Weissherbst.

VILLAGE	VINEYARD
Michelfeld	Michelfelder Himmelberg
Zulzfeld	Burg Ravensburger
Durbach	Durbacher Schlossberg

Saale-Unstrut

The Müller-Thurgau, Silvaner, Bacchus and Riesling vines are grown on small terraces along the course of the Saale and Unstrut Rivers, producing light, soft, flowery, dry white wines. A little red wine is also made from the Portugieser grapes.

VILLAGE	VINEYARD
Freyburg	Weingut Decker
	Weingut Pawis
Bad Kösen	Weingut Lützkendorf

Sachsen

These vineyards are sited along the Elbe River between Pillnitz and Diesbar. The Müller-Thurgau, Weissburgunder, Traminer, Gutedel, Riesling and Ruländer vines are grown on very steep terraces, producing dry, white wines with fruity acidity. Elbtal Sekt is a local speciality sparkler.

VILLAGE	VINEYARD
Meissen	Weingut Proschwitz
Radebeul	Weingut Klaus Seifert
Diesbar	Weinbau Jan Ulrich

Summary of German regions and wine styles

REGION	SOIL	GRAPE	WINE STYLE
Ahr	Volcanic slate	Spätburgunder, Portugieser, Müller-Thurgau, Riesling	Velvet smooth to light reds, lively refreshing whites
Mittelrhein	Slate, clay	Riesling, Müller-Thurgau, Kerner	Fruity, flavoursome whites and sparkling
Mosel-Saar-Ruwer	Slate	Riesling, Müller-Thurgau, Elbling	Light, steely flavoured white; balanced acidity
Rheingau	Loess, loam	Riesling, Spätburgunder	Elegant, slightly honeyed whites, fullsome reds
Nahe	Loess, loam, quartzite	Müller-Thurgau, Riesling, Silvaner	Light, subtle, crisp whites
Rheinhessen	Loess, limestone, sand	Müller-Thurgau, Silvaner, Riesling	Soft, mild, rounded whites
Pfalz	Loam, sand, limestone	Müller-Thurgau, Silvaner, Portugieser	Vivacious, spicy whites, deep flavoured, earthy red wines
Franken	Loess, sandstone, limestone	Müller-Thurgau, Silvaner	Earthy, dry white wines
Hessische Bergstrasse	Loess	Riesling, Müller-Thurgau, Silvaner	Fruity, acidic white wines
Württemberg	Limestone, marl, loess	Trollinger, Müllerrebe, Spätburgunder, Riesling, Müller-Thurgau, Silvaner	Light, tannic reds, vigorous fruity whites
Baden	Loess, loam, volcanic	Müller-Thurgau, Ruländer, Riesling, Gewürztraminer, Spätburgunder	Fragrant, spicy whites, velvet smooth to raw fiery reds
Saale-Unstrut	Limestone, sandstone	Müller-Thurgau, Silvaner, Weissburgunder, Bacchus	Soft, flowery, dry whites
Sachsen	Sand, porphyry, loam	Müller-Thurgau, Weissburgunder, Silvaner, Traminer	Dry whites with high acidity, good sparklers

GREECE

With the integration of Greece into the European Union, general standards of wine production will have to improve and the producers must become more quality conscious. Until recently, good quality wines were the exception rather than the rule, but now the better wines are being subjected to an appellation system in harmony with EU requirements. Quality wines produced in a specified region (QWPSR) are divided into:

- *Appellation d'Origine de Qualité Supérieur* (AOQS) for light table wines.
- *Appellation d'Origine Contrôlée* (AOC) for liqueur wines.

Furthermore, there is a Traditional Appellation (TA) designated to Retsina wine and another category 'Country Wine' covers local table wines.

Of all the wines produced, Retsina, which can be white or rosé, is the most famous. The wine is flavoured with pine-tree resin obtained from the Aleppo pines of Attica. The bark of the pine tree is cut to obtain the resin. This is allowed to solidify before being cut into pieces and added at an early stage to the fermenting wine. The resin is left with the wine until the first racking and by that time it will have imparted flavour, character and preserving qualities to the wine. Retsina, because of its slightly turpentine flavour, is an acquired taste, but with its fine cutting edge it is a good foil for some of the more spicy, oily, Greek foods.

Other Greek wines of note are the dry whites Demestica, Antika, Santa Helena, Pallini, Mantineia and Zitsa (which can be dry or semi-sweet). Côtes de Meliton make good red, white and rosé wine with the red Château Carras being exceptionally fine. Other good reds are Naoussa, Lion de Nemea and Demestica. Of the dessert wines, the golden Muscat of Samos is the classic. Also fine are Mavrodaphne (red), Muscat of Patras (golden) and Muscat of Rhodes (golden).

HUNGARY

All Hungarian wines marketed for export are controlled by the state monopoly called Monimepex. The wines are usually named after their production zones: Eger, Balaton, Pécs, Sopron, Mór, Badacsony and Somló. The principal grapes for white wines are Olaszrizling, Furmint, Hárslevelü, Leanyka and Muscat; and for reds Kadarka, Kékfrankos, Merlot and Cabernet Sauvignon. The best known table wine is the robust red Egri Bikavér, also known as 'Bull's Blood of Eger'. The name dates from 1552 when the Magyars, severely outnumbered, were defending the fortress of Eger against the Turks. Throughout the battle the Magyars fortified their courage with the local wine and their red-stained beards were mistakenly identified by the non-drinking Muslims as the blood of bulls. They fled the battle. Besides Bull's Blood, other flavoursome reds such as Kadarka, Sopron, Hungarian Merlot and Vilany are made. They are all good foils for the highly seasoned local food. Many of the white wines are simply sold as Hungarian Rizling, Balatoni Rizling and most, like Egri Leáyka, are medium sweet.

The greatest wine produced in Hungary is Tokay (also spelt Tokaji). It is made around the town of Tokay. The vineyards lie on the foothills of the Carpathian mountains and along the Bodrog, a tributary of the Danube. Here climatic conditions encourage the development of *Botrytis cinerea* (noble rot) on the Furmint, Hárslevelü and Muscat grapes. There are three styles of Tokay.

TOKAY SZAMORODNI

Tokay Szamorodni means 'as it comes'. That is to say, the wine has nothing added to it and it can be dry (*szaraz*) or sweet (*edes*) depending on the percentage of botrytis-affected grapes in the blend.

TOKAY ASZÚ

One of the great dessert wines, *aszú* (pronounced ossu) refers to a paste of handpicked, botrytis-affected, over-ripe grapes which is kept aside to be added to the dry base wine made from non-botrytised Furmint, Hárslevelü and Muscat grapes. The dry wine ferments in a 140-litre (30-gallon) cask called a *gönc*. The Aszú grapes are kneaded or mashed into a paste in *puttonyos*; these are hods or small wooden barrels which hold 25 kg (55 lb) of grapes or 35 litres (8 gallons) of paste. The sweetness of a Tokay is determined by the number of *puttonyos* added to the fermenting wine in the *gönc*. Three is usual, so that would mean that 105 litres (23 gallons) of paste would be added to the 140 litres (31 gallons) of the basic wine. There are, of course, sweeter versions when four, five or even six *puttonyos* of paste are added. The new wine is allowed to mature for many years and even to oxidise a little to intensify the flavours and develop the rich, raisin character and sherry-like bouquet.

TOKAY ASZÚ ESSENCIA

Also known as Royal Tokay, this wine is made entirely from specially selected noble rotting grapes. The grapes are pressed by their own weight over six to eight days and the trickle of syrup that oozes out is so rich in sugar that a special strain of yeast has to be added to help with the fermentation. Even then, the grape essence seldom reaches in excess of 2% alcohol. It is matured for years and years and can remain at its glorious best for a hundred years or more. Sometimes it is used to give a boost to some Aszú styles. On its own, Essencia has the reputation of being an aphrodisiac. Its legendary health-giving properties once made it a favourite with royalty throughout Europe.

INDIA

India has been making wine for many centuries. Both red and white table wines are produced but the most prestigious product is the sparkling wine sold under the Omar Khayyam label. This notable wine is made by the classic champagne method using the Ugni Blanc, Pinot Blanc and Chardonnay grapes. These are grown at high altitude on lime-rich soil on the slopes of the Sahyadri mountains in the state of Maharashtra near Bombay. The wines are cultivated using the Lenz Moser system (grown high on trellises and widely spaced).

ISRAEL

The *Société Coopérative Vigneronne des Grandes Caves* is the major producer of wine in Israel, acounting for 75% of the output. It markets its wines under the brand name Carmel. The modern wine industry was founded in the 1880s by Baron Edmond de Rothschild. He planted vineyards and established wineries which he later generously donated to the growers. Much of the wine is Kosher, made under Rabbinical supervision, and the main export market is to the USA. In 1957 the Israeli Wine Institute was formed at Rehovat, and since then there has been a gradual improvement in all aspects of wine-making. The wines range from dry to sweet, reds and whites, with some fortified and sparkling wines also made. Of the table wines, the white Carmel Hock, Château Montagne, Yarden Sauvignon Blanc and Palwin are of a good standard. The best reds are Gamla Cabernet Sauvignon, Château Windsor, Adom Atic, Yarden Cabernet Sauvignon, Yarden Merlot and Golan Cabernet Sauvignon.

Of the dessert wines, Yarden Late Harvested Sauvignon Blanc made from botrytis-affected grapes is really fine. The better sparkling wines, such as Yarden Brut, Yarden Blanc de Blancs and Gamla Rosé, are made by the *méthode traditionnelle*.

For a wine to be considered Kosher there are two basic requirements:

1   Only Kosher items may be used in the wine-making process.

2   Only religiously observant Jews may touch the product or equipment at the winery.

Nothing in the production affects wine quality. Traditional methods regarding fermentation, maturation, blending and bottling are adhered to.

ITALY

All the regions in Italy from Trentino-Alto Adige in the Dolomites to the toe of Sicily in the south, make wine. It has long been considered that the wines of Italy were carelessly made and were more noted for their inconsistency than for their reliability.

Italy was synonomous with low cost *vino* in screw-capped bottles. Wine laws were introduced in 1963 to improve quality and regulate standards of production. The Government piled in money to assist in the development of all aspects of viticulture and vinification and to improve the public image of the wine. These endeavours have been rewarded. Italy is now the largest producer of wine, accounting for up to one-fifth of the world's total. It is also the largest exporter of wine. The Italians themselves consume 62 litres (13.6 gallons) per capita annually. However, as with all wines, it is best to follow a producer's name or a particular brand. The wine laws were revised in 1992 and controls tightened for all categories. These easy-to-drink and sometimes very fine wines are classified as follows. The gradations are in ascending order.

Vino da Tavola (VT)   Table wine. A basic wine with no pretensions – basic plonk in other words – but it can be quite agreeable.

Indicazione Geografica Tipica (IGT)   These wines are generally superior to the above and reference to colour, grape, place or typology will appear on the label. It is on the same level as the German *Landwein* or the French *Vin de Pays*.

Denominazione di Origine Controllata (DOC)   This is supposedly the equivalent of the French AOC. When DOC appears on the label it indicates that the wine was made from specified grapes grown in a demarcated area and that the wine was vinified and aged according to prescribed high standards.

Denominazion de Origine Controllata e Garantita (DOCG)   This category guarantees authenticity of origin, controls the grape variety used and has more stringent restrictions on yield, alcohol content, vinification and ageing. These wines have to be tasted and officially approved by a panel of experts. This top-tier ranking only includes a few wines. Within this quality group are Chianti; Brunello di Montalcino; Vino Nobile di Montepulciano; Carmignan; all reds from Tuscany, Barbaresco; Barolo; Gattinara; all reds plus the white and sparkling Moscato d'Asti/Asti Spumante from Piedmont; Taurasi a red from Campania; Torgiano Rosso Riserva and Sagrantino de Montefalco reds from Umbria; Albana di Romagna, a white wine from Emilia-Romagna.

PRINCIPAL GRAPES
For red wines, the main grapes are: Aglianico, Nebbiolo, Lagrein, Dolcetto, Sangiovese, Barbera, Lambrusco, Merlot, Cabernet Sauvignon, Schiava.
    For white wines, the grapes used are: Trebbiano, Malvasia, Moscato, Pinot Grigio, Verdicchio, Müller-Thurgau, Vernaccia, Rheinriesling, Traminer.

UNDERSTANDING THE LABEL

Abboccato or amabile	Slightly sweet
Annata	Vintage
Azienda	Estate
Bianco	White

Casa vinicola	Wine company
Chiaretto	Deep rosé
Classico	Classical or best zone of a wine area
Consorzio	Voluntary association of producers who ensure high standards above the minimum requirements
Imbottigliato da	Bottled by
Metodo Classico or Tradizionale	Champagne method for making sparkling wine
Nero	Dark red
Riserva	Wine received additional ageing
Rosata	Pink
Rosso	Red
Secco	Dry
Spumante	Foaming or sparkling
Superiore	Wine of superior quality
Vecchio	Old
Vendemmia	Harvest or vintage
Vino Novello	New wine usually made by *macerazione carbonica*

Reading the label

Producers

FATTORIA DEL CERRO

Name of wine

Vino Nobile di Montepulciano

Denominazione di Origine Controllata e Garantita

Control of origin and guarantee of quality

Vintage — 1989

Bottled at source by the producer

Imbottigliato all'origine dal produttore Saiagricola SpA Montepulciano - Italia

Produce of Italy

Volume content complies with EU bottling regulations — 750 ml.℮   PRODOTTO IN ITALIA   13% vol. — Alcoholic strength

Regions and principal wines

ITALY

1   *VALLE D'AOSTA*
2   *PIEDMONT*
3   *LOMBARDY*
4   *TRENTINO-ALTO ADIGE*
5   *FRIULI-VENEZIA GIULIA*
6   *VENETO*
7   *LIGURIA*
8   *EMILIA ROMAGNA*
9   *TUSCANY*
10 *UMBRIA*
11 *THE MARCHES*
12 *LAZIO*
13 *ABRUZZI*
14 *CAMPANIA*
15 *MOLISE*
16 *PUGLIA*
17 *BASILICATA*
18 *CALABRIA*
19 *SICILY*
20 *SARDINIA*

Valle d'Aosta

This French-speaking region with its capital at Aosta is the smallest viticultural zone in Italy. Most vineyards lie in the shadows of Mont Blanc and the wines are mostly consumed locally. The best examples are the reds Donnaz and Enfer d'Arvier and the whites La Salle and Morgex.

Piedmont

This region bordering Switzerland and France is best known for it sweet effervescent wine Asti Spumante (Asti is the town where the foaming, sparkling wine is made). The capital is Turin. Using the Nebbiolo grape, fabulous reds like Barolo, Barbaresco and Gattinara have even more prestige. Barbera is a grape making notable reds Barbera d'Alba, Barbera d'Asti and Barbera di Monferrato. Another red grape Dolcetto is used to make Dolcetto d'Acqui and other good reds. Of the whites, Moscato d'Asti and Cortese di Gavi are best.

Lombardy

The Appenines in the south and the beautiful lakes Como, Garda, Iseo and Maggiore in the north, all have an influence on this Alpine climate. Oltrepó Pavese is the largest producing area, with good reds from the Pinot Nero and Barbera grapes and lively, fruity whites from the Riesling and Muscato grapes. One of the special wines of the area is the sparkling Santa Maria della Versa. Brescia also produces some fine wines, such as the dry white Lugana and Riviera del Garda. Also good are Bresciano Rosso, Bianco and Chiaretto (pink). Perhaps the real star of the region is in the bottle-fermented sparkling wine Franciacorta. Up in the mountains near Sondrio, a good red wine Valtellina is made from the Nebbiolo grape. The capital of the region is Milan.

Trentino-Alto Adige

This region in the south Tyrol borders Austria and Switzerland and its capital is Trento. It once was part of Austria but was ceded to Italy in 1919 as a result of the Treaty of St Germain. The wines are promoted in Italian and German and the ones to look out for are the reds Lago di Caldaro, Santa Maddalena, Colli di Bolzano and Lagrein; the whites, Traminer Aromatico, Terlaner and the Riesling Renano; the rosé Lagrein Kretzer, and the sparkling wine Gran Spumante. This last is made by the *metodo classico* from the Riesling and Pinot Bianco grapes.

Friuli-Venezia Giulia

This region bordering Austria, Slovenia and Croatia has two zones of exceptional merit, Collio Goriziano and Colli Orientali. The reds Refosco, Aquileia, Carso, Cabernet Sauvignon, Cabernet Franc, Merlot and Pinot Nero and the whites Traminer Aromatico, Ribolla Gialla, Pinot Grigio and Tocai Friulano are all fine wines. The sweet whites Picolit and Verduzzo are lovely dessert wines. The best sparklers are made by the *metodo classico* using Pinot Bianco, Chardonnay and Ribolla grapes. Trieste is the region's capital.

Veneto

The best known wines of Veneto, whose capital is Venice, are the dry, white Soave, the dry, light-red Bardolino and the immensely popular red Valpolicella, of which the opulent style Recioto della Valpolicella Amarone is truly magnificent. Bianco di Custoza, a fruity dry white, and the sparklers Lessini Durello and Prosecco, are all well-made wines.

Liguria

There is only a limited wine production in this region by the sea. Cinqueterre (five lands, in reality five fishing villages) produces dry white wine called Cinqueterre and a sweet white version called Sciacchetrà. Colli di Luni makes Vermentino, a really good dry white wine. Rossese di Dolceacqua and Ormeasco from Riviera Ligure di Ponente are classy dry reds. Genoa is the capital.

Emilia-Romagna

The most popular wine in this region around the capital Bologna is Lambrusco Frizzante, a frothy, fizzy wine which may be red or rosé in colour. Fifty million bottles are produced annually. The most famous wine is Albana di Romagna which was granted DOCG status in 1987 – the first white wine in Italy to be so graded. Other good whites are Bianco di Scandiano, Bosco Eliceo, Colli di Parma and Trebbiano di Romagna. Good table reds are Colli Bolognesi, Colli Piacentini and Sangiovese di Romagna.

Tuscany

Centred, of course, on Florence, this region is renowned for its truly great red wines Brunello di Montalcino, Carmignano, Chianti and Vino Nobile di Montepulciano, all graded DOCG. They all use the Sangiovese grape or a local clone such as Brunello or Prugnolo Gentile as the prime grape. Chianti used to be marketed in a globular-shaped, wicker-covered bottle called a *fiasco* (flask). Modern technology has made it impractical to continue with such presentation. More emphasis nowadays is on the quality of the wine. Chianti has seven sub-districts including Classico, Colli Fiorentini and Rufina. Classico is the heartland or historic centre of the zone. Its consortium of producers is symbolised by a black rooster on the neck label of each bottle. Of the Tuscan white wines, Vernaccia di San Gimignano and Galestro are fresh with an attractive fruit flavour. Vin Santo, made from semi-dried grapes, is an excellent dessert wine.

Umbria

The region was once synonomous with Orvieto, the semi-sweet (*abboccato* or *amabile*) white wine. The modern version, also popular, is Orvieto Secco, though *amabile* (meaning soft in the mouth) is still available. The best wine, however, is Torgiano Rosso Riserva, closely followed by Sagrantino di Montefalco. Both are quality red wines. The capital is Perugia.

The Marches

These wines come from the Adriatic coastal area, around its capital Arcona. The best examples are the whites, Verdicchio Dei Castelli di Jesi (Jesi is the town) and Verdicchio di Matelica. Traditionally these light, dry wines, made from Verdicchio grapes, were sold in green amphora bottles. The red wines are made from the Sangiovese or Montepulciano grapes. Rosso Piceno and Rosso Conero are good examples.

Lazio

This region is famous for Frascati, a white wine that can be dry or sweet and sometimes sparkling, and the equally well-known white wine called Est! Est!! Est!!! di Montefiascone. The latter got its fanciful name because of a German bishop who was on his way to the capital, Rome, in AD IIII for the coronation of Emperor Henry V. Bishop Fugger sent his servant Martin in advance to mark the door of various inns en route, with the word '*est*' (it is) when the wine was particularly good and '*non est*' when the wine was bad. At Montefiascone, Martin marked the door '*Est! Est!! Est!!!*'. The story goes that the bishop was so enchanted with the wine he never got to Rome, but settled happily in Montefiascone until he died. The reds Aprilia, Cerveteri, Cori and Velletri are worth trying too.

Abruzzi

The capital of this region is l'Aquila. The two best wines here are the red Montepulciano d'Abruzzo and the dry, white Trebbiano d'Abruzzo.

Campania

The wines made here around Naples read like a holiday brochure: Capri (red and dry white), Ischia (red and dry white) and Vesuvio especially Lacryma Christi (tears of Christ) del Vesuvio, which may be red, white, rosé or sparkling. However, the best wines are the reds Taurasi and Anglianico del Taburno, and the whites Greco di Tufo and Fiano di Avellino.

Molise

Most Molise wines are consumed locally. Biferno and Pentro di Isernia which can be red, white or rosé are the most popular examples. The capital is Campobasso.

Puglia

Puglia or Apulia forms the heel of the Italian boot. It is a prolific producer of wine – it was once known as 'Europe's wine cellar'. Negroamoro, Castel del Monte, Primitivo, Rosso Canosa, Rosso Barletta and Rosso di Cerignola are good red wines. The better whites are Locorotondo and Martina Franca. The capital is Bari.

Basilicata

The wine to note from this arid region is Aglianico del Vulture, a big, powerful red wine, one of the best in southern Italy. Some good dessert wines like Moscato and Malvasia are also made. The capital is Potenza.

Calabria

This mountainous region surrounding the capital, Catanzaro, is the toe on Italy's boot. Although the wines are unremarkable, Cirò Rosso, Melissa (red and white), Pollino, Donnici and Savuto (all red) are good with food. Greco di Bianco, a sweet white wine, is one of the best of its kind in all Italy.

Sicily

The largest Mediterranean island, Sicily produces good table wines and an exceptional fortified wine, Marsala. The best table wines are Corvo (red and white), Regaleali (red and white), Cerasuolo di Vittoria (red), Bianco d'Alcamo (dry white), and the sweet whites Malvasia delle Lipari, Moscato di Pantelleria and Moscato di Siracusa. Look out for the Q symbol on labels. This *Marchia di Qualitá* is awarded by the Sicilian Government when a wine has passed a tasting and analysis test. The capital is Palermo.

Sardinia

The wine industry on this island is dominated by co-operatives. Traditionally it produces excellent dessert wines such as Vernaccia di Oristano, Nasco di Cagliari, Girò di Cagliari, Moscato di Sardegna and the red port-like Anghelu Ruju. The best table wines are the whites Vermentini di Sardegna and Nuragus di Cagliari, and the reds Cannonau di Sardegna, Monica di Cagliari and Monica di Sardegna. Cagliari is the capital.

Summary of Italian regions and wine styles

REGION	SOIL	GRAPE	WINE STYLE
Valle d'Aosta	Stony, alluvial, sandy-clay, gravel	Nebbiolo, Dolcetto, Pinot Noir, Gamay, Müller-Thurgau	Red and white wine of local repute.
Piedmont	Calcareous clay and silica tufa	Nebbiolo, Barbera, Dolcetto, Moscato, Cortese	Fine, fullsome red wines, fresh, balanced whites, some excellent sparkling wines.
Lombardy	Alluvial, limestone, clay, gravel, sand	Pinot Nero, Barbera, Nebbiolo, Riesling, Moscato	Good reds, pleasant fruity whites and rosés, top quality sparkling.
Trentino-Alto Adige	Alluvial, light stony clay, gravel	Schiava, Lagrein, Teroldego, Gewürztraminer, Pinot Grigio, Riesling Renano, Pinot Bianco	Light soft reds, clean, fresh rosés. Flowery, spicy whites, fine sparkling wines.
Friuli-Venezia Giulia	Alluvial, sand, clay, marl	Refosco, Merlot, Cabernet Franc, Pinot Nero, Tocai Friulano, Pinot Grigio, Pinot Bianco, Chardonnay, Ribolla	Light fruity reds, fresh fruity whites with crisp acidity, refined sparklers, good dessert wines.

REGION	SOIL	GRAPE	WINE STYLE
Veneto	Alluvial, clay, sand, gravel	Corvina, Rondinella, Molinara, Merlot, Cabernet Sauvignon, Cabernet Franc, Raboso, Pinot Grigio, Sauvignon, Chardonnay, Tocai, Torcolato	Light to full fruity red wines. Crisp dry whites, light sometimes sweet sparklers. A little sweet white.
Liguria	Alluvial, calcareous, marl	Rossese, Bosco, Albarola, Vermentino	Fine dry reds, dry crisp whites, sweet whites.
Emilia Romagna	Alluvial, granite, limestone	Sangiovese, Barbera, Bonarda, Cabernet Sauvignon, Merlot, Lambrusco, Trebbiano, Sauvignon, Chardonnay	Zesty reds, frothy pink or red sparklers. Dry to sweet white wine.
Tuscany	Limestone, clay, gravel, schist, tufa	Sangiovese, Barbera, Cabernet Sauvignon, Brunello, Merlot, Chardonnay, Sauvignon Blanc, Pinot Bianco, Pinot Grigio, Vernaccia,	Classical reds, fresh fruity whites, good dessert wine.
Umbria	Gravel, limestone, clay	Sangiovese, Barbera, Merlot, Cabernet Sauvignon, Trebbiano, Malvasia, Grechetto, Chardonnay Sauvignon Blanc, Passito	Modern well-made red, quality dry to medium whites. Sweet Vin Santo.
The Marches	Marl, sandy-clay, chalk	Sangiovese, Montepulciano, Verdicchio, Malvasia	Smooth, fresh-flavoured reds, light dry whites.
Lazio	Volcanic, tufa, chalk	Sangiovese, Montepulciano, Cabernet Sauvignon, Merlot, Trebbiano, Malvasia	Sturdy rustic reds. Dry to semi-sweet white wine. Also sparkling.
Arbruzzi	Calcareous clay, sand, gravel	Montepulciano, Trebbiano, Pinot Grigio, Riesling Renano, Moscato	Inky, strong-flavoured reds, refreshing slightly acidic whites.
Campania	Black volcanic	Anglianico, Sangiovese, Barbera, Trebbiano, Malvasia	Dry, balanced velvet-smooth reds. Straw-coloured aromatic dry whites.
Molise	Alluvial sand, gravel, clay	Montepulciano, Trebbiano, Moscato	Dry red, white, rosé and some sweet white.
Puglia	Volcanic, granite, clay, chalk	Montepulciano, Sangiovese, Bombino Nero, Verdeca, Malvasia, Trebbiano, Bombino Blanco	Full-bodied red wines, dry, fruity whites.
Basilicata	Volcanic	Anglianico, Sangiovese, Montepulciano, Moscato, Malvasia	Powerful red wines. Sweet dessert wines.
Calabria	Granite, sand, clay, limestone	Gaglioppo, Greco	Dry red wines, dry acidic whites, some sweet whites.
Sicily	Volcanic, granite, tufa, limestone	Calabrese, Inzolia, Malvasia, Moscato, Chardonnay, Sauvignon Blanc, Catarratto	Dry reds and whites. Sweet whites and fortified.
Sardinia	Red, sandy stone, granite, limestone	Cannonau, Monica, Vernaccia, Moscato, Vermentino, Nuragus	Dry to sweet reds, dry to sweet whites. Good dessert wines.

Note   Fortified wines are detailed in chaper 6

JAPAN

Japan, which is prone to monsoons and typhoons, does not have a climate conducive to vine cultivation. Yet the country produces some good red and white wines, for instance those sold under the Château Lumière label and good sweet wine from Château Lion.

The main grapes used are Labrusca, Delaware, Campbell's Early and the indigenous Koshu. Some European vines like the Cabernet Sauvignon, Merlot, Chardonnay and Sémillon are also cultivated.

The principal wine districts are Honshu, Kyushu and Hokkaido, which enjoy some favourable micro-climates.

The best known wine companies are Suntory, Mercian, Mann's and Sanraku.

The Japanese are not averse to blending native wines with imported wines and selling them as the genuine article.

LEBANON

War-torn and scourged with political upheaval, Lebanon, with its Muslim background, still manages to produce some very good wines. Most of the vineyards are located in the Bekáa Valley, which is cradled between Mount Lebanon and the Syrian border.

The vines, grown 1,000 metres above sea level, have the advantage of a favourable micro-climate. The soil is mainly gravel covering a limestone base. The principal grape is the Cabernet Sauvignon, with the Cinsault and Syrah also used. Red wines are the speciality, with Château Musar – made predominately from the Cabernet Sauvignon – enjoying a worldwide reputation. From the same 140-hectare (346-acre) vineyard a second string wine Cuvée Musar is also made. Both wines are in style close to clarets. Of the other wines, Domaine des Tournelles has quality potential.

LUXEMBOURG

Luxembourg vineyards stretch for some 64 km (40 miles) along the banks of the River Mosel. These light, flowery, white wines, low in alcohol and high in acidity, have an affinity with the sharper, thinner style of Mosel wines. Made from the Rivaner (Müller-Thurgau), Elbling, Riesling, Auxerrois and Gewürztraminer grapes, they are classified in ascending order of quality as Marque Nationale, Vin Classé, Premier Cru and Grand Premier Cru. Sparkling wines such as Crémant de Luxembourg are made principally by the *méthode traditionnelle* and there is also a *pétillant* wine produced called Edelperl.

MALTA

With the climate alternating between scorching sunshine and torential rain, the cultivation of the vine for fine wines is virtually impossible here. Malta and its neighbouring island of Gozo produce average quality wines mainly from vines native to these islands. Marsovin is the largest and most important winery producing red, white and rosé table wines. Other wines to note are Verdala Rosé, Lachryma Vitas (red and white), the Wine Farmers' Co-operative (red and white), and Coleiro (red and white). The dessert wines are pleasant to drink when made from the Muscat grape.

MEXICO

Spanish missionaries first started to cultivate the vine in this torrid climate around 1520. Nowadays nearly all the vineyards are located in the cooler locations about 1,500 m above sea level. The main areas are Baja California, Saltillo/Parras, Torreon and Aguascalientes. About 90% of the wine made (mostly from the Ugni Blanc grape) is converted into brandy. However, as it is a requirement that Mexican table wines should be on offer in all restaurants, the following producers are endeavouring to make good quality wine: Bodegas de Santo Tómas, Casa Madero, Casa Martell, Casa Pedro Domecq, Cavas de San Juan, Antonio Fernandez y Cia, Marqués de Aguayo, and the largest winery Vinicola de Aguascalientes. *Vitis vinifera* vines are used – Cabernet Sauvignon, Malbec, Merlot, Grenache and Zinfandel for reds, and the Ugni Blanc, Chenin Blanc, Sauvignon Blanc, Riesling and Chardonnay for white wines.

MOROCCO

When France gained control of Morocco in 1912, emphasis was directed towards upgrading existing vineyards and establishing new ones. By the time Morocco regained her independence in 1956 a quality system had been established. Morocco now produces the best wines in north Africa with the better wines graded as Appellation d'Origine Garantie (ADG) by the state body Sodevi. Meknés – Fes is the largest wine region with vineyards situated on the northern slopes of the Atlas mountain. Oujda – Taza and Rabat – Casablanca are the other wine regions. Wines for export must have an alcoholic strength of at least 11 per cent. Red and white wines are made in abundance with reds such as Tarik and Chante Bled having the better reputations. A speciality blush wine, Gris de Boulaouane, is very popular in Casablanca. It is made by the bleeding method. The grapes are picked and then left suspended on sheets of white linen. The grapes are crushed by their own weight and the juice slowly drips through the linen into collecting containers. The new wine is aged in bottle, not in cask. It is drunk thoroughly chilled.

NEW ZEALAND

Traditionally New Zealand was associated with big, heavy sherry-style fortified wines. Since the 1980s all that has changed. Now New Zealand has a new and clear identity, producing table wines of excellent quality which people really appreciate. With a cool climate and a long growing season, the country is becoming a champion producer of light, aromatic, zesty, fruity, white wines. Although the Müller-Thurgau is still the main grape cultivated, it is the Sauvignon Blanc and Chardonnay grapes that are now propelling New Zealand wine up the quality league table. So far, the red wines are not in the same class, but they are improving, especially the Cabernets and Merlots from Hawkes Bay. Some outstanding sparkling wines are made by the classic *méthode traditionnelle*. Fine examples are Montana Lindauer Brut and Deutz Marlborough Cuvée.

The major wine regions are Aukland, Hawkes Bay, Poverty Bay and Gisborne in the North Island and Marlborough and Canterbury in the South Island.

The principal wineries are Babich, Cloudy Bay, Collard Brothers, Cooks, Coopers Creek, Delegat's Vineyard, Hunters Wines, Martinborough Vineyard, Matawhero, Mission Vineyards, Montana, Morton Estate, Neudorf, Nobilo's, Penfolds Wines, St Helena, Selak Wines, Te Mata Estate, Vidal and Villa Maria Estate.

PORTUGAL

Besides the classic fortified wines port and Madeira already discussed in chapter 6, Portugal produces a wonderful array of good quality, full-flavoured table wines. The vineyards are spread throughout the country in the following regions: Alentejo, Algarve, Bairrada, Beiras, Bucelas, Carcavelos, Colares, Dáo, Douro, Estremadura, Minho, Setúbal and Trás-os-Montes.

The soil, amazingly fertile, is predominantly decomposed granite with deposits of schistous rock, chalk, limestone, slate, sand and alluvial substances. A wide variety of grapes are cultivated. The red wine grapes include Agua Santa, Ramisco, Alvarelhão, Tinta Pinheira, Bastardo and Touriga. The white wine grapes include Alvarinho, Malvasia, Arinto, Moscatel, Galego Dourado and Rabigato

The climate in the northern regions is influenced by the Mediterranean, having hot, generally dry summers, with occasional torrential downpours. Proceeding southwards, the Atlantic brings warm summers and also the winds and rain. Winters are usually cold, wet and blustery.

Modern temperature-controlled fermentation techniques are producing lighter, fresher more appealing red and white wines with plenty of fruit character. The wine-growers are subject to a controlling system known as *Denominacã de Origem Controlada* (DOC), similar to the French *Appellation Contrôlée*. Another classification – *Indicacao de Provenienca Regulamentada* (IPR) – was introduced in

1989 to cover wine below DOC standards. Wines in this category may eventually, with improvement, be elevated to DOC status.

Understanding the label

Adega	winery
Colheita	vintage
Engarrafado	bottled by
Garrafeira	vintage dated wine with an alcohol content above the minimum requirement
Quinta	estate
Região demarcada	legally demarcated region
Reserva	quality, aged wine
Selo de origin	seal of origin
Denominaçao de Origem Controlada	guarantee of origin and quality
Vinho espumante	sparkling wine
Vinho generoso	fortified dessert wine

Reading the label

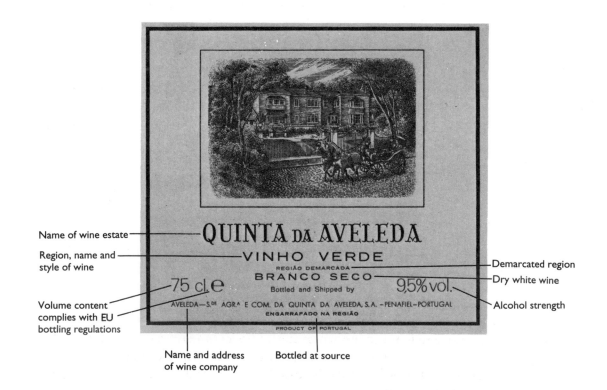

Name of wine estate

Region, name and style of wine

Volume content complies with EU bottling regulations

Name and address of wine company

Bottled at source

Demarcated region

Dry white wine

Alcohol strength

Regions and Principal Wines

Alentejo

The vineyards in this huge territory are sited on flatlands, producing red, white and rosé wines. The reds have the best quality potential. Most of the wine is made by co-operatives.

Algarve

This holiday resort is more famous for its sun and fun than for its wines. The wines, which can be red or white, are produced around Lagoa. The whites, when aged in wood, sometimes develop a sherry-like flor and make a refreshing apéritif when well chilled. The reds are for swilling or for forming the base for sundry wine cups and coolers.

Bairrada

South of Oporto is best known for its tannic red wines, which mature to a soft mellowness if given time. These wines can age up to 20 years and beyond. The whites are of average quality and are mostly drunk locally. Most of the country's sparkling wine is made within the region. Produced by the *méthode traditionnelle*, a particularly good example comes from the Quinta do Ribeirinho.

Beiras

This province lies between Dão and the Spanish border. Some good rosé wine is produced in the Pinhel district, but the white wines generally are very ordinary and slightly acidic. Red wines dominate in the region with the excellent Buçaco (Bussaco) being a prime example. Good sparkling wines like Raposeira are made by the *méthode traditionnelle*.

Bucelas

These white wines used to be sold as Portuguese Hock. They are made mainly from the Arinto grape and are usually oak-aged before being bottled. The wines are almost straw coloured and are light and refreshing to taste.

Carcavelos

This small region is situated at the mouth of the Tagus between Lisbon and Estoril. Formerly these white and red wines were imported into England under the name of Lisbon. Today the wine is mostly white, fortified, almond-flavoured and varying in taste from sweet to medium dry.

Colares

This region, west of Lisbon, lies by the sea at the foot of the towering mountains of Sintra. Due to the nature of the sandy soil these vineyards have always been phylloxera-free. The aphid or vine louse could not penetrate through the sand to get at the vine roots, which are planted deep in the clay subsoil. These dark, tannic red wines are made from the tough-skinned, scented Ramisco grape and are considered to be very fine indeed when they receive additional ageing. The white wines are undistinguished.

Dão

Named after a small river within the region, Dão has a great many vineyards scattered around the town of Viseu. To escape the scorching intensity of the summer sunshine, the vines are planted at high altitude, mostly on terraces amongst the granite hills. Predominately a red wine region, Dão produces long-lasting, deep-coloured wines that are full bodied with a glycerine-rich smoothness. The traditional whites are an acquired taste especially when aged in oak. The modern style of white is dry, fruity and fragrant and much more palatable.

Douro

The Douro Valley is renowned for its port wine, but the region also produces an abundance of red, white and rosé table wine. The full-flavoured, fruity reds such as Barca Velha are best.

Estremadura

This prolific region, 113 km (70 miles) north-west of Lisbon, produces fairly ordinary wines. The Torres Vedras whites and the Cartaxo reds are about the best.

Minho

This region is renowned for Vinhos Verdes – green wines. The green refers to the youth and invigorating, precocious personality of the wine and not to its colour, which may be white or red. The vines are grown very high on pergolas or trained on trees or on trellis work supported by pillars. Often the vines are undergrown with other crops such as vegetables and maize. Grown so high, the grapes do not get reflected heat from the soil and are protected from the fierce sun rays by the foilage from above. Consequently these barely ripe grapes have less sugar and more malic acid than grapes grown on low-pruned vines. Their characteristic *pétillance* results from a malolactic fermentation which is sustained in bottle after normal fermentation. The wine is ready for drinking immediately. In Portugal, red Vinho Verde is much more popular than the white style. For the export market the preference is reversed.

Setúbal

Pronounced 'Shtoobal', this region is located on the opposite side of the River Tagus from Lisbon. It is renowned for its great dessert wine Moscatel de Setúbal. Made from two grapes, Moscatel de Setúbal (Muscat d' Alexandria) and Moscatel de Málaga, the wine is fortified with brandy during fermentation (like port) when much sugar still remains in the wine. This golden coloured, luscious wine is left to mature, sometimes with additional Moscatel grape skins, for six to 25 years. As the wine evaporates the colour, sugar, alcohol and bouquet intensify. In old age the wine develops an attractive honeyed flavour. At Azeitâo, the firm of Fonseca bottles some excellent table wines such as the dry, fresh, fruity white Joâo Pires, Lancers rosé and the stylish reds Periquita Pasmados and Quinta da Bacalhoa.

Trás-os-Montes

'Across the mountains' is located north of the River Douro. This mountainous area produces largely red and rosé wine – with the latter giving the region its vinous fame. Mateus Rosé, a lightly carbonated medium sweet rosé wine, is traditionally made here at Vila Real and is the biggest seller of its kind worldwide.

Summary of Portuguese regions and wine styles

REGION	SOIL	GRAPES	WINE STYLE
Alentejo	Granite, clay	Periquita, Touriga Nacional, Arinto	Easy to drink reds, agreeable whites and rosés.
Algarve	Sand	Bastardo, Negra Mole, Periquita, Crato Branco, Boais	Undistinguished red, dry, sometimes flabby whites.
Bairrada	Clay	Baga, Bastardo, Tinta Pinheira, Arinto, Maria Gomes, Chardonnay, Bical	Tannic to soft mellow reds, whites of average quality, good sparkling wine.
Beiras	Alluvial, sand	Pinot Noir, Baga, Bastardo, Pinot Blanc, Chardonnay, Arinto	Dry reds, light acidic whites, some good sparklers.
Bucelas	Loam	Arinto, Cerceal	Fine, dry delicate white.
Carcavelos	Limestone	Arinto, Galega Dourado, Boais	Medium dry to sweet white wine and fortified.
Colares	Sand, loam, clay	Ramisco	Dark tannic reds.

REGION	SOIL	GRAPES	WINE STYLE
Dão	Weathered, crumbled granite	Touriga Nacional, Alvarelhão, Tinta Pinheira, Arinto, Cerceal, Encruzado	Dark oak aged reds, fruity, fragrant whites, some with a dry flinty flavour.
Douro	Schist, granite	Tinta Francisca, Touriga Nacional, Bastardo, Mourisco Tinta Cão, Rabigato, Donzelinho Branco, Arinto	Port, fruity reds, whites and rosés.
Estremadura	Slatey-clay, quartz, granite	Baga, Camarate, Periquita, Arinto, Bual, Malvasia	Clean, fruity reds, fresh, crisp whites.
Minho	Granite, schist	Amaral, Loureiro, Trajadura, Alvarinho, Azal	Young, fresh red and white Vinho Verde with a slight pétillance.
Setúbal	Clay, limestone, sand	Periquita, Muscat d'Alexandrie, Moscatel de Málaga	Much red wine, fresh fruity white but especially sweet golden dessert wines.
Trás-os-Montes	Granite, schist	Bastardo, Alvarelhão, Tinta Francisca	Some reasonable red wines, famous for pétillant rosés.

Note   Fortified wines are detailed in chaper 6

ROMANIA

Romania is a large producer of wine, most of which is heavy, strong and sweet. Much of the wine is consumed domestically. Whatever is exported is sold to adjoining countries such as Russia. The vineyards are well established and are cultivated mainly in the following regions: Banat, Dealul Mare, Moldavia, Murfatlar, Oltenia and Transylvania.

Both native and classical grapes are used. For white wines they use Bābeaskă, Chardonnay, Fetească Albā, Gewürztraminer, Grasā, Muscat Ottonel and Riesling. For red wines, the grapes are: Bābeaskă Neagrā, Cabernet Sauvignon, Fetească Neagrā, Cadarca (Kadarka), Merlot and Pinot Noir.

The country's most esteemed wine is Cotnari, a rich, golden dessert wine made from the Grasă grape. Other luscious wines made from late-gathered, botrytis-affected grapes are Gewürztraminer de Murfatlar and Rosé Edelbeerenlese, the latter made from the Feteasca Neagra grape. The best red wines are Valea Calugareasca (valley of the monks), Valea Lunga, Focsani, Nicoresti, Simburesti and Tohani. In Translyvania some good crisp, fresh, fruity white wines are now being made.

SLOVAKIA

This used to be the most important wine province of the former Czechoslovak Federation, accounting for two-thirds of the total production. Now the Republic is producing even better wines under its own banner. The main vineyard area is located near Bratislava in the district of the Little Carpathians and around the towns of Modra and Nitra.

Most of the wine is white – still or sparkling – and made from the following grapes: Rheinriesling, Vlässkyrizling, Grüner Veltliner, Sylvaner, Müller-Thurgau, Gewürztraminer and Rulandské. The Limberger and Spätburgunder (Pinot Noir) are the main red wine grapes. In the southern corner around Malá Trna some golden, sweet, Tokay-style wines are made using the Furmint, Härslevelü and Muscat grapes.

SOUTH AFRICA

South Africa is the oldest of the New World wine-producing countries. In 1652, Jan Van Riebeck, commander of the earliest Dutch settlement, planted the first vines. During the eighteenth and nineteenth centuries, a dessert wine called Constantia was regarded as the equal of any in the world. Unfortunately, towards the end of the nineteenth century, over-production diminished quality and when in 1861 Gladstone reduced the tax on French wines, South African wines no longer enjoyed their customary preferential tariff on British markets. The dreaded vine disease, phylloxera, followed in 1885 and South African wines virtually disappeared. A resurgence came when in 1918 the Co-operative Winegrowers Association (*Ko-operatiewe Wijnbouwers Vereniging*) was formed for the purpose of rationalising the making and marketing of South African wines. Now about 90% of the wine exported is produced by members of this Association. The KWV cellars at Paarl extends over 10 hectares (25 acres) and is capable of holding 136 million litres (30 million gallons) of wine. In recent years political pressure has curtailed the sale of South African wines worldwide, but with political changes the situation is improving for South African wines and their good to fine wines are now being sold on merit, like all other wines.

The main wine producing regions are:

The Coastal Region   This comprises Constantia, Durbanville, Stellenbosch and Swartland.

Boberg Region   This includes Paarl and Tulbagh.

Breede River Valley   Worcester, Robertson and Swellendam make up this region, which adjoins Klein Karoo.

The main grape varieties used are:

For Red Wines   Cabernet Sauvignon, Shiraz, Gamay, Cinsault (Hermitage), Pinot Noir and Pinotage (Pinot Noir × Cinsault) and Tinta Barocca.

For White Wines   Steen (Chenin Blanc), Sémillon, Cape Riesling, Sauvignon Blanc, Chardonnay, Gewürztraminer.

THE WINES

White Wines   The best known whites come from Stellenbosch, Paarl, Tulbagh and Constantia. Paarl and Tulbagh have especially hot climates and many growers harvest their crop at night, under floodlight, when the grapes are coolest. This, along with cool fermentation techniques, contributes towards quality and freshness. The wines are meant to be drunk young, when they are vigorous and lively. Good examples are:

- Danie De Wet Chardonnay sur Lie
- Fleur du Cap Sauvignon Blanc
- KWV Chenin Blanc
- Groot Constantia Gewürztraminer
- Twee Jongegezellen
- Chardonnay Buitenverwachting
- Theuniskraal Riesling
- L'Ormanines Chardonnay
- Zonnebloem Sauvignon Blanc
- Langoed Le Bonheur Sauvignon Blanc
- Boschendal Estate produces good sparkling wines made by the *méthode traditionnelle*.

Red Wines   The red wines, which can be light or full bodied, are mainly produced in Constantia, Durbanville, Stellenbosch, Swartland, and Robertson.
   Some good examples are:

- Beyerskloof Cabernet Sauvignon
- Zonnebloem Cabernet Sauvignon
- Culemborg Pinotage
- Nederburg Cabernet
- KWV Roodeberg
- Château Libertas
- Backsberg Cabernet Sauvignon
- Hamilton Russell Pinot Noir
- Rust-en-Vrede (Rest and Freedom) Cabernet Sauvignon
- Meerlust Cabernet Sauvignon

Dessert and fortified wines

The Klein Constantia area produces a wonderful, luscious dessert wine called Vin de Constance made from the Muscat de Frontignan grape. The fortified port-style and sweeter sherry-style wines are mainly produced in the Breede River Valley and in the

Boberg and Klein Karoo regions. Port-style wines are made from the Tinta Barocca, Souzão and Muscat grapes and are mostly consumed locally. Sherry-style wine, made from the Palomino, Steen and Sémillon grapes, are really excellent – the best outside Spain. Especially fino is the Pale Dry variety which develops *flor* and is made in Paarl, Stellenbosch and Tulbagh. As in Spain, sherry-style wines are matured and blended by the solera system. A great quantity of wine is distilled into brandy. The best brand is Oude Meester (Old Master). An exceptional, fine, tangerine-flavoured liqueur, Van der Hum, is one of South Africa's prime products.

THE BUS TICKET

Wines of origin have a numbered seal on the neck label which will have either a white background or, if the wine is superior, a gold background. This is known locally as the bus ticket. The Wine and Spirit Board awards one to four horizontal coloured bands and these will appear against the appropriate background.

- Blue (origin) guarantees the wine comes from the region stated.
- Red (vintage) guarantees that the wine is made from at least 75% of grapes grown in the year stated on the label.
- Green (cultivar) certifies that 75% of the wine was made from the indicated grape.
- Black (estate) shows the wine was made from grapes grown and vinified on the indicated estate.

SPAIN

The pre-eminence of sherry has overshadowed the considerable merits of Spanish table wines. In the past, bulk wines from Spain were sold in Britain as French pretenders, labelled Spanish Sauternes, Spanish Chablis and so on. All that did was to diminish the general reputation of all Spanish wines. That dubious marketing ploy has long been abandoned and the wines of export significance are now promoted under estate names, geographical regions or brand names. Today there is also more stringent control on standards of production. That, and the use of modern equipment and cool fermentation techniques ensure that most Spanish wine is well made. The variety offered is enormous. The quality control system introduced in 1970 is known as *Denominación de Origen* (DO), similar to the French *Appellation d'Origine*. Each region has its own *Consejo Regulador*, a regulating body, which controls vine varieties, situations of the vineyards, viticulture, vinification, yields, alcohol strengths, authenticity and so on. In 1991 a higher quality grade, *Denominación de Origen Calificada* (DOCa) was introduced initially for Rioja wines.

In a country as large as Spain, climatic conditions vary enormously, ranging from torrid heat in the central plateau to maritime conditions in the western and northern coastal areas. Generally northern locations get much more rainfall than the southern regions.

Much of the soil is chalk or limestone or decomposed rock with alluvial silt deposits. The grapes used are chosen to suit the climate and the soil conditions.

For red wines, Tempranillo, Garnacha, Graciano, Mazuelo, Cabernet Sauvignon, Cabernet Franc, Monastrell and Merlot grapes are used.

For white wines, Viura, Airen, Chardonnay, Sauvignon Blanc, Malvasia, Garnacha Blanco, Parellada, Xarello and Macabéo grapes are used.

UNDERSTANDING THE LABEL

Abocado	Medium sweet
Bodega	Winery
Cava	Cellar or generic name for sparkling wines made by the *méthode traditionnelle*
Cosecha	Harvest suggests a vintage which would be indicated on the label
Denominación de Origen	Designation of origin
Dulce	Sweet
Embotellado por	Bottled by
Espumoso	Sparkling
Granvas	Sparkling wine made by the tank method
Reserva, Grand Reserva	Mature quality wine (see Rioja)
Rosado	Rosé
Seco	Dry
Semi-seco	Medium dry
Tinto	Red

Reading the label

Name of wine company/producer

Highest quality grade guaranteeing the geographical origin

Regional appellation

Trademark symbol

Name of brand, 'The Golden Letter'

Vintage year

Official seal of guarantee showing the stamp of the regulating body

Volume content

Name and address of the winery

Bottled by

Vendimia	The gathering of the grape, the vintage
Viejo	old
Viña	vineyard
Vino	wine
Vino de calidad	Quality wine

Regions and Principal Wines

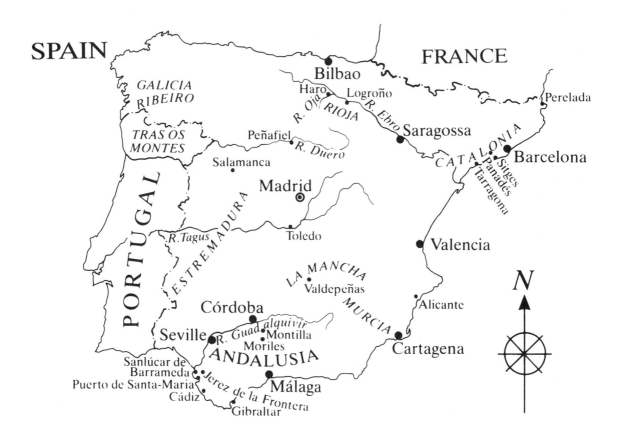

La Mancha

This large arid plateau in south-eastern Spain produces huge quantities of cheap and cheerful red and white table wines. In terms of output, it can be compared to the Midi of France. Much of this vast wine lake is made from the white Airen grape, used for distilling into brandy. Valdepeñas (valley of stones) is the largest centre of production, making sound red wine used as a base for Sangria, and white wines which are similarly popular in the general Madrid area.

Montilla-Moriles

These wines have an affinity to sherry. The principal grape used to make them is the Pedro Ximénez. The *must* is fermented in *tinajas* – earthenware containers – and the new wine is put through the solera system of maturing and blending. These white wines from Andalucia are usually not fortified and have a natural strength of about 15% alcohol. Rueda is a good white table wine with about 14% alcohol.

Ribera del Duero

This region east of Valladolid and centred around Peñafiel and Pesquera produces some of the truly great red wines of Spain. Exceptionally fine is the classic Vega Sicilia 'Unico' Reserva, reputedly the most expensive wine on the market. Made from the Cabernet Sauvignon, Malbec, Merlot, Tinto del Pais (Tempranillo) and Garnacha grapes, this wonderful wine is aged in wood usually for ten years. It can continue to improve in bottle for another 20 years or more. The same bodega also produces Tinto Valbuena which is matured for three or five years in cask. This is also a fine quality wine but a little lighter in body which some people prefer. They also appreciate the price difference. Other good red wines from the region are Bodegas Alejandro, Fernandes Tinta Pesquera and Bodegas Hermanos Perez Viña Pedrosa. Two other speciality wines from the Duero Valley are the big alcoholic Red Toro and the distinctive white Rueda made from the Verdejo grape.

Rioja

The name is a diminutive of Rio (river) Oja, one of seven tributaries of the Ebro. The best table wines of Spain are made here. All three colours of wine are made, with the big, soft, mellow reds being especially fine. They have a characteristic vanilla flavour due to their traditional ageing in *barriques* (50 gallon/225 litre) of American oak. With the towns of Logroño and Haro as commercial centres, Rioja is divided into three zones: Rioja Alta, Rioja Alavesa and Rioja Baja. The finest wines are found in the first two zones, with the rustic, unsubtle Baja wine mainly used for blending.

Tempranillo is the classic red grape and it is used in tandem with the Garnacha Tinta, Graciano and Mazuelo to produce Rioja's finest reds and rosés. White Rioja used to be oak-aged as well, but modern styles made from the Viura and Malvasia grapes get little cask ageing. Some examples of outstanding Riojas are:

- Marqués de Cáceres (red, white and rosé)
- Marqués de Murrieta (red, white and rosé)
- Marqués de Riscal (red and white)
- López de Heredia (red and white)
- Vina Tondonia (red, white and rosé)
- Viña Ardanza Reserva 904 (red)
- Compañiá Vinicola del Norte de España (CVNE) (red and white)
- Viña Solidad (white)

AGEING OF RIOJAS

Sin Crianza A young wine, usually white or rosé, bottled within a year of the vintage.

Con Crianza The wine has been matured for at least one year in cask if red, and usually six months in bottle.

Reserva The wine has matured for one year in cask and two years in bottle.

Gran Reserva The wine has spent at least two years in cask and three years in bottle.

Navarra

Lying in the shadow of Rioja, Navarra uses virtually the same grapes. Although the wines are not yet as good as Riojan wines they are less expensive and offer good value. Of the wines produced, the reds are, so far, the best. The following are good examples of a style which is usually lighter in body than the reds from Rioja.

- Bodegas Magaña
- Bodegas Villafranca Monte Ory
- Julián Chivite Gran Feudo Tinto
- Agro Navarra Camponuevo Tinto
- Señorió de Sarria Viña Ecoyen Tinto
- Viña del Perdon Tinto
- Cenalsa Agramont

Catalonia

Tarragona is the largest wine region in Catalonia and best known for its sweet red dessert wine which used to be called the 'poor man's port'. A big, heavy, robust, red table wine, Priorato, is also well considered locally. Eleven kilometres (7 miles) north of Barcelona is Alella, which produces red, white and rosé wines of reasonable quality. Ampurdán-Costa Brava in the province of Gerona makes good rosé wines and some good sparkling wines such as Perelada, made by the *méthode traditionnelle*. The classic region of Catalonia is Penedès, which makes really fine red and white wines and excellent sparkling wines. The best examples are:

Red Wines Masía Bach Tinto Reserva, Torres Gran Coronas Black Label, Jean León Cabernet Sauvignon and Raimat Cabernet Sauvignon.

White Wines Torres Gran Viña Sol Green Label, Torres Viña Esmeralda, Torres Waltraud, Masía Bach Viña Extrísima, Jean León Chardonnay.

Sparkling Wines More than 90% of Spanish sparkling wines are produced in Catalonia. The best styles are made by the *méthode traditionnelle* and are marketed under the name of *cava*. The finest cavas are made in San Sadurnui da Noya, Penedès.

Made from a combination of Xarello, Macabéo and Parellada grapes, those with particularly good reputations are Castellblanch, Codorníu, Freixenet, Marqués de Monistrol, Mestres, Mont Marcal, Segura Viudas and Jean Perico.

Levante

This region is primarily associated with bulk wines produced mainly in two zones.

Valencia   This area is not renowned for its table wines, which may be red, white or rosé. The standard bearer here is the luscious Moscatel de Valencia, a dessert wine which may or may not be fortified. Further south, Utiel-Requena, Jumilla and Yecla all make big heavy red wines.

Alicante   Good rosé wines are made here, and the dark, unique, heavy, red wine Vino de Doble Pasta. This VDP wine is made by adding a double quantity of grape skins to the fermenting must which gives a wine rich in extract with a deep, dark red colour. The wine is mainly used as a blender.

Summary of Spanish regions and wine styles

REGION	SOIL	GRAPES	WINE STYLE
La Mancha	Red, brown, sandy clay, limestone, chalk	Airén, Pardilla, Moravia, Cencibel, Garnacha	Bulk good value, red and white wines.
Montilla-Moriles	Chalk, sand	Pedro Ximénez, Airén	Sherry-style wines and fragrant white table wines.
Ribera del Duero	Alluvial with sand, clay, limestone, chalk, marl	Tinto del Pais, Cabernet Sauvignon, Malbec, Merlot, Garnacha, Verdejo	Classic red wines, less fine rosés and whites.
Rioja	Limestone, sandstone, chalk, iron rich clay	Tempranillo, Graciano, Mazuelo, Garnacha, Viura, Malvasia, Garnacha Blanca	Big tannic reds with a characteristic vanilla-oak taste. Some rosés and light fruity whites also made.
Navarra	Clay, gravel, chalk, sand	Tempranillo, Garnacha Tinta, Graciano, Mazuelo, Viura, Malvasia, Garnacha Blanca	Robust oak-flavoured reds. Some reasonable whites.

REGION	SOIL	GRAPES	WINE STYLE
Catalonia	Sand, clay, granite, limestone, chalk	Tempranillo, Garnacha Tinta, Monastrell, Cabernet Sauvignon Samsó, Parellada, Xarello, Macabeo	Fast improving reds, fine whites and some excellent sparkling wines.
Levante	Alluvial with limestone clay, sand	Monastrell, Garnacha Tinta, Tempranillo, Bobal, Merseguera, Moscatel Romano, Malvasia Riojana, Pedro Ximénez	Dark heavy reds, placid whites and rosés. Luscious dessert wines.

Note   Fortified wines are detailed in chaper 6

SWITZERLAND

Most Swiss wines are consumed domestically. Whatever arrives in Britain is very expensive and is fast losing ground, especially against the keenly priced, good quality, New World wines. Of the 25 cantons (districts) capable of producing wine, the French-speaking cantons produce the best quality wines.

Regions and principal wines

Vaud

This is the largest wine-producing district. It is divided into three sub-regions: La Côte, Chablais and La Vaux. The vineyards are sited along the shores of Lake Geneva (Lac Léman) and produce some really lovely white wines from the Chasselas grape, known locally as Dorin. The best examples of these wines are Dézaley, Mont-sur-Rolle, Saint Saphorin and the elegantly fine Aigle Clos de Murailles. Some red and rosé wines of fair quality are made from the Gamay grape.

Valais

This wine-growing region extends from Viège to Martigny along the upper valley of the Rhône. Good white wines are produced from the Chasselas grape, known here as the Fendant. The region also produces Switzerland's best red wine, Dôle, made in no precise proportions from the Pinot Noir and Gamay grapes. Another good red, Petite Dôle, is made entirely from the Pinot Noir grape. A speciality white wine Vin du Glacier is made in the Anniviers Valley. When young it is taken up near the glaciers where in mountain caves it is matured in larchwood casks for some 15 years. Another 'special' of the region is the estate-bottled Malvoisie, a golden dessert wine made from late-gathered, botrytis-affected grapes.

Neuchâtel

This canton north of Geneva produces lovely, crisp, fragrant, white wine made from the Chasselas grape and sometimes bottled *sur lie*. Some of these wines can also be *pétillant*, they make a star of tiny bubbles when poured from a height into the glass. The Pinot Noir makes the good red wine Cortaillod and a pink wine called Oeil de Perdrix (partridge's eye).

TUNISIA

The vineyards of Tunisia are located in the north of the country. Mostly reds and rosé wines are made from the Alicante Bouchet, Carignan, Cabernet Sauvignon, Mourvèdre and Grenache grapes. The Clairette and Ugni Blanc are the grapes used for the less fine white wine. If the country has a speciality it is the big, strong, dessert wines made from the Muscat grape.

TURKEY

The bulk of Turkish grapes are eaten and not made into wine. Nevertheless, there is also some reasonable wine vinified, such as the reds Villa Doluca, Hosbag, Busbag, Anatolia, Dikmen, Yakut and Trakya Kirmisi. Of the white wines, Trakya, made from the Sémillon grape is best. Tekel, the state monopoly, dominates the industry.

UNITED STATES OF AMERICA

It is estimated that 43 of the 50 American States cultivate the vine for making wine. Of these, California is the prime region producing 95% of the crop, New York State 2% and Washington State and its neighbour Oregon 1.8%. The other states output totals 1.2%. The Bureau of Alcohol, Tobacco and Firearms (BATF) is the controlling body for the drinks industry. In 1978 it conceived a form of appellation known as Approved Viticultural Areas (AVAs). Briefly it stipulates that:

- Varietal wines must use a minimum of 75% of the grape named on the label.
- When a geographical source is indicated, at least 75% of the wine must come from there.
- Wines from a specific vintage or from a nominated particular estate, must have at least 95% of that wine in the bottle.

It must be said that not all wineries adhere to these restrictions. They blend in whatever proportions suits their needs.

Basically there are two qualities of wine made in America.

TABLE WINE

These popular table wines are reliable, attractive, cheap and made in huge quantities by the ultra-modern, fully automated wineries. Technically sound, the wines are blended to a recipe. We would call them carafe wines. In America they are known as 'jug wines' as they are traditionally sold by the jugful in diners and restaurants throughout the US.

PREMIUM WINE

The best quality is known as premium wine, made by proprietors working on a smaller scale. These designer wines are crafted to the highest standard in boutique wineries, especially in California. A few of the owners are hippy wine-makers – having had a previous professional occupation before dropping out and opting for wine-making. Most, however, are graduates of the Wine College of the University of California at Davis. These masters of cultured yeast use meticulous control of fermentation temperatures and technical innovations to help nature in making good wines great. They are now producing wines of real quality, concentrating on elegance and subtlety rather than on alcohol and powerfully dominating flavours. Some of the sparkling wines being made are also outstanding. It is just a pity that some producers persist in calling the bubbly product – which can be made by the traditional method or closed tank method or the transfer method – champagne, which it is not.

The most important wine-producing regions in America are California, New York State, Washington State and Oregon.

Regions and principal wines

California

Spanish missionaries first brought the vine to California towards the end of the eighteenth century. By 1831 Jean Louis Vignes, a Frenchman from Bordeaux, was producing good wine and distilling good quality brandy. With the arrival of Agoston Haraszthy, a Hungarian political exile, in 1849 a real wine industry began to develop. By 1857 Haraszthy had established his own, now famous, Buena Vista vineyard in Sonoma County. In 1861 he was sent to Europe by the Governor of California, charged with bringing back the widest selection of European vines. He returned with over 100,000 cuttings of 1,400 varieties. By 1875, California was producing 18 million litres (four million gallons) of wine annually, based on the classical *Vitis vinifera* stock.

With its benign climate, accommodating soil and ideal aspects, California is a natural home for the vine. Many of the vineyard sights are also blessed by a unique micro-climate. The Californian coastal fog shrouds the vines throughout the summer from the fierce morning sun rays. This benefits the quality of the grapes by slowing down and prolonging the ripening process. The main grapes used are the European varieties Cabernet Sauvignon, Pinot Noir and Merlot, as well as the indigenous Zinfandel for red wines. The Chardonnay, Sauvignon Blanc (Fumé Blanc) and Johannisberg Riesling are the principal white grapes in use.

The major areas of production are the classic Napa Valley, the Sonoma Valley, Mendocino and the central coast from Monterey to Santa Barbara.
Some of the best producers are listed by their speciality grape variety below.

RED WINES

Zinfandel   Ridge Vineyards, Buena Vista, Joseph Phelps, Ch. Montelena.

Cabernet Sauvignon   Robert Mondavi, Trefethen, Jordan, Joseph Phelps, Heitz (Martha's Vineyard and Bella Oaks especially), Freemark Abbey, Stags Leap, Ridge Vineyards, Mayacamas, Jekel, Iron Horse, Clos du Val, Buena Vista, Almeden.

Pinot Noir   Chalone, Acacia, Trefethen, Robert Mondavi (the Reserve wines especially), Kalin, Saintsbury.

Merlot   Clos du Bois, Firestone Vineyard, Stags Leap, Sterling Vineyards, Clos du Val, Rutherford Hill, Inglenook, Jordan.

WHITE WINES

Chardonnay   Robert Mondavi, Trefethen, Stags Leap, Acacia, Ch. St. Jean, Mark West, Monticello, Freemark Abbey, Ch. Montelena, Mayacamas, Chalone, Edna Valley, Firestone Vineyard, Alexander Valley, Buena Vista.

Sauvignon Blanc (Fumé Blanc)   Dry Creek, Robert Mondavi, Sterling Vineyards, Matanzas Creek.

Johannisberg Riesling   Château St Jean, Joseph Phelps, Jekel, Firestone Vineyard.

Sparkling wines – méthode traditionnelle   Schramsberg, Domaine Chandon, Piper Sonoma, Iron Horse, Ch. St. Jean, Mumm Cuvée Napa.

THE RETURN OF PHYLLOXERA
Tragically the vine louse has re-emerged and is destroying a substantial number of Californian vineyards. Rootstock previously thought to be immune to the aphid has been found wanting and has succumbed to this new strain of phylloxera known as Biotype B. A huge re-planting programme is in progress using aphid-resistant rootstock.

New York State

Traditionally, the New York wine industry was based on the use of *Vitis labrusca* vines (Concord, Catawba, Delaware, Dutchess, Ives and Niagara) Although those produced reasonable fortified and sparkling wines, their table wine had a distinctive musky aroma and flavour – generally described as 'foxy'. The flavour is so exotic it is not really appreciated outside New York. The Labrusca vines were chosen initially to withstand the arctic conditions of winter. Later it was discovered that other species can also cope with the extremes of climate. Recently hybrids based on *labrusca* and *vinifera* vines (Vidal Blanc, Seyval Blanc, Chelois, Baco Noir, De Chaunac, Aurore, Maréchal Foch) were developed to temper the notorious taste. Even more recently the classic *vinifera* vines have also been successfully planted, as anybody who has tasted Wagner's Chardonnay will realise.

The main areas of production are Finger Lakes, Long Island and the Hudson River Valley. Some of the best producers are Vinifera Wine Cellars, Wiemer, Wagner, Hargrave Vineyard, Pindar, Lenz, Gold Seal, Heron Hill and Bridgehampton. Some of these concentrate entirely on *vinifera* vines such as Chardonnay, Riesling and Sauvignon Blanc for white wines, and the Cabernets for reds. Some excellent sparkling wines are made such as Gold Seal and Great Western.

Oregon

Oregon's vineyards are concentrated in the Willamette Valley, Umpque Valley and Rogue Valley. Although the general climatic conditions are cool, the coastal range in the west and the Cascade mountains in the east prevents them from being extreme. Mostly *Vitis vinifera* vines are cultivated: Chardonnay, Müller-Thurgau, Sauvignon Blanc and Pinot Gris for white wines, and Pinot Noir, Merlot and Cabernet Sauvignon for reds. The best producers are Sokol Blosser, Eyrie Vineyards, Peter F. Adams, Amity Vineyards, Knudsen Erath, Tualatin Vineyards, Elk Cove and Arterberry Winery (noted for its sparkling wine).

Washington State

Washington vineyards are phylloxera-free and so the vines in cultivation are ungrafted. With a hot, arid climate, irrigation is necessary. The sweltering summer days are counterbalanced by cool temperatures at night, so the grapes have a healthy acidity. *Vitis vinifera* vines were first introduced in the 1950s. Chardonnay, Sauvignon Blanc, Sémillon for white wine, and Cabernet Sauvignon and Merlot for reds are all cultivated successfully. The main vineyards are grouped in Yakima Valley, Columbia Valley, Walla Walla Valley and Spokane. Château Ste Michelle, Associated Vintners, Hinzerling, Preston Wine Cellars, the Hogue Cellars and Leonetti Cellar are the best known producers.

WINES FROM THE FORMER SOVIET UNION

With modern technology and expertise and greater awareness of the international market requirements, these wines are bound to improve. At the moment, they are on the sticky, sweet side, which suits the Russian palate well. Moldova, on the Romanian border, produces Negru de Purkar, a high strength red wine with good ageing potential. It is made from the Cabernet Sauvignon, Saperavi and Rara Neagra grapes. Fetjaska is the principal grape for white wines. Massandra in the Crimea is the dessert wine centre, using mainly the Muscatel grape. Good sparkling wines such as Kaffia and Krim are made by the *méthode traditionnelle*. Georgia, with its vineyards in the valley of the River Rion, makes decent red wines like Mukuzani and Saperavi and straw-coloured whites such as Tsinandal and Rkatsiteli. Some sparkling wine is made and marketed as Champanski. Russia produces mainly white and sparkling wine from around Krosnador. Stavropol, east of Krosnador, makes dryish white as well as the good dessert wine Muscatel Praskoveiski. In Armenia, port and sherry-style wines are made as well as table wines like the red Norashen, the white Echmiadzin and the pink Pamid. Perla (white) and Iskra (red) are the sparklers.

WINES FROM THE FORMER YUGOSLAVIA

With the political situation in such confusion, it is best to deal with the wine-growing provinces as we now know them.

Regions and principal wines

Slovenia

The most important white wine-producing province, Slovenia has Ljutomer, Maribor and Ptuz as the commercial centres. Lutomer Riesling is the best known wine, followed by Lutomer Welschriesling (Laski Riesling) and the sweet Spätlese wine Ranina Radgona (tiger's milk). There is also a small amount of Renski Riesling made using, as the name suggests, the Rhine Riesling grape.

Croatia

This is mostly a red wine region, with the black Plavac Mali grape widely cultivated. One of the best wines is the full-bodied Dingač made from semi-dried grapes. Other good reds are Postup, Faros, Bolski Plavač and Motovunski Teran. Inland there is a light, straw-coloured wine called Kutjevacka Graševina. Near the Hungarian border in Kontinentalna Hrvatska the Laski Riesling grape makes an abundance of semi-sweet white wines. GRK is a sherry-style wine made in the island of Korčula.

Bosnia-Herzegovina

This region produces two well known dry varietal wines: Zilavka, a pungent dry white wine, coming from vineyards around the city of Mostar, and a mild flavoured red wine called Blatina.

Macedonia

This region produces mainly red wines from the Vranac and Kratošija grapes; the deep red earthy Kratošija and Teran have the best reputations.

Montenegro

This is also a red wine region with the Vranac grape dominant. The best wine is Crnogorski Vranac.

Serbia

This large region makes red, white and rosé wines. The reds and rosés are made mostly from the Prokupac grape, Smederevka is the principal white grape. The better vineyards are located around Zupa, south of Belgrade, but many of the best white wines come from grapes grown on the cool hillsides of Fruška Gora. German commercial sources have helped Kosova to develop dry to sweetish red wines, which sell under the brand name Amselfeld (German for Kosova). Made from the Pinot Noir grape, these wines are extremely popular in Germany and are now beginning to make wine waves in Britain.

10

WINE AND FOOD HARMONY
—

INTRODUCTION

Wine needs the dimension of food to bring out its true flavours. The art of choosing
the best combinations is not too difficult to master and the learning process is usually
very enjoyable. Expertise comes with practice, trial and error. You make mistakes but
you quickly learn the flavours that harmonise and those that do not. The
combinations that work successfully are those that please the individual. As they say
in France, '*tout les goûts sont dans la nature*' – there is room for everybody's likes and
dislikes. The partnership of wine and food depends principally on four factors:

1   The style of wine
2   The style of food
3   The personal preference of the diner
4   The financial constrictions

Complications set in when:

•   other people's tastes have to be considered;
•   the choice has to be appropriate to suit a particular occasion.

A further complication arises from the knowledge that some foods are the enemies of
wine. Foods unkind to wine are those with a high vinegar or sulphur content and
those with strong acidity or overpowering hot spicy flavours. Examples of such foods
are:

- hors d'oeuvre, globe artichoke, avocado when served with vinaigrette dressing;
- smoked mackerel, kippers, anchovies;
- brined or pickled fish;
- lamb swimming in mint sauce;
- very hot curries and chillies;
- grapefruit, tart apples, oranges, lemons;
- many egg dishes because their sulphur content and their characteristic coating of the mouth neutralises the taste of wine;
- chocolate, again because its mouth-coating effect reduces to an almost imperceptible state the flavour of wine.

If you must have wine with these 'problem foods', let it be an inexpensive bottle.

However, most wine and food have a beneficial effect on each other. The general principles, still broadly valid, are that:

- white wine should be served with white meat, fowl and fish;
- red wine should be served with red meat, game and cheese;
- sweet white wine should be served with sweets, pudding and dessert.

Of course there are exceptions to these generalities. Red wine, because of its tannin content, makes most fish taste metallic. Yet it accompanies strong-flavoured fish such as salmon, red mullet and lamprey very well indeed – especially when these foods are cooked in red wine, as they often are. So when contemplating wine and food partnerships, no combinations exist to which there are not exceptions. The main aim, as always, should be for compatibility and balance of flavour. Here are some guidelines – they are not rules.

- Most food can be successfully accompanied by several styles of wine.
- White and rosé wines are usually more versatile than red wines. This is an important consideration if one wine is being chosen to accompany the complete meal.
- Regional pairings are normally very successful.
- The simpler the food, the more the wine is likely to shine.
- The finer the food, the more it is likely to show up inferior wine.
- Look at the complete dish and not just at the main food component. Identify the principal flavours. Often the sauce will decide the wine.
- The weight and body of the wine should match the character and flavour intensity of the food.
- Serve light wine with delicate food.
- Serve medium-bodied wines with medium-flavoured foods.
- Serve full-bodied wines with full-flavoured, assertive foods.
- Food with an element of acidity, oily foods and fatty foods require wines with good healthy acidity.
- Match dry with dry, rich with rich.
- Food flavoured with spices go best with aromatic or aggressively brash wines.

- With sweets and puddings the food nearly always come off better than the wine. Botrytised wines and the *vins doux naturels* are probably the best bet.
- When a particular food is served hot, it requires a more assertive wine than it does when served cold.

Besides the important matters of food, wine, personal preference and financial constraints, the following factors should also be considered:

- time of day – lunch or dinner;
- time of year – summer or winter;
- the weather – dull, cold, bright, warm, hot, humid;
- mood – bad, good, celebratory, experimental;
- occasion – formal, cosy, business;
- theme of occasion – re-union, birthday;
- style of service – sit-down meal, buffet, carvery;
- style of restaurant – Italian, Greek, French;
- ambience of occasion and location;
- previous experience of your party and the party mix;
- the logical progression of the wines during the meal:
  dry wine before sweet wine,
  light wine before heavy wine,
  young wine before older wine,
  simple wine before more complex wine,
  white wine before red wine, except in the case of sweet white wine,
  good wine before better wine.

SUGGESTIONS

Although innovation and experimentation should be encouraged, the following suggestions may be worth trying out before endeavouring to improve on them. Remember, they are only intended to be used for initial guidance – they are conventional combinations which are popular because they work successfully.

Drinks before the meal

Apéritifs are meant to stimulate the appetite, cleanse the palate and help people to unwind and relax. The trend nowadays is to abandon numbing spirits and potent cocktails before a meal in favour of the perceived healthier drinks – sherry, Madeira, apéritif ports, champagne and sparkling wines, Buck's Fizz, Kir, light white wines and blush wines.

Wine with the meal

FOOD	STYLE OF WINE REQUIRED	WINE EXAMPLES OR TRY SIMILAR STYLES FROM OTHER COUNTRIES
HORS-D'OEUVRE	Clean, sharp white or fortified	Muscadet, Sylvaner, Fino, Manzanilla
HORS-D'OEUVRE SUBSTITUTES		
Artichoke with Hollandaise	Full-bodied dry or medium white	Mâcon Lugny, Frascati, Chablis, Vouvray
Asparagus	Soft, flowery whites	Chardonnay, Côtes de Gascogne, Liebfraumilch
Avocado with prawns	Dry to medium white or rosé	Australian Chardonnay, Cape Steen, Tavel Rosé
Caviar	Sparkling wines	Champagne, Yarden Brut, Lindauer, Cuvée Napa
Gravlax	Medium sweet whites	Vouvray, Gran Viña Sol, Californian Chardonnay
Melon	Sweet fortified	Port, Madeira, Olorosa Sherry
Mushroom à la Greque	Big whites with some acidity	Demestica, Sancerre, Verdicchio
Oysters	Sparkling or dry white	Champagne, Chablis, Muscadet, Soave
Pâté	Sweet white or light red	Sauternes, Cru Beaujolais, Kalterersee
Prawn cocktail	Sauce difficult, medium white	Graves, Chardonnay, Riesling
Prosciutto with melon	Full-bodied, dry or medium white	Frascati, Orvieto, Gumpoldskirchner
Salade Niçoise	Full-bodied, dry white or rosé	Müller-Thurgau, Mâcon Viré, Provence Rosé
Smoked salmon	Smoky, oaky whites	Rioja Blanco, Pouilly Fumé, New World Chardonnay
Snails	Spicy wines	Côtes de Provence, Gewürztraminer, Verdicchio
Whitebait	Whites with good acidity	Muscadet, Welsch Riesling, Frascati
SOUP	A liquid does not need another liquid, but if you must!	
Bisques	Full-bodied, dry white	Montilla, Pinot Gris, Rioja Blanco
Consommé	Medium dry, fortified	Amontillado, Verdelho, Palo Cortado
Bortsch	Medium sweet white	Vouvray, Liebfraumilch, Oppenheimer Goldberg
Cream, velouté, vegetable	Full-flavoured white	Aligoté, Sancerre, Pouilly Fumé
EGG DISHES	Difficult, perhaps sparkling	Crémant d'Alsace, Cava, Sekt, Great Western
FARINACEOUS	Red or white, depends on sauce	
With cream sauce	Mild-flavoured whites	Frascati, Orvieto, Lacryma Christi
With tomato sauce	Light reds	Valpolicella, Santa Maddelena, Beaujolais

FOOD	STYLE OF WINE REQUIRED	WINE EXAMPLES OR TRY SIMILAR STYLES FROM OTHER COUNTRIES
With meat sauce	Bigger reds	Chianti, Barolo, Vino Nobile de Montepulciano
With seafood sauce	Fresh whites	Verdicchio, Soave Classico, Pinot Grigio
FISH		
Cod, smoked	Whites with crispness	Muscadet, Aligoté, Chablis
Coquille St Jacques	Dryish, medium whites	Chardonnay, Riesling, Chenin Blanc
Crab salad	Dry medium white	Frascati, Aligoté, Sauvignon Blanc
Haddock	Mild, acidic whites	Soave, Meursault, New World Chardonnay
Kedgeree	Aromatic whites	Gewürztraminer, Sancerre, Traminer Aromatico
Lobster, plain	Soft whites	German Riesling, Pouilly Fuissé, Condrieu
Lobster in rich sauce	Richer whites	Rully, Graves, Australian Chardonnay
Mackerel	Sharp whites	Vinho Verde, Rioja Blanco, Sauvignon Blanc
Moule marinière	Most clean crisp whites	Muscadet, Chablis, Soave
Plaice	Fine whites	Montrachet, Pouilly Fuissé, Alsace Riesling
Salmon	Fine dry whites, light red	German Kabinett, White Burgundy, Beaujolais
Sardines	Very dry whites	Vinho Verde, Muscadet, Aligoté
Scampi	Mild flavoured whites	Frascati, Côtes de Gascogne, Moselle
Skate	Dry white with body	Pinot Gris, Chablis, Albana di Romagna
Sole (grilled)	Fine whites	Montrachet, Pouilly Fuissé, Meursault
Sole (Véronique)	Reasonably rich whites	Vouvray, Jurançon, Oppenheimer
Trout	Dry white	Sauvignon Blanc, Seyssel, Chablis
Turbot	Dry to medium fine white	Château Grillet, German Riesling, Condrieu
MEAT		
Beef		
boiled	Young light reds	Modern Shiraz, Pinotage, Zinfandel
casseroled	Sturdy reds	St Emilion, Côte du Rhône, Australian Hermitage
roast	Fine reds	Margaux, Brunello, Nuits St. Georges
stroganoff	Flavoursome reds	Barolo, Hermitage, Amarone
Steak		
Fillet	Good medium to heavy reds	Chénas, Beaune Villages, Côte Rôtie
Tournedos	Medium-bodied reds	Barbera, Dão, Graves
T-bone	Full, fruity reds	Fitou, Bulgarian Cabernet, Rioja

FOOD	STYLE OF WINE REQUIRED	WINE EXAMPLES OR TRY SIMILAR STYLES FROM OTHER COUNTRIES
Lamb		
Cutlets	Good solid reds	Gattinara, St. Julien, Egri Bikaver
Roast	Soft flavoursome reds	St Émilion, Pomerol, St Nicolas-de-Bourgueil
Stews	Vigours reds	La Mancha, Corvo, Barbaresco
Kebabs	Spicy reds	Cahors, Taurasi, Demestica
Pork		
Chop	Full-bodied reds	Australian Shiraz-Cabernet, Chianti, Barolo
Stuffed roast	Big alcoholic reds	Châteauneuf-du-Pape, Gigondas, Hermitage
Ham, gammon	Light reds	Beaujolais crus, Mâcon, Mercurey
Veal		
Roast	Medium bodied reds or rosé	Fitou, Corbières, Rosé d'Anjou
Wienerschnitzel	Light to medium, white and red	Grüner Veltliner, Gumpoldskirchner, Kalterersee
Ossobuco	Medium to full dry reds	Barbera, Rosso Conero, Gattinara
Offal		
Kidneys	Soft reds	Merlot, Valpolicella, St Émilion
Liver	Flavoursome reds	Taurasi, Cousiño-Macul, Bull's Blood
Ox tongue with Madeira sauce	Fortified	Nothing better than a glass of Verdelho
Sweetbreads	Fruity young reds, dry white	Beaujolais, Chinon, Pouilly Fumé
Tripe	Whites with acidity	Pinot Grigio, Mâcon Lugny, Breaky Bottom
POULTRY		
Chicken		
Cordon bleu	Light reds	Bandol, Roussillon, Fleurie
Kiev	Good acidic whites	Chablis, Aligoté, Mâcon Viré
Roast	White, red, rosé	Graves, Côtes de Beaune, Anjou or Tavel Rosé
Tikka masala	Medium to full reds	Australian Shiraz, Californian Cabernet, Graves
Coq-au-vin	Full-bodied reds	Chambertin, Rioja, Merlot
Chicken curry	Aromatic Whites	Traminer Aromatico, Gewürztraminer, Verdicchio
Duck		
Roast	Strong reds	Rioja, Barbera, Vosne Romanée
Duckling à l'orange	Medium sweet, white, full reds	Vouvray, Brunello, Châteauneuf-du-Pape

FOOD	STYLE OF WINE REQUIRED	WINE EXAMPLES OR TRY SIMILAR STYLES FROM OTHER COUNTRIES
Goose		
Roast	Full-flavoured reds	Gidondas, Cousiño Macul, Barolo
GAME		
Grouse	Full-bodied reds	Fine Burgundy, Australian Cabernet, Pomerol
Hare	Strong-flavoured reds	Châteauneuf-du-Pape, Cahors, Madiran
Partridge	Light, fruity reds	young Pinotage, Santa Maddalena, Beaujolais
Pheasant	Medium-bodied reds	Bergerac, Californian Cabernet, Bourgueil
Quail	Delicate whites and rosé	Frascati, Soave, Anjou Rosé
Rabbit	Young reds	Beaujolais, Kalterersee, Zinfandel
Snipe, woodcock	Fine reds	Claret, Gevrey-Chambertin, Grange Hermitage
Wild duck or wild goose	Big reds	Brunello, Crozes-Hermitage, Chianti
Venison	Big heavy reds	Barolo, Rioja, Gigondas
CHEESE		
Soft creamy cheese	Light to full reds	Beaujolais, Corbières, Mâcon Rouge
English cheese	Light red and fortified	Moulin à Vent, Claret, Port
Semi-hard cheese	Full-bodied reds	St Émilion, Burgundy, Cahors
Hard cheese	Dryish white or rosé	Alsace Riesling, Pouilly Fuissé, Anjou Rosé
Blue-veined cheese	Full red, port or sweet white	Châtauneuf-du-Pape, Port, Sauternes
SWEET, PUDDING		
Apple pie	Sweet, luscious	Sauternes, Tokay, Beerenauslese
Bread and butter pudding	Less sweet whites	St Croix-du-Mont, Coteaux du Layon, German Auslese
Cheesecake	Very sweet white	Sauternes, Tokay, Trockenbeerenauslese
Christmas pudding	Celebratory, sparkling	Asti Spumante, Blanquette de Limoux, Clairette de Die (semi-sweet)
Crème brulée	Rich, creamy whites	Sauternes, Vins Doux Naturels, Barsac
Crêpes Suzette	Luscious golden	Monbazillac, Sauternes, Tokay
Fruit salad	Golden delicious	Quarts de Chaumes, Bonnezeaux, Barsac
Profiteroles	Rich white or sparkling	Jurançon, Crémant d'Alsace, Kriter
Strawberries and cream	Sparkling or sweet white	Asti Spumante, Sauternes, Monbazillac

FOOD	STYLE OF WINE REQUIRED	WINE EXAMPLES OR TRY SIMILAR STYLES FROM OTHER COUNTRIES
Summer pudding	Luscious, sweet whites	Sauternes, Monbazillac, Tokay
Trifle	Fortified	Sherry or Madeira
Zabaglione	Fortified	Only one wine: Marsala
SAVOURIES		
Highly seasoned food on toast	Sweet fortified or none	Sherry, Port, Madeira, Marsala
Dessert – Fresh fruit	Sparkling or sweet white	Pink Champagne, Asti Spumante, Clairette de Die (semi-sweet), Sauternes
Dried fruit and nuts	Sweet fortified	Port, Madeira, Málaga
Coffee	Sundry liqueurs and spirits	Kümmel, Malt Whisky, Cognac, Armagnac, Calvados

VEGETABLE AND VEGETARIAN DISHES

Most vegetables have some natural sweetness, so the wines need to be fruity or spicy to match them. Frascati, Vinho Verde, Vouvray, Sancerre and Gewürztraminer are good partners.

Light, fruity reds also go well, for example Beaujolais, Mercurey, Valpolicella and Bouches-du-Rhône. For pasta-influenced dishes see farinaceous above.

INDIAN, CHINESE AND JAPANESE

Oriental food is hard to match, but not impossible.

For the spicy Indian foods try Gewürztraminer, Anjou Rosé, Mateus Rosé, Sancerre, Australian Sémillon and the red Shiraz-Cabernet.

With Chinese foods the sweetness of the dishes can be a problem. Try Vouvray, Liebfraumilch, Vinho Verde, Jurançon, Mateus Rosé, Lambrusco Frizzante and German Spätlese.

Japanese food is noted for its stark simplicity and purity of flavour. Uncomplicated New World white wines go best. Try New Zealand Sauvignon Blanc, South African Steen, Australian Sémillon and Californian Chardonnay.

SALES AND SERVICE

BAR PREPARATION

Bars may be either for dispense purposes only or places where customers give an order, are served and make payments.

A dispense bar is any bar situated within a food and beverage service area that dispenses only wine or other alcoholic drinks to be served to a guest consuming a meal. Wine and other alcoholic drinks for consumption without meals are sold from bars situated outside the food and beverage service area itself.

Equipment

In order to carry out efficiently the service of all forms of drink requested, a bar should have available all the necessary equipment for making cocktails, decanting wine, serving wine correctly, making fruit cups and so on. The equipment includes:

- assorted glasses
- assorted measures
- ice buckets and stands
- small ice buckets and tongs
- wine baskets
- soda syphons
- water jugs
- cutting board and knife
- optics/spirit measures
- bottle openers
- cork extractors
- ice crushing machine
- ice pick
- muslin and funnel
- ice-making machine

- lemon squeezing machine
- drinking straws
- swizzle sticks
- cocktail sticks
- strainer and funnel
- carafes
- coasters
- cooling trays
- refrigerator
- small sink unit
- bar glass washing machine
- service salvers
- wine and cocktail lists
- wine knife and cigar cutter
- plentiful supply of glass cloths, serviettes and service cloths

Food items include:

- olives
- maraschino cherries
- Worcestershire sauce
- Tabasco sauce
- salt and pepper
- cinnamon
- nutmeg
- cloves
- assorted bitters: angostura, peach, orange

- assorted sugars: cube, caster, demerera and coloured
- eggs
- cream
- mint
- cucumber
- borage
- orange
- lemon
- coconut cream

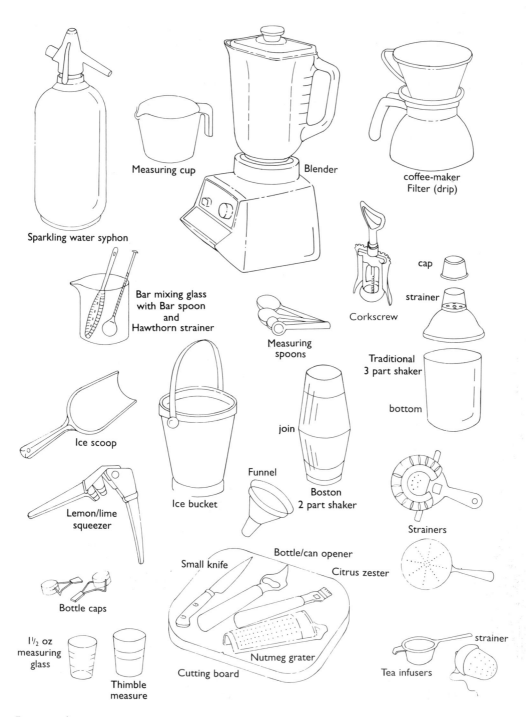

Measuring cup

Blender

coffee-maker
Filter (drip)

Sparkling water syphon

Bar mixing glass
with Bar spoon
and
Hawthorn strainer

Measuring
spoons

Corkscrew

cap

strainer

Traditional
3 part shaker

bottom

Ice scoop

join

Lemon/lime
squeezer

Ice bucket

Funnel

Boston
2 part shaker

Strainers

Bottle caps

Small knife

Bottle/can opener

Citrus zester

1½ oz
measuring
glass

Thimble
measure

Cutting board

Nutmeg grater

Tea infusers

strainer

Bar equipment

Glassware

TYPES AND SIZES OF GLASSWARE

Glasses are measured in terms of capacity by fluid ounces (fl oz), out , or centilitres (cl). An 18.93 cl (6⅔ fl oz) goblet denotes that this particular goblet holds 18.93 cl (16⅔ fl oz) or one-third of a pint.

Except in certain speciality restaurants or other establishments, where either coloured glassware or cut glassware may be used, glassware is usually plain.

Lager   Straight beer   Dimple   Worthington

Standard tulip   Traditional Mosel   Champagne flûte   Paris goblet   Traditional hock

Sherry Copita   Cocktail   Cognac   Liqueur (Elgin)   Port (Dock)

Some common glass shapes

Table 11.1   *Types and sizes of glassware*

GLASS	SIZE
Wine goblets	14.20, 18.93, 22.72 cl (5, 6⅔, 8 fl oz)
German/Alsace	18.23 cl (6, 8 fl oz)
Flute	18.23 cl (6, 8 fl oz)
Saucer champagne	18.23 cl (6, 8 fl oz)
Cocktail glasses	4.7 cl (2, 3 fl oz)
Sherry, port	4.735 cl (3 out)
Highball	23, 28 cl (9, 10 fl oz)
Worthington	28, 34 cl (10, 12 fl oz)
Lager glass	28, 34 cl (10, 12 fl oz)
Brandy balloon	23, 28 cl (8, 10 fl oz)
Liqueur glass	2.367 cl (6 out)
Tumbler	28.40 cl (½ pint)
Beer	25, 50 cl (½, 1 pint)

STORAGE

Glasses are normally stored in single rows on paper-lined shelves, upside down to prevent dust settling in them. An alternative to this is to have plastic-coated wire racks made specifically for the purpose of stacking and storing the glassware. This cuts down on breakages. Tumblers should not be stacked inside one another as this may result in heavy breakages and cause accidents.

CONSIDERATION IN THE PLANNING OF THE BAR

Area   The bar staff must be given sufficient area or space in which to work and move about. There should be a minimum of 1 m from the back of the bar counter to the storage shelves and display cabinets at the rear of the bar.

Layout   Careful consideration must be given to the layout in the initial planning. Everything should be easily to hand so that the bar staff do not have to move about more than necessary to give a quick and efficient service.

Plumbing and power   It is essential to have hot and cold running water for glass washing. Power is necessary to provide the effective working of cooling trays, refrigerators and ice-making machines.

Storage   Adequate storage must be provided in the form of shelves, cupboards and racks, for all the stock required and equipment listed.

Safety and hygiene   Great care must be observed so that the materials used in the make up of the bar are hygienic and safe. Flooring must be non-slip. The bar top should be of a material suited to the general decor that is hard wearing, easily wiped down and has no sharp edges. The bar top should be of average working height, approximately 1 m, with a width of 60 cm (20 in).

Site of the bar   The position should be chosen so that the bar is convenient for stocking as well as for staff and guests.

Hygiene

Bar hygiene standards can vary greatly, the main reasons being as follows.

- Many casual staff are employed in this area of work and training can be difficult.
- Less overall supervision is possible by the Public Health Inspector due to the irregular hours worked.
- Standards are allowed to fall because of peak demands in business for which no adequate staffing provision is made.

For the purpose of the Food Hygiene (General) Regulations 1970, drink is food. However, special exemptions are given to some of the provisions, provided that only drink (that is beers, spirits, liqueurs and such like) is dispensed.

Some aspects of the provisions that should be given particular attention by management are:

- provision of suitable overclothing;
- avoidance of possible contamination through smoking when handling food and drink;
- adequate glass washing facilities together with the important process of glass drying;
- dealing with 'spillage' to avoid the possibility of contamination;
- correct use of materials in bar design to facilitate easy cleaning.

All staff concerned with the service of food and drink should be made aware of the importance of hygiene in the bar. This may be achieved by adequate staff training at all levels.

Bar preparation

Bar opening duties may include:

- completing the requisition for bar stocks for the day's trading;
- carrying out housekeeping duties;
- cleaning one area of the bar shelves thoroughly on each day of the week, so that over the seven-day period every part of the bar receives attention;
- requisitioning food items which may be required from the stores;
- wiping and polishing bar and table tops where appropriate;
- collecting clean linen before service;

- restocking the shelves in the bar behind the bottles which are already there; labels should always face the customer with each bottle wiped clean as it is put in place; old stock is put in front of the new stock;
- checking that an adequate supply of ice is available;
- checking the cash float;
- laying out cocktail equipment where needed;
- checking the optics are in working order;
- attending to the beer casks in the cellar and turning on the beer taps; a small sample of each beer should be tasted;
- polishing the glassware.

Bar closing duties may include:

- check and clear the tills;
- complete bar summary sheet;
- remove empty bottles from the bar;
- attend to the beer casks in the cellar and turn off the beer taps;
- collect all glasses and ashtrays from the bar tables;
- brush out the ashtrays into a metal bin with a 4–5 cm (2½–3 inch) paintbrush;
- make the bar ready for early cleaning the next morning by placing the chairs on the tables;
- start a requisition list of known items of stock which will be required the next day; the list will be completed by the next day's opening team;
- wash all glassware;
- return useable fruit to the fridge;
- disconnect electrical equipment, except for tills and refrigeration or cooling cabinets, by removing the plugs from the sockets;
- pull down and secure all grills, hatches and windows.

TAKING ORDERS

Methods of order taking

Essentially there are four methods of taking beverage orders from customers. These are summarised in table 11.2.

Table 11.2 *Methods of taking beverage orders*

METHOD	DESCRIPTION
Triplicate	Order is taken: top copy goes to the supply point; second copy is sent to the cashier for billing; third copy is retained by the waiter as a means of reference during service
Duplicate	Order is taken; top copy goes to the supply point; second copy is retained for service and billing purposes
Service with order	Order is taken: customer is served and payment received according to that order. This method is most common in bar service
Pre-ordered	• Individually, for example room service • Functions

All order-taking methods are based upon these four concepts. Even the most sophisticated electronic system is based upon either the duplicate or triplicate methods, even though the actual checks may not be written but communicated to VDUs or print-out machines.

Taking orders for dispense bar beverage service

An efficient system must operate here to ensure that:

- the correct drinks are served at the right table;
- the service rendered is charged to the correct bill;
- a record is kept of all drinks issued from the dispense bar;
- management is able to assess sales over a financial period and make comparisons.

The usual system of control is a duplicate check pad (figure 11.3). The colour of the check pad may be pink or white, but is generally pink. This acts as an aid to the cashier and the control and accounts department in differentiating quickly between food (white) and drink (pink) checks.

When the wine order is taken it is written in duplicate. The wine service staff must remember to fill in the four items of information required, one in each corner of the check. These are:

- table number or room number
- number of covers
- date
- signature

Abbreviations are allowed when writing the order as long as they are understood by the dispense bar staff and the cashier. When wines are ordered only the bin number, together with the number of bottles required and the price, should be written down.

The bin number is an aid to the dispense bar staff and cellar staff in finding, without delay, the wine required by a customer. Each wine in the wine list will have a bin number printed against it. All drinks ordered should also have the price written against them. At the base of the check, the total amount of cash owing for the order given should then be written and circled. This is an aid to the cashier who must check all prices before entering them on the bill.

On taking the order, the wine staff should hand both copies to the dispense bar staff, who retain the top copy, put up the order and leave the duplicate copy with the order. This enables the wine staff to see which is their order when they come to collect their drinks, and after serving them the duplicate copy is handed to the cashier.

	Name of Establishment	
Table No.		**Covers**
Date	**Signed**	

Figure 11.3   *Wine check (pink): top copy to dispense bar*

SERVICE OF COCKTAILS

Equipment

Professional bar staff will have to hand all the essential equipment necessary to create drinks that will please the eye and excite the palate. Their panache, flamboyance and skill will add another dimension to the drink and another degree of excellence to the taste. Below is a reasonably selective list of equipment.

Cocktail shaker   The ideal utensil for mixing ingredients that will not easily blend together well by stirring. This is a three-part utensil.

Boston shaker   This consists of two cones, one of which overlaps the other to seal in the 'mix'. It is made of stainless steel, glass or plated silver. The mix is strained using a Hawthorn strainer.

Mixing glass   This looks like a glass jug without a handle, but it has a lip and is used for mixing clear drinks which do not contain juices or cream.

Strainer   There are many types, the most popular being the Hawthorn. This is a flat, spoon-shaped utensil with a spring coiled round its edge. It is used in conjunction with the cocktail shaker and mixing glass to hold back the ice after the drink is prepared. A special design is available for use with liquidisers and blenders.

Bar spoon   For use with the mixing glass when stirring cocktails; the flat 'muddler' end is used for crushing sugar and mint in certain drinks.

Bar liquidiser or blender   Used for making drinks that require puréed fruit.

Drink mixer   Used for drinks that do not need liquidising, especially those containing cream or ice cream. If ice is required, use only crushed ice.

Other equipment
This includes:

- ice trays, bucket, tongs and crusher;
- corkscrew and crown cap opener;
- bottle sealer (for champagne and sparkling wines);
- fruit juice squeezer;
- sharp knife and cutting board;
- measure/jigger
- glasses.

Cocktail decorations

Cocktails can very often look overdressed which is off-putting and may also cause difficulties for the drinker. Below is a list of garnishes which can be used in a creative manner to complement the basic flavour of the drink:

- mint and/or borage;
- cucumber;
- celery stick;
- fresh fruit: orange, lemon, lime, pineapple, mango, banana, peach, maraschino cherry;
- green olive stuffed with pimento;
- pearl onions;
- cinnamon or nutmeg (for cream-topped cocktails);
- caster sugar or fine salt for frosting glasses.

Glassware

Cocktail glasses should be plain and brilliantly clean. Table 11.3 gives the most popular glasses and their uses.

Table 11.3   *Cocktail glasses and their uses*

GLASS	USE
1. Cocktail	Pink Lady, White Lady, Martinis and Manhattens
2. Saucer	Champagne cocktails, Daisies
3. Tulip	Brandy Alexander, Kir Royale
4. Flûte	Buck's Fizz, Grasshopper
5. Paris goblet	Cobblers, Pina Colada, Green Blazer, Whisky Toddy
6. Liqueur	Layered drinks, e.g. Rainbow Cocktail
7. Worthington	Pimms, Coolers, long drinks such as Fruit Cups
8. Rocks/Old Fashioned	Old Fashioned, Negroni, Bronx, Blue Monday
9. Highball/Collins	Highballs, John Collins, Tom Collins, Mint Julep, Tequila Sunrise, Spritzers
10. Brandy balloon (small)	B & B and as an alternative for brandy- and liqueur-based cocktails
Brandy balloon (large)	Pimms, long drinks such as Sangria
11. Sour	Sours and as an alternative to rocks glasses

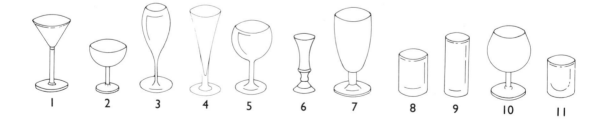

Frosting glasses

Sometimes a cocktail – such as Tequila Sunrise – calls for the glass to be frosted by way of presentation. Glasses can easily be frosted by dipping the rim into a saucer of egg white and then quickly into a saucer of caster sugar. The frosting must be allowed to dry before using the glass. Coloured sugar, made by adding a few drops of food colouring to the caster sugar and blending well, can also be used. If the idea of egg white does not appeal, simply cut an orange or lemon in half and wipe it over the glass rim, then dip the rim into the sugar as before.

Tips to ensure success in cocktail making

1 Ice should be clean and clear and should be the first item to be placed in the shaker or mixing glass.

2 The cocktail shaker should not be filled to more than four-fifths of its capacity (less is better) to allow sufficient room for efficient shaking.

3 Put plenty of ice in the shaker as this helps to chill the drink instantly, as well as giving better balance for a more rhythmic shaking action.

4 When using eggs, check that they are fresh before adding them to the other ingredients. (The use of eggs since the salmonella scare is now a matter of personal choice. The inclusion in this book of drinks containing egg looks forward to a time when the risks associated with eggs, especially raw eggs, have diminished).

5 Do not put effervescent drinks in a shaker or mixing glass.

6 Handle glasses round the base or stem, never the rim.

7 Never fill glasses to the brim in case of spillage.

8 Whenever possible, serve cocktails in chilled glasses as this helps retain the temperature of the drink.

9 Use the best possible ingredients.

10 Keep to the recipe.

11 When shaking, use a short snappy action. Do not prolong the shaking as this merely melts the ice and dilutes the drink. The professionals use the figure of eight, piston, hip and on-shoulder styles of shaking.

12 When stirring cocktails, the action should be quick and continuous until the drink is well chilled.

13 Cocktails should be made to order and served immediately when they are at their peak of perfection. Cocktails left standing around will soon separate.

14 Do not over-decorate.

SERVICE OF APÉRITIFS

The term apéritif covers a wide range of drinks which may be served before a meal.

Aerated waters

All aerated waters may be served on their own, chilled, and in either Slim Jim tumblers, Paris goblets, Highball glasses or 34.08 centilitre short-stemmed beer glasses, depending on the requirements of the guest and the policy of the establishment. They may also accompany other drinks as mixers, such as whisky and dry ginger, gin and tonic, vodka and bitter lemon, rum and cola.

Natural spring waters/mineral waters

Natural spring or mineral waters are normally drunk on their own as a pleasant-tasting and refreshing drink. However, some mineral waters may be mixed with other alcoholic beverages to form an appetising drink. In all cases, they should be drunk well chilled, at approximately 7–10°C (42–48°F). If drunk on their own they should be served in a 18.93 cl (6⅔ fl oz) Paris goblet or a Slim Jim tumbler.

Squashes

A measure of squash should be poured into a tumbler or 34.08 centilitre (12 fl oz) short-stemmed beer glass containing ice. This is topped up with iced water or water from the soda syphon. The edge of the glass may be decorated with a slice of fruit where applicable and drinking straws may be added.

Juices

All juices should be served chilled in for example, a 14.2 centilitre (5 fl oz) goblet.

Tomato juice
This should be served chilled in a 14.2 centilitre (5 fl oz) goblet on an underplate with a teaspoon. The Worcestershire sauce should be shaken, the top removed, placed on an underplate and offered as an accompaniment. The goblet may also have a slice of lemon placed over the edge.

Fresh fruit juice
This is normally served chilled with no additions.

Syrups/cordials

Syrups and cordials are not normally served as drinks in their own right but generally as flavourings in such items as cocktails, fruit cups, long drinks and milk shakes.

Fortified wines

Sherry
Fino, Manzanilla and Amontillado sherries are best served chilled or on the rocks. Others styles may be served straight from the bottle, ideally into a copita – the traditional sherry glass.

PORT

The better ports are normally served as an after-meal drink. They are usually served in a port or Dock glass and rarely chilled. For some good ports, cut glass can be used as it really does show off the myriad of colours within it.

Lesser ports are often served as apéritifs by themselves or mixed with lemonade as in port and lemon. White ports are served chilled much in the same way as dry sherry but also sometimes with the addition of ice and a lemon slice.

OTHER FORTIFIED WINES

Service is similar to the above but in a Paris goblet or other stemmed glass. Drier varieties are usually served chilled.

VERMOUTHS

Use a Paris goblet or any stemmed glass. Serve a measure either chilled or with ice, soda water, tonic water or lemonade. It mixes well with sundry spirits and is an important ingredient for many cocktails. A lemon slice is the garnish for the dry varieties and a cherry on a cocktail stick for the sweet styles.

For dry vermouths, especially Martini, a twist of lemon may be used and/or an olive on a cocktail stick.

Spirits

Spirits may be served on their own or mixed with other drinks such as minerals, juices and squashes.

GIN

Normally served as a gin and tonic with the addition of ice and lemon, gin also forms the base of a variety of mixed drinks and cocktails.

WHISKY

Whisky is usually served in a Paris goblet or tumbler. Whisky is at its best when served neat, but personal preference dictates whether it is served on the rocks (with ice), with soda water, mineral water or tapwater or with mixers such as lemonade, tonic water and so on. Scotch whisky with ginger wine is Whisky Mac. Irish whiskey with ginger wine is Whiskey Mick.

VODKA

Vodka is best served neat in small tumblers which have come straight from the freezer ('with a tear', as the Russians say). The outside of the glass has therefore become frosted over with the intense cold. Served like that, vodka is best drunk in one gulp (no need to smash the glass).

A more leisurely way to drink vodka is with ice and a mixer in a Paris goblet or with fresh orange juice (Screwdriver), tomato juice (Bloody Mary) or with ginger beer (Moscow Mule).

Rum
Dark rum is normally served neat, or with ice, juices, squashes or minerals added. Light rum is normally served iced with or without lemon and other drinks added.

Brandy
Brandy should be served at room temperature in thin glasses that can be easily warmed in the hand to enhance the bouquet and flavour. There is no need for the gimmicky glass heaters that you see in some establishments. Brandy balloons are the best glasses to use as they curve in narrowly at the top to contain the aroma. Over-large balloons are wasteful, pretentious and make the measure appear stingy. Ginger ale, soda water or 7-Up may be added to brandy, but only the cheaper varieties of spirit should be so adulterated.

Pastis
Pastis should be served with iced water. The usual proportion is three parts water to one part pastis, but extra water can be added if it is preferred weaker.

Other spirits
Generally spirits may be served by themselves or as additions to mixed drinks. Most are served chilled and some with ice and various garnishes according to the customers taste.

SERVICE OF BEERS

To allow for a good, attractive head or collar, glasses should be larger than the amount of beer to be dispensed. Under the EU hygiene regulations, a clean glass should be used for each new order. This does not please people who prefer their old glasses to be refilled. Glasses should be clean and brilliant in appearance, free from chips, cracks, smudges such as lipstick marks and other blemishes. They should be handled by the base, around the centre or by the handle – never by the rim.

Draught beers are dispensed in four ways:

- by a manual pull-beer engine;
- through a free-flow tap;
- through measured beer dispensers;
- through taps with a back-action creaming device.

Beers are usually served within the temperature range 12.5–15.5°C (55–60°F), with lagers generally cooler than other beers at 8.9–10.5°C (48–51°F). However, some people prefer to drink certain stouts at room temperature (18°C/65°F).

Glassware

All glasses used should be spotlessly clean with no finger marks, grease or lipstick on them. Examples of glassware are:

- half pint/pint tankards for draught beer;
- pint tumblers for draught beer;
- tumblers for any bottled beer;
- 34.08 cl (12 fl oz) short-stemmed beer glass for Bass/Worthington/Guinness;
- lager glass for lager: 22.72, 28.40, 34.08 cl (8, 10, 12 fl oz);
- Paris goblets for brown/pale/strong ales.

Bottled beers are available in the following sizes:

- nips   22.72 cl (7–8 fl oz)
- half pint   28.40 cl (10 fl oz)
- pints   56.80 cl (20 fl oz)
- quarts   113.60 cl (40 fl oz)

Pouring

Hold the glass at an angle and control the head of the beer by pouring against the inside of the glass. Lower and straighten the glass when a head needs to be encouraged. Never allow the tap or bottle neck to come in contact with the beer when pouring.

Certain bottle beers such as light ales and pasteurised beers can be poured straight into the glass. Others which have been bottle-conditioned must be poured very carefully. A typical example of a sediment beer is Worthington White Shield. The skill is not to disturb the sediment when pouring so that only the brilliance of the beer can be seen in the glass: hold the tilted glass at eye-level and pour the beer very carefully down the inside of the glass, keeping the bottle absolutely steady. As the glass fills, lower it from the bottle to ensure an attractive head. When the sediment reaches the shoulder of the bottle, stop pouring.

The perfect glass of beer should look good enough to photograph; it should be star-bright in appearance, taste true to type and lace the glass (with froth) as it is drunk.

Faults in beer

Although thunder has been known to cause a secondary fermentation in beer thereby affecting its clarity, faults can usually be attributed to poor cellar management.

Cloudy beer   This may be due to too low a temperature in the cellar or, more often, may result from the beer pipes not having been cleaned properly.

Flat beer   Flat beer may result when a wrong spile has been used – a hard spile builds up pressure, a soft spile releases pressure. When the cellar temperature is too low, beer often becomes dull and lifeless. Dirty glasses and those that have been refilled for a customer who has been eating food will also cause beer to go flat.

Sour beer   This may be due to a lack of business resulting in the beer being left on ullage for too long. Sourness may also be caused by the filthy habit of adding stale beer to a new cask or by beer coming in contact with old deposits of yeast which have become lodged in the pipeline from the cellar.

Foreign bodies   Foreign bodies or extraneous matter may be the result of productional or operational slip-ups.

SERVICE OF WINES

Opening techniques for still wines

Firstly cut away the top of the capsule to expose the cork. Above all, use a corkscrew with a wide thread so that the cork can be levered out without any crumbling. The cork should leave the bottle with a sigh as if sad to depart after such long contact. Smell the cork, which should smell of wine. Sometimes a wine may have a bit of bottle stink due to stale air being lodged between cork and wine, but this soon disappears as the wine is exposed to air.

Red wine bottles are usually placed on a coaster beside the host, whereas sparkling, white, blush and rosé bottles should be placed in a wine bucket holding ice and water up to the neck of the bottle. In a restaurant it is very important to show the host the bottle with the label uppermost and to say the name of the wine so there is no confusion regarding the wine or vintage ordered.

Pour, twist and take

When pouring wine, the neck of the bottle should be over the glass, but not resting on the rim in case of an accident. Care should be taken to avoid splashing and, having finished pouring, the bottle should be twisted as it is being taken away. This will prevent drips of wine falling on the tablecloth or on someone's clothes. Any drips on the rim of the bottle should be taken away with a clean service cloth or napkin.

The host gets a little taster and decides that the wine is perfectly sound for drinking. Service proceeds on the right from the right around the table with the label clearly visible and with the host's glass being finally topped-up to the customary two-thirds full. Later, if another bottle of the same wine is ordered, the host should be given a fresh glass from which to taste the new wine.

Opening and serving champagne and sparkling wines

Champagne and sparkling wines can be a bit of a problem. The bottle should not be shaken on its journey to the table and the wine must be well chilled. This helps control the effervescence and imparts the refreshing qualities associated with such wines.

Loosen or take off the wire muzzle. Holding the bottle at an angle of 45° in one hand and the cork in the other, twist the bottle only and, when the cork begins to move, restrain it by pushing it almost back into the neck. Soon the cork will leave the bottle quietly (never with a loud pop or bang). Should the cork prove stubborn and reluctant to leave the bottle, soak a napkin in hot water, wrap it around the neck of the bottle and movement will quickly occur.

Be extra careful when opening sparkling wines. Always keep the palm of your hand over the cork to prevent any accidents. Hold the bottle with your thumb in the punt and pour the wine against the inside of the glass – there should be a nice mousse but no frothing over.

Decanting

The main reasons for decanting an old red wine are

- to separate it from the sediment;
- to allow the wine to breathe;
- to develop its bouquet.

Fine old red wines and some ports which have spent most of their lives maturing in bottle throw a deposit or crust which, if allowed to enter the glass, would sully the appearance of the wine. This deposit forms as the wine ages and consists of tannins, bitartrates of calcium and magnesium and colouring matter. It makes the wine cloudy and can cause it to taste of lees.

Decanting is the movement of wine from its original container to a fresh glass receptacle, leaving the sediment behind. It is best to stand the bottle upright for two days before decanting to give the sediment a chance to settle at the bottom.

1 Extract the cork carefully – it may disintegrate because of long contact with alcohol, so be wary.

2 Place a light behind the shoulder of the bottle, a candle if you are decanting in front of guests, but a torch, light bulb or any light source at home or in the cellar will do.

3 Carefully pour the wine (through a funnel) into an absolutely clean decanter. The light will reveal the first sign of sediment (known as beeswing in port) entering the neck of the bottle.

4   At this stage stop pouring into the decanter but continue pouring into a glass which should be handy. This wine when it settles can be used as a taster or for sauces in the kitchen.

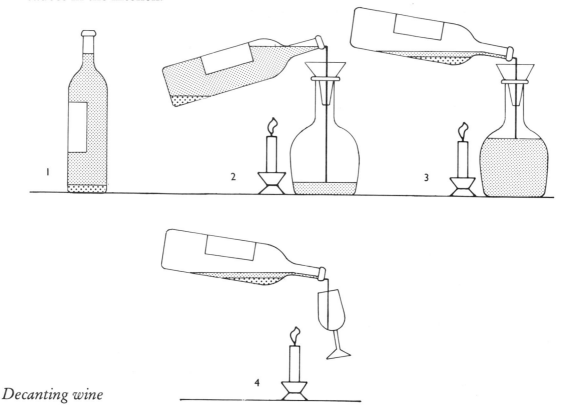

Decanting wine

A quick method for decanting is to place a coffee filter or perfectly clean muslin in a funnel which should be in the neck of the decanter as the wine flows in. The vogue nowadays is also to decant younger red wines, simply because exposure to air improves the bouquet, and softens and mellows the wine. Of course, the host's permission must always be given before decanting a wine in a restaurant. Decanting also enhances the appearance of the wine, especially when presenting in a fine wine decanter.

Very old red wine breaks up with too much exposure to air. It is best to stand such a bottle for a few days to allow the sediment to settle in the bottom. Then open the bottle just before the meal is served and pour the wine very carefully straight into the glass with the bottle held in the pouring position as each glass is approached. This prevents the wine slopping back to disturb the sediment. Sufficient glasses should be available to finish the bottle, thereby ensuring that the wine does not re-mingle with its sediment at the end of service.

Wine cradles or wine baskets are useful when taking old red wines from the cellar as they hold the bottle in the binned position, thus leaving the sediment undisturbed.

If great care is taken when pouring, you can avoid disturbing the sediment by using the cradle, but the skill requires expertise and a large hand to span the cradle. It has become fashionable to serve red wines in a wine basket or cradle. Whilst this practice appeals to some, there is no technical argument for doing so.

Suitable glasses for wines

Recommended service temperatures

Champagne and sparkling wines (red, white, rosé)	4.5–7°C (40–45°F)
Sweet white wines	7–10°C (45–50°F)
White and rosé wines	10–12.5°C (50–55°F)
Young light red wines	12.5–15.5°C (55–60°F)
Full-bodied red wines	15.5–18°C (60–65°F)

Wines can be chilled quickly by placing a bottle in a wine bucket containing salt, ice and water. The salt quickly melts the ice and drastically reduces the temperature. Another way is to place the wine in the freezer for about 10 minutes. Wines can also now be chilled quickly by using a pre-frozen reusable ice collar. These will cool a wine within about five to ten minutes. A cool red wine can be brought to room temperature by being poured into a warmed decanter or by microwaving it for about 45 seconds. Remember these are extreme situations – nothing beats traditional methods of chilling and chambering wine to a perfect temperature.

Service of wine by the glass

Wine left in a bottle, even when securely corked, becomes lifeless and unpalatable after a couple of days. To prevent this, a neat piece of equipment exists called a Vacu-vin which will reseal an opened bottle of wine, keeping the contents in perfect condition for several days. It extracts the air from the bottle and then reseals it with a special reusable stopper that preserves the natural freshness of the wine for a longer period.

SERVICE OF LIQUEURS

Liqueurs are most often served after meals and are offered together with port or brandies. Liqueurs can be served from a bar but are commonly served in restaurants from a designated trolley. The trolley is brought to the customer's table and liqueurs are offered from it. It is important for presentation purposes to ensure that bottles are clean and that the labels are facing the customers. In addition an adequate supply of glasses and equipment should be place on the trolley. Almost empty bottles should have replacements to hand to ensure that service is speedy.

The basic equipment required on the liqueur trolley is as follows:

- assorted liqueurs;
- assorted glasses – liqueur/brandy/port;
- draining stand and appropriate measures;
- service salver;

- jug of double cream;
- teaspoon;
- drinking straws;
- cigar cutter;
- wine list and check pad;
- box of matches.

Liqueurs are traditionally served in small, skimpy Elgin glasses which, when filled to the very top, just hold a single measure. A much more practical glass is a small brandy balloon which is sufficiently roomy to allow for the swirling of the drink so that the aroma can be appreciated without getting your nose dunked. Such glasses give options for double measures and for additions such as:

- crushed ice – as in Crême de Menthe Frappé;
- ice cubes – as in Bailey's Irish Cream or Cointreau on the rocks;
- cream – as in Tia Maria with cream;
- coffee beans – as in flambéed Sambuca.

We know that liqueurs come in a galaxy of colours and for glamour and sheer eye appeal no presentation can compare to the spectacular Rainbow Cocktail sometimes called Pousse Café. This is a combination of seven floated liqueurs, layered according to their specific gravity, each being carefully poured into the glass over the back of a teaspoon so that they do not mix. The sequence of pouring is vital as the lighter product must always float on the denser. Here is a classical recipe, although there are many other variations and combinations:

⅐ Crème de cacao
⅐ Crème de violette
⅐ Yellow chartreuse
⅐ Maraschino
⅐ Bénédictine
⅐ Green chartreuse
⅐ Brandy

For a more colourful alternative you could start with Grenadine (a rich red syrup made from pomegranate) and leave out one of the other ingredients.

Liqueur frappé

If a person asks for a liqueur to be served frappé, then it is served on crushed ice. A larger glass will then have to be used. The glass should be two-thirds filled with crushed ice and then the measure of liqueur is poured over. Two short drinking straws should be placed into the glass and then served. An example of this is Crême de Menthe Frappé.

Liqueurs with cream

If a liqueur is requested with cream (for example Tia Maria with Cream), then the cream is slowly poured over the back of a teaspoon to settle on the top of the selected liqueur. Under no circumstances should the liqueur and cream be mixed together.

SERVICE OF TEA AND COFFEE

Fairly rigid guidelines used to exist for the service of tea and coffee.

- Morning coffee was traditionally served in tea cups, with hot milk and white sugar only.
- In the evening demi-tasse (half cups) were used for coffee, and cream might have been offered. Brown sugar was available as well as white.
- Similarly with tea, breakfast cups were used in the morning and the smaller tea cup in the afternoon and in the evening.
- Lemon was offered only with China tea and milk with other teas

Both tea and coffee are now more commonly available throughout the day with a choice of milks, creams (including non-dairy creamers) and sugars (including non-sugar sweeteners). The use of the demi-tasse for coffee is also on the decline.

Equipment

The following are examples of the equipment used for the service of tea and coffee.

TEA TRAY

- Tray or salver
- tray cloth
- teapot
- hot water jug
- jug of cold milk
- slop basin
- tea strainer (for leaf tea)
- stands for teapot and hot water jug
- sugar basin and tongs
- teacup and saucer
- teaspoon

COFFEE TRAY

- Tray or salver
- tray cloth/napkin
- cup and saucer
- teaspoon
- sugar basin and tongs or a teaspoon according to the type of sugar offered
- coffee pot
- jug of hot milk or cream
- stands for the coffee pot and hot milk jug

Variations of the above basic equipment will depend on the type of tea or coffee offered. The following points should be observed in laying up a tea or coffee tray.

- Position the items to ensure an evenly balanced tray for carrying.
- Position the items for the convenience of the guest: beverage on the right with handles facing the guest for ease of pouring.
- Ensure the beverage is placed on the tray at the last moment so that it is served piping hot

When serving coffee, the waiter must remember to ask the guest if he or she would prefer black coffee or coffee with milk or cream (not 'black coffee' or 'white coffee'). As there are a number of alternatives for the service of coffees, it is important to be precise as to what it is.

Remember certain coffees have flavourings added either in the blend or during the process of making:

- Turkish coffee contains vanilla;
- French coffee contains chicory;
- Viennese coffee contains fig.

Tea

The quantities of dry tea used per pot, per litre or per gallon may vary slightly with the type of tea used but, as an approximate guide, the following may be adhered to:

- 42.5–56.7 g (1½–2 oz) dry tea per 4.546 litres (1 gallon);
- ½ litre (1 pint) of milk will be sufficient for 20–24 cups;
- ½ kg (1 lb) loaf sugar for approximately 80 cups.

When brewing smaller amounts such as a pot for one or two, it is often advisable to install a measure. This then ensures standardisation of brew and control on the commodity in use. Other means of pre-portioning tea may be used, such as tea bags. When making tea in bulk and calculating quantities of tea required for a party, allow approximately 190 ml (⅓ pint) per cup or 24 cups per 4.546 litres (1 gallon). If breakfast cups are used, capacity of 280 ml (½ pint), then allow only 16 cups to 4.546 litres.

Because tea is an infusion and therefore the maximum flavour is required from the brew, a few simple rules carefully observed will obtain satisfactory results.

- Heat the pot before putting the dry tea in so that the maximum heat can be obtained from the boiling water.
- Measure the dry tea and freshly drawn cold water exactly.
- Use freshly boiled water.
- Make sure the water is boiling on entering the pot.
- Stir and allow to brew for three to four minutes to obtain maximum strength from the brew.
- Remove the tea leaves at the end of this period if making in multipot insulated urns.
- Ensure all the equipment used is scrupulously clean.

INDIAN OR CEYLON
Indian or Ceylon tea may be made in either china or metal tea pots. Usually both are offered with milk in Britain. Sugar is offered separately.

CHINA
Tea is made in the normal way. The tea is served in 280 ml (½ pint) glasses, which stand in a silver holder with a handle, and on a side plate with a teaspoon. A slice of lemon may be placed in the glass, and a few slices of lemon served separately on a side plate with a small sweet fork. Sugar would be served separately.

ICED
Make a strong tea and chill well. This iced tea may then be strained and stored chilled until required. It should be served in a tumbler, on a side plate, and with a teaspoon. A slice of lemon may be placed in the glass and some lemon should be served separately as for Russian tea.

SPECIALITY TEAS
These are a variety of special tea blends, some examples of which are listed in table 11.4, together with the appropriate accompaniment.

Coffee

When making coffee in bulk, 283.5–340 g (10–12 oz) of ground coffee is sufficient to make 4.5 litres (1 gallon) of black coffee. Assuming that tea cups with a capacity of 200 ml (⅓ pint) will be used, then 283.5–340 g (10–12 oz) of ground coffee is sufficient to provide 24 cups of black coffee or 48 cups if serving half coffee and half milk. When breakfast cups are used then 16 cups of black coffee or 32 cups of half coffee and half milk will be available. Capacity, at a dinner where demi-tasse, 75 ml (3½ fl oz), are used, is 48 cups of black coffee or 96 cups half black coffee and half milk. Methods of making coffee are given on pages 111 and 112.

Table 11.4   *Service of tea*

TEA	ACCOMPANIMENT	
	MILK	**LEMON**
Assam: a rich full and malty flavoured tea, suitable for service at breakfast.	x	
Ceylon: a pale golden colour with a good flavour.	[If preferred]	x
Darjeeling: a delicate tea with a light grape flavour.	[Very little]	x
Earl grey: a blend of Darjeeling and China flavoured with Bergamot.	[If preferred]	x
Jasmine: fragrant with a scented flavour		x
Lapsang Souchong: a smokey, pungent and perfumed tea, delicate to the palate, that may be said to be an acquired taste		x
Orange pekoe: similar to Lapsang Souchong, but with a slightly fruity aroma and flavour		x

The following rules should be observed when making coffee.

- Use freshly roasted and ground coffee.
- Buy the correct grind for the type of machine in use.
- Ensure all equipment is clean before use.
- Use a set measure of coffee to water: 283.5–340 g per 4.5 litres (10–12 oz per gallon).
- Add boiling water to the coffee and allow to infuse.
- The infusion time must be controlled according to the type of coffee being used and the method of making it.
- Control the temperature, since to boil coffee is to spoil coffee: the coffee develops a bitter taste.
- Strain and serve.
- Add milk or cream separately.
- The best serving temperatures are: coffee 82°C (180°F) and milk 68°C (155°F).

BAD COFFEE
These are the reasons why bad coffee is produced:

Weak coffee

- Water has not reached boiling point;
- insufficient coffee;
- infusion time too short;
- stale or old coffee used;
- incorrect grind of coffee used for equipment in operation.

Flat coffee

- Coffee left in urn too long before use, or kept at wrong temperature;
- dirty urn or equipment;
- water not fresh, or boiled too long;
- coffee reheated.

Bitter coffee

- Too much coffee used;
- infusion time too long;
- coffee not roasted correctly;
- sediment remaining in storage or serving compartment;
- infusion at too high a temperature;
- coffee may have been left in urn too long before use.

INSTANT COFFEE

This may be made in individual coffee or tea cups or in large quantities. It involves the mixing of soluble coffee solids with boiling water. When making instant coffee in bulk, approximately 71 g (2½ oz) to each 4.5 litres (1 gallon) of water should be allowed. This form of coffee may be made very quickly, immediately before it is required, by pouring freshly boiled water onto a measured quantity of coffee powder. Stir well. Hot or cold milk, cream and sugar may be added to taste.

IRISH AND OTHER SPECIALITY COFFEES

The following equipment is required:

- silver salver;
- serviette;
- 18.93 cl (6⅔ fl oz) Paris goblet on an underplate;
- teaspoon;
- jug of double cream;
- 25 ml measure;
- coffee pot;
- sugar basin of coffee sugar with a teaspoon;
- bottle of Irish whiskey.

Order of ingredients in the glass
1 sugar
2 black coffee
3 spirit or liqueur
4 double cream

An 18.93 cl (6⅔ fl oz) Paris goblet should be used and sugar added as required by the guest. (A certain amount of sugar is always required when serving this form of coffee as it is an aid to floating the double cream on the surface of the hot coffee; the server must ensure the guest realises this). A teaspoon is then placed in the goblet to conduct the heat and avoid cracking the goblet as the piping hot, strong black coffee is poured in. The coffee should be stirred well to dissolve the sugar and then one measure of Irish whiskey added. At this stage it is important to ensure that everything is thoroughly blended. The liquid should now be within 2.5 cm (1 in) of the top of the goblet. Double cream should then be poured slowly over the back of a teaspoon onto the surface of the coffee until it is approximately 19 mm (¾ in) thick. The coffee must not be stirred; the best flavour is obtained by drinking the whisky-flavoured coffee through the cream.

When the Irish coffee has been prepared, the goblet should be put on a side-plate and placed in front of the guest.

OTHER SPECIALITY COFFEES
There are a range of speciality coffees containing specific liqueurs or spirits:

- **Monks Coffee** (Bénédictine)
- **Russian Coffee** (vodka)
- **Jamaican Coffee** (rum)
- **Calypso Coffee** (Tia Maria)
- **Highland Coffee** (Scotch whisky)
- **Seville Coffee** (Cointreau)

Different catering outlets may put a different name to a speciality coffee containing the same liqueur or spirit. For example:

- **Café Royal** (brandy)
- **Café Parisienne** (brandy)
- **Caribbean** (rum)
- **Jamaican** (rum)

CIGARS

Although cigars are nowadays made in a host of countries like the USA, Puerto Rico, the Philippines, Japan, the Dominican Republic, and the East Indies, the true home of the cigar is Cuba and, to a lesser extent, Jamaica.

Cigar components

There are three parts to a good cigar: the filler, the binder and the wrapper.

Filler   The filler comprises the bulk of the cigar and is made of a blend of leaves to form the inner core. This blend gives the cigar most of its flavour, so quality here is important.

Binder   The binder, the inner covering of the cigar, is made of a single quality leaf which binds the filler. These together form what is known as the bunch.

Wrapper   The wrapper is an exceptionally fine single leaf which must have elasticity, strength and a fine appearance. The wrapper leaf is classified according to colour.

- **Claro**   (CCC) light coloured
- **Colorado Claro**   (CC) medium
- **Colorado**   (C) dark
- **Colorado Maduro**   (CM) very dark
- **Maduro**   (M) exceptionally dark

Storage

Cigars should be stored at a temperature of 15–18°C (59–64°F), (16.5°C (61°F) is best), with a relative humidity of between 53% and 57%. Cedar wood boxes or cedar-lined containers are ideal, as cedar, being porous, allows the cigar to breathe and the aroma of cedar blends well with that of a cigar. Using a humidor is also a good way of keeping cigars in condition. Sometimes when cigars are badly stored a greyish mildew or grey specks may appear on the wrapper. These can be wiped away quite easily with a soft brush. They are not harmful and neither are the yellow and green spots which you sometimes see. The yellow spots occur through the sun-drying raindrops on the tobacco leaves as they grow and the green indicates an over abundance of oil. Both demonstrate the authenticity and naturalness of the tobacco leaf.

Service

Cigar boxes should be opened carefully with a blunt instrument. In a box of 25, 13 cigars should be on the top and 12 on the bottom layer. To extract a cigar, press the rounded head and the cigar will tilt upwards for easy extraction. The band or identification tag is best removed immediately as it can damage the outer leaf if moved up and down.

When cigars are not pre-cut, a V-shaped cigar cuter is required to cut the end thereby facilitating maximum free draught and ease of smoking. Do not make a small hole with a match or cocktail stick as this will leave a moist tar concentrate which imparts a very bitter flavour as you approach the end of your smoke.

Light cigars with a broad flame of a match, a cedar wood spile or a gas lighter, rotating the cigar to effect even burning. Should the cigar need re-lighting, first remove all excess ash and then blow through it onto the flame.

When a cigar is being carried for smoking later, it is best to use a tube or a special leather case with separate tubing. Some people carry cigars along their inner leg, inside their sock.

Cigar sizes

- **Corona:** 14.5 cm (5½ in) with a round top;
- **Petite Corona (Corona Chica):** 13 cm (5 in) with a round top;
- **Trés Petite Corona:** as Corona but 11.5 cm (4.5 in) in length;
- **Half Corona:** as Corona but 9.5 cm (3.75 in) in length;
- **Lonsdale:** as Corona but about 16.5 cm (6.5 in) in length;
- **Idealess:** torpedo-shaped, about 16.5 cm (6.5 in) in length;
- **Londres:** straight cigar, 12 cm (4.5 in) in length;
- **Panatella:** long and thinnish and open at both ends, 12.5 cm (5 in) in length;
- **Stumpen (Cheroot):** stubbier than a Panatella but slightly tapered, open at both ends;
- **Whiff:** usually small and open at both ends, about 8.9 cm (3.5 in) in length.

SALES AND PROMOTION

Sales promotion involves activities designed to promote temporary sales – mainly to increase business at slack periods such as Mondays, early evenings (happy hours) or during January and February.

Also included are special product sales – mainly to increase sales by promoting particular products. For example, festival promotions, wine and spirit promotions (in association with suppliers, perhaps), taste of England, Scotland and so on; products to complement calendar dates.

For beverage operations three aspects of sales promotion are considered, these are:

- sales promotion through advertising;
- sales promotion through merchandising;
- sales promotion through personal selling.

Advertising

'Advertising is that function of an organisation concerned with contacting and informing the market of an operation's product and persuading it to buy.'

Food and Beverage Management, Davis and Stone

ADVERTISING MEDIA

The following are examples of advertising and media:

- **Broadcast**: radio and television.
- **Print**: newspapers, consumer publications, directories such as Yellow Pages and Thompsons, guides, business publications, and other magazines.
- **Other media**: transport, posters, hoardings and cinema.
- **Postal advertising**: direct mail (some consider this to be a form of direct selling rather than advertising) and hand drops (not really postal as such but may be useful on a very local basis).

In addition it is worth considering the use of mailing lists to advise existing customers of special events. Retaining existing customers is always less costly than finding new ones.

Merchandising

Merchandising is related mainly to point-of-sale promotion. Its main role is to improve the average spend per head of the customer. However, it is also used to promote particular services or goods.

Examples of beverage merchandising tend to be mainly visual, but may also be audio, such as instore broadcasts or hotel audio systems, or audio-visual, such as hotel room videos.

Beverage merchandising stimuli can include:

- aromas
- bulletin/blackboards/brochures
- directional signs
- display cards and brochures
- displays of food and drinks
- trolley (apéritifs, liqueurs etc.)
- drinks/placemats
- facia boards
- illuminated panels
- menus/drinks and wine lists
- posters
- tent cards

However, most merchandising stimuli must also be supplemented by good personal selling techniques by all restaurant and bar staff in order to achieve the improvement in customer spending.

Personal selling

Personal selling refers specifically to the ability of the staff in a food and beverage operation to contribute to the promotion of sales. This is especially important where specific promotions are being undertaken. The promise of a particular type of menu or drink, a special deal or the availability of a particular service can often be devalued by the inability of the staff to fulfil the requirements as promised. It is therefore important to involve service staff in the formulation of particular offers and to ensure that briefing and training are undertaken so that the customer can actually experience what has been promised.

However, personal selling does not solely relate to supporting special promotions. The service staff contribute to the customers' perception of value for money, hygiene and cleanliness, the level of service and the perception of atmosphere that the customer experiences.

Within the context of selling the service staff should be able to carry out the following tasks.

- Detail the drink on offer in an informative way and also in such a way as to make the product sound interesting and worth having.
- Use the opportunity to promote specific items or deals when seeking orders from the customer.
- Seek information from the customer in a way that promotes sales. For example, rather than asking if drinks are required with the meal, ask which drinks are to be required with the meal.
- Use opportunities for the sale of additional items, such as a dessert wine with a sweet course.
- Provide a competent service of the items for sale and seek customers' views on the acceptability of the drinks and the service.

Good beverage service staff must therefore have a detailed product knowledge, be technically competent, have well developed social skills and be able to work as part of a team.

Appendix
COCKTAILS

Cocktails are an American invention, the direct result of Prohibition in the United States (1919–35) During this period, the distillation and sale of alcohol was illegal. However, enterprising entrepreneurs soon started making bathtub gin and bootleg whiskey, known as moonshine, in their own homes and selling the dreadful stuff to an eager public. To disguise the appearance and improve the flavour of these crude spirits, barmen started adding fruit juices, syrups and other mixtures. So the Cocktail Era (1920–37) was born.

Many theories are propounded as to the origin of the name 'cocktail'. Here is just one of them. Apparently in 1779, a buxom Irish lady called Betsy Flanagan, widow of a revolutionary soldier, kept a tavern much frequented by French and American officers during the American War of Independence. One day, she stole some chickens from her pro-British neighbour and prepared them for dinner. She kept to one side the feathers from the cock's tail and, as the officers entered the tavern, they were served with their favourite mixed drink decorated with a feather. The officers were so impressed, one of them proposed the toast 'Vive le cocktail'.

Cocktails have always been popular in America. In Britain, towards the end of the 1930s, excesses in this drinking pattern brought the cocktail into disrepute. World War II brought deprivation and its own discipline. Afterwards the social pattern changed. Sherry parties and the comforting gin and tonic came into vogue, although the two classic cocktails Dry Martini and Manhattan still managed to maintain popularity.

In the 1980s nostalgia for a bygone era revived the interest in cocktails. Mass taste sought the cult and instant sophistication of cocktails. Once again, the cocktail bar and home bars flourished and continue to do so. The following are the more common recipes for cocktails and mixed drinks.

COCKTAIL RECIPES

Whisky based cocktails and mixed drinks

FLYING SCOTSMAN
2 measures malt whisky
1 measure green chartreuse
½ egg white
Ice

Shake vigorously with ice and strain into a cocktail glass. Decorate with cherries.

OLD-FASHIONED
1 measure bourbon whiskey
1 teaspoon caster sugar
1 teaspoon water
2 dashes Angostura bitters
Ice

Stir all the ingredients with ice in a mixing glass. Strain and pour into a rocks glass. Decorate with cherry and orange.

MINT JULEP
2 measures bourbon whiskey
Soda water
1 tablespoon caster sugar
6 mint leaves
Crushed ice

Put sugar and mint into a highball glass. Add a little soda water and thoroughly mash the mixture until the sugar is dissolved. Add the bourbon and fill the glass with crushed ice. Stir until the outside of the glass is well frosted. Decorate with mint. Serve with two straws.

RUSTY NAIL
1 measure Scotch whisky
1 measure Drambuie
Ice

Stir with ice in a mixing glass. Strain and pour into a cocktail glass.

HIGHBALL
1 measure whiskey
Dry ginger ale
Ice

Put ice into a highball glass. Add the whiskey and ginger ale to taste. Decorate with lemon peel.

MANHATTAN
2 measures rye whiskey
1 measure sweet red vermouth
1 dash Angostura bitters
Ice

Stir all together with ice. Strain into a cocktail glass. Decorate with a cherry and lemon peel.

BOBBY BURNS
1 measure Scotch whisky
1 measure sweet vermouth
3 dashes Bénédictine
Ice

Shake all together with ice. Decorate with lemon or orange peel.

ROB ROY
2 measures Scotch whisky
1 measure sweet vermouth
1 dash Angostura bitters
Ice

Stir in a mixing glass with ice. Decorate with a cherry.

GREEN BLAZER
2 measures Irish whiskey
2 teaspoons lemon juice
2 teaspoons clear honey
1 wedge lime or lemon studded with cloves
1 very small cinnamon stick
1 teaspoon caster sugar
Boiling water

Put all the ingredients in a 250 ml (8 oz) Paris goblet. Add the boiling water. Stir until honey and sugar are dissolved.

SHAMROCK
½ measure Irish whiskey
½ measure dry vermouth
3 dashes green chartreuse
3 dashes green crème de menthe
Ice

Stir with ice and strain into a cocktail glass. Decorate with a sprig of mint.

WHISKY TODDY
3 measures Scotch whisky
2 teaspoons caster sugar
Boiling water

Put sugar and a little boiling water into a warmed 250 ml (8 fl oz) Paris goblet. Add 2 measures Scotch whisky, more boiling water, stir and top up with more Scotch.

WHISKY SOUR
2 measures whisky
1 measure lemon juice
1 teaspoon caster sugar
1 dash egg white
Ice

Shake all the ingredients with the ice and strain into a rocks glass. Decorate with a slice of lemon.

Gin-based cocktails and mixed drinks

JOHN COLLINS
1 measure gin
1 teaspoon sugar
Juice of 1 lemon
1 dash Angostura bitters
Soda water

Put ingredients except soda water into a highball glass. Stir until sugar is dissolved. Add soda water to taste. Decorate with lemon slice.
    Tom Collins is made in the same way as a John Collins but uses Old Tom Gin, which is sweeter.

PINK GIN
1 measure Plymouth gin
1 dash Angostura bitters
Iced water

Roll Angostura around a (5 fl oz) Paris goblet until the inside is well coated. Shake out surplus. Add gin and iced water to taste. Some prefer a couple of ice cubes instead of water.

MAIDEN'S BLUSH
2 measures gin
1 measure Pernod
1 teaspoon grenadine
Ice

Shake with ice and strain into a cocktail glass. Decorate with a slice of strawberry.

HORSE'S NECK
2 measures gin
Dry ginger ale
Ice

Place ice cubes and gin into a highball glass. Add ginger ale to taste. Decorate with twisted lemon peel.

GIN SLING
1 measure gin
2 teaspoons lemon juice
2 teaspoons caster sugar
1 dash Angostura bitters
Soda water
Ice

Put all ingredients, except soda water, into a highball glass with ice. Stir until sugar is dissolved. Add soda water to taste. Decorate with lime and an olive.

DRY MARTINI
2 measures gin
½ measure dry vermouth
Ice

Stir ingredients in a mixing glass. Strain into a cocktail glass and decorate with an olive. The amount of vermouth added is a source of constant debate. Some add just a little, others a lot.

CLOVER CLUB
2 measures gin
1 measure grenadine
Juice of ½ lemon
¼ egg white
Ice

Shake thoroughly with ice in a Boston shaker. Strain into large cocktail glass. Decorate with lemon peel and a cherry.

ORANGE BLOSSOM
1 measure gin
1 measure fresh orange juice
Ice

Shake with ice and strain into a cocktail glass. Decorate with orange peel.

PINK LADY
2 measures gin
1 teaspoon grenadine
¼ white of egg
Ice

Shake with ice and strain into a large cocktail glass.

NEGRONI
1 measure gin
1 measure sweet vermouth
1 measure Campari
Ice

Stir all ingredients together in mixing glass with ice. Strain into a rocks glass. Decorate with lemon peel.

GIBSON
1 measure gin
1 measure dry vermouth
Ice

Shake together with ice. Decorate with an olive and a slice of lime and lemon or with a cocktail onion.

GIMLET
2 measures gin
1 measure lime juice
Ice

Shake with ice and strain into a cocktail glass. Decorate with a slice of lime.

BRONX
1 measure gin
½ measure dry vermouth
½ measure sweet vermouth
1 measure fresh orange juice
Ice

Shake with ice and strain into a rocks glass. Decorate with a slice of orange.

SINGAPORE SLING
½ measure gin
1 measure cherry brandy
2 teaspoons lemon juice
Ice
Soda water

Shake with ice. Strain into a highball glass and add soda water to taste. Decorate with lime or lemon peel and a cocktail cherry.

CLARIDGE
⅓ measure gin
⅓ measure dry vermouth
⅙ measure Cointreau
⅙ measure apricot brandy
Ice

Stir with ice and strain into a cocktail glass. Decorate with orange peel.

WHITE LADY
2 measures gin
1 measure Cointreau
1 measure lemon juice
Ice

Shake with ice. Strain into a cocktail glass.
Decorate with a cherry on a cocktail stick.

Rum-based cocktails and mixed drinks

DAIQUIRI
2 measures white rum
1 measure lime juice
½ teaspoon caster sugar
Ice

Shake with ice. Strain into a cocktail glass.
Decorate with lemon or orange peel.

BLUE HAWAIIAN
½ measure white rum
½ measure blue curaçao
3 tablespoons cream
3 tablespoons coconut cream
3 measures pineapple juice
Ice

Shake with ice and strain into a highball
glass. Decorate with pineapple and cherry.

VIRGIN'S PRAYER
(serves 2)
2 measures light rum
2 measures dark rum
2 measures Kahlúa (or other coffee-
   flavoured liqueur)
2 tablespoons lemon juice
4 tablespoons orange juice
Ice

Shake with ice and strain into two highball
glasses. Decorate with a grape or strawberry.

MAI TAI
½ measure dark rum
1 measure light rum
½ measure tequila
½ measure Curaçao or Cointreau
1 measure apricot brandy
1 measure orange juice
2 dashes grenadine
1 dash Angostura bitters
Ice

Shake with ice. Put two ice cubes in a Paris
goblet and strain in the cocktail. Decorate
with pineapple and cherries.

PLANTERS
½ measure golden rum
½ measure fresh lemon juice
1 dash fresh lime juice
Ice

Shake with ice and strain into a cocktail
glass. Decorate with slices of lime and
lemon.

BACARDI
1 measure Bacardi or white rum
Juice of 1 lime
½ teaspoon caster sugar
Ice

Shake with ice. Strain into a cocktail glass.
Decorate with a slice of lime.

CUBA LIBRE
1 measure white rum
juice of ½ lime
Cola

Place rum with lime juice and ice in a
highball glass. Add cola to taste. Decorate
with slices of lime and lemon.

PINA COLADA
2 measures white rum
2 measures pineapple juice
2 teaspoons coconut milk or coconut liqueur
2 dashes Angostura bitters
1 pinch salt
Ice

Shake with ice. Pour into a highball glass.
Decorate with pineapple, coconut and
cherries.

XYZ
1 measure dark rum
½ measure Cointreau
½ measure lemon juice
Ice

Shake with ice and strain into a cocktail
glass. Decorate with orange and lemon peel.

Vodka-based cocktails and mixed drinks

FRENCH LEAVE
1 measure vodka
1 measure orange juice
1 measure Pernod
Ice

Shake with ice. Strain into a cocktail glass.
Decorate with orange peel.

MOSCOW MULE
1½ measures vodka
Juice of ½ lemon
Ginger beer
Ice

Fill a highball glass with ice, add vodka and
lime juice. Top up with ginger beer to taste.
Stir and decorate with lime.

BLACK RUSSIAN
2 measures vodka
1 measure Kahlúa or other coffee liqueur
Ice

Stir with ice. Strain and serve in cocktail
glass.

VODKATINI
1 measure vodka
1 dash dry sherry
Ice

Stir with ice. Strain into a cocktail glass and
decorate with lemon peel.

HARVEY WALLBANGER
(SCREWDRIVER WITH GALLIANO)
2 measures vodka
Galliano
Fresh orange juice
Ice

Fill highball glass with ice. Add vodka and
enough orange juice to fill the glass to within
12 mm (½ in) from the top. Float over the
Galliano on the back of a spoon. Decorate
with an orange slice.

SCREWDRIVER
1 measure vodka
Fresh orange juice
Ice

Fill a rocks glass with ice. Add vodka, top up
with orange juice and stir. Decorate with a
slice of orange.

BLOODY MARY
2 measures vodka
150 ml (5 fl oz) tomato juice
2 dashes Worcestershire sauce
2 dashes lemon juice
1 dash Tabasco sauce
1 pinch celery salt
Slight sprinkle of cayenne pepper
Ice

Stir together all the ingredients in a highball
glass with ice. Decorate with mint and a
celery stick.

BLUE MONDAY
2 measures vodka
1 measure blue Curaçao
Ice

Shake with ice and strain into a rocks glass.

Tequila-based cocktails and mixed drinks

ACAPULCO
1 measure tequila
1 measure Tia Maria
1 measure dark rum
150 ml (5 fl oz) coconut cream
Ice

Shake with ice and strain into a rocks glass.

TEQUILA SUNRISE
2 measures tequila
Orange juice
1 teaspoon grenadine
Ice

Fill a highball glass with ice cubes. Add tequila and enough orange juice to within 12 mm (½ inch) of the top. Add the grenadine and decorate with orange and a cherry. Add straws.

MARGARITA
1 measure tequila
1 measure Cointreau or Curaçao
2 teaspoons lime juice
Lemon
Salt

Shake. Rub rim of cocktail glass with lemon to moisten. Dip into a saucer of fine salt. Strain cocktail into the prepared glass.

Brandy-based cocktails and mixed drinks

BRANDY ALEXANDER
1 measure brandy
1 measure crème de cacao
1 measure cream
Ice

Shake with ice and strain into a champagne glass. Sprinkle nutmeg on top.

BRANDY SMASH
1 measure brandy
1 teaspoon caster sugar
3 sprigs mint
Soda water
Ice

Crush mint with sugar in a rocks glass. Add a little soda water, ice and brandy. Decorate with a sprig of mint.

B & B
1 measure brandy
1 measure Bénédictine

Stir in a small brandy balloon. Ice is optional.

CORPSE-REVIVER (A)
1 measure brandy
1 measure Fernet Branca
1 measure white crème de menthe
Ice

Shake with ice and strain into a cocktail glass.

CORPSE-REVIVER (B)
1 measure brandy
½ measure Calvados
½ measure sweet vermouth
Ice

Stir with ice and strain into a cocktail glass. Add twist of lemon.

COPACABANA
½ measure brandy
1 measure apricot brandy
½ measure Cointreau
2 teaspoons lemon juice
Ice

Shake with ice and strain into a cocktail glass. Decorate with slices of orange and lemon.

BETWEEN THE SHEETS
½ measure brandy
½ measure white rum
½ measure Cointreau
1 dash lemon juice
Ice

Shake with ice and strain into a cocktail glass. Decorate with a strawberry.

SIDECAR
½ measure brandy
½ measure Cointreau
½ measure lemon juice
Ice

Shake with ice and strain into a cocktail glass. Decorate with lemon peel.

PRAIRIE OYSTER
2 measures brandy
1 egg yolk
1 teaspoon wine vinegar
1 dash Worcestershire Sauce
1 dash Tabasco Sauce
1 pinch Cayenne pepper

Stir all the ingredients gently in a wine glass without breaking the egg yolk. Drink in one gulp.

Liqueur-based cocktails

GRASSHOPPER
½ measure crème de menthe
½ measure white crème de cacao
½ measure cream
Ice

Shake with ice and strain into a champagne glass.

WIDOW'S KISS
½ measure Bénédictine
½ measure chartreuse
1 measure Calvados
1 dash Angostura bitters
Ice

Shake with ice and strain into a cocktail glass. Decorate with a slice of strawberry and apple.

HONEYMOON
1 measure Bénédictine
1 measure Calvados
juice of ½ orange
Ice

Shake with ice and strain into a cocktail glass. Decorate with a slice of orange and apple.

Mixed drinks

The main types of alcoholic mixed drinks produced are: flips, fizzes, noggs, grogs, cobblers, coolers, cups, sours and daisies.

FLIPS

BRANDY FLIP
2 measures brandy
1 egg yolk
2 teaspoons caster sugar
Ice

PORT FLIP
2 measures port
1 egg yolk
2 teaspoons caster sugar
Ice

SHERRY FLIP
2 measures sherry
1 egg yolk
2 teaspoons caster sugar
Ice

Put the ingredients of the desired flip into a Boston shaker with ice. Shake vigorously, strain, and pour into a cocktail glass, sprinkling nutmeg on top. Serve with a straw.

FIZZES

GIN FIZZ
2 measures gin
2 teaspoons sugar
Juice 1 lemon
Soda water

GOLDEN FIZZ
2 measures gin
1 teaspoon grenadine
2 teaspoons sugar
Juice 1 lemon
1 egg yolk
Soda water

SILVER FIZZ
2 measures gin
2 teaspoons sugar

2 teaspoons fresh cream
Juice 1 lemon
Soda water

Put the ingredients of the desired fizz into a shaker with ice. Shake vigorously and strain into a Paris goblet. Top up with soda water and serve with a straw.

EGG NOGG
2 measures spirit (whisky, rum, brandy, etc.)
1 egg
2 teaspoons caster sugar
75 ml (3 fl oz) milk
Grated nutmeg

Put desired spirit, egg and sugar into a shaker with ice. Shake vigorously and strain into a 250 ml (8 fl oz) Paris goblet. Stir in milk and sprinkle grated nutmeg on top.

GROG
2 measures spirit (whisky, rum, brandy, etc.)
2 sugar lumps
2 cloves
1 small stick cinnamon
Lemon juice
Boiling water

Put the desired spirit, sugar, cloves and cinnamon stick into a Paris goblet with a little lemon juice. Top up with boiling water and stir.

COBBLER
2 measures spirit (whisky, rum, brandy etc.)
2 teaspoons sugar
4 dashes Curaçao
Crushed Ice

Half-fill a Paris goblet with crushed ice. Add the ingredients, stir and decorate with fruit and a sprig of mint.

COOLERS
RUM COOLER
2 measures dark rum
4 dashes grenadine
juice 1 lemon or lime
Soda water
Ice
Soda water

Shake all the ingredients together with ice and strain into a highball glass. Add more ice and top up with soda water.

WINE COOLER
1 small glass red or white wine
4 dashes grenadine
Soda water
Ice

Place the wine and grenadine in a highball glass. Add ice and top up with soda water.

CUPS
CLARET CUP
(serves 8)
1 bottle claret (red Bordeaux wine)
2 tablespoons sugar
Juice 1 orange
Juice 1 lemon
2 measures orange
Curaçao 150 ml (¼ pint)
water
Rind of orange and lemon
Ice

Boil the sugar and the lemon and orange rinds in the water. Put these into a container along with the claret, Curaçao and fruit juices. Stir and leave in the fridge until ready to serve. Put ice into a glass bowl and pour over the Claret Cup. Decorate with very thin slices of cucumber, apple and orange. Ladle into glasses and decorate with a sprig of mint.

FRUIT CUP
(serves 6)
3 measures orange squash
3 measures lemon squash

3 measures lime juice
4 teaspoons grenadine
Soda water/sparkling mineral water
Ice

Half fill a jug with ice and add the fruit squashes, lime juice and grenadine. Top up with soda or sparkling mineral water and stir gently. Decorate with slices of fruit, cherries and a sprig of mint, borage or cucumber rind.

PIMMS CUP
Large measure Pimms No 1
Lemonade/tonic water
Ice

Pour the Pimms into a large bowl-shaped glass such as a brandy balloon or a 300 ml (½ pint) tankard or Worthington glass. Add ice and top up with lemonade or alternative. Decorate with a cherry and slice of apple, orange, lemon, lime and borage or a twist of cucumber peel. A stirrer and two straws are optional.

HOCK CUP
(serves 6)
½ bottle Rhine wine
2 measures medium sherry
1 measure Curaçao
Soda water
Ice

Pour the wine, sherry and curaçao into a jug. Add ice, top up with soda water and decorate with a slice of lemon and cucumber rind.

CIDER CUP
(serves 6)
2 bottles cider
2 measures brandy
1 measure Maraschino
Soda water
Ice

Pour the cider, brandy and Maraschino into a glass jug. Add ice and slices of assorted fruit. Top up with soda water. Stir slightly and decorate with apple slices and cucumber rind.

SOURS

PISCO SOUR

2 measures Pisco brandy
4 measures lime juice
2 teaspoons caster sugar
1 dash Angostura bitters
1 dash egg white
Ice

Shake thoroughly with ice. Strain into a rocks glass. Decorate with a slice of lemon and lime.

FRISCO SOUR

2 measures bourbon whiskey
1 measure Bénédictine
1 measure fresh lime juice
1 measure fresh lemon juice
Ice

Shake with ice and strain into a rocks glass. Decorate with a slice of lemon and lime.

DAISIES

2 measures spirit or liqueur (rum, whisky, brandy, cherry brandy etc.)
1 measure grenadine
juice of ½ lemon
Ice

Put all the ingredients into a shaker, together with some ice. Shake and strain into a champagne saucer.

Top up with a little soda water and decorate with cherries.

Wine-based cocktails and mixed drinks

BLACK VELVET

½ chilled champagne
½ Guinness

Pour the champagne and Guinness simultaneously into a chilled silver tankard, taking great care to avoid frothing over.

KIR

Chilled dry white Burgundy, traditionally Aligoté
1 teaspoon crème de cassis

Put the crème de cassis in a goblet and pour over the chilled white wine.

KIR ROYALE

As above, but substitute chilled champagne for white wine.

CHAMPAGNE COCKTAIL

Champagne
1 sugar lump
Angostura bitters
1 teaspoon Cognac/orange Curaçao

Dampen the sugar lump with Angostura and place in a champagne glass (the saucer style if you prefer). Pour over well chilled champagne and float the Cognac or orange Curaçao over the back of a teaspoon. Decorate with a slice of orange and a cocktail cherry or, more simply, with a strip of orange peel.

BUCK'S FIZZ

1 measure chilled, fresh orange juice
1 dash grenadine
chilled champagne

Stir the orange juice and grenadine together in a wine glass. Top up with champagne (it *should* be Bollinger, but other brands can be substituted). Decorate with a slice of orange or a strip of orange peel.

SANGRIA

(serves 12)
1 bottle reasonable quality Spanish red wine
3 measures brandy
150 ml (¼ pint) orange juice

600 ml (1 pint) lemonade
Ice

Pour all the ingredients, together with some ice, into a glass bowl or other glass container. Stir until cold. Decorate with thin slices of orange, lemon and lime.

SPRITZER
½ glass white wine
Soda water or sparkling mineral water

Put the wine and ice into a highball glass. Top up with soda water or mineral water and stir gently.

MULLED WINE AND WINTER WARMERS

In the absence of a suitable serving bowl, the mulled wines and winter warmers can be stored in bottles placed in a basin of hot water. When serving, a clean napkin should be wrapped around each bottle.

MULL OF MAYO
(serves 20)
2 bottles Burgundy/Rhône red wine
¼ bottle dark rum
½ bottle Dubonnet
½ bottle water
1 orange liberally studded with cloves
2 cinnamon sticks
25 g (1 oz) sultanas
2 lemon halves
5 g (¼ oz) mixed spice
140 g (1 lb) clear honey

Heat the orange in the oven at 180°C/350°F for 10 minutes to bring out the full flavours. Tie the mixed spices securely in a muslin bag to prevent cloudiness, so that only the flavour will be released. Then place all the ingredients, except the rum, in a large pot – do not use all the honey so the flavour can be adjusted later. Place the pot on a low heat and stir occasionally. Bring the mixture to boiling point, but do not allow to boil. Add

the rum, stir, taste and add more honey if necessary. Return to boiling point and then serve into goblets using a ladle with a lip. Sprinkle a little nutmeg over each drink.

Serve immediately whilst it is fresh and hot. (Tepid mulled wine is insipid.)

DR JOHNSON'S CHOICE
(serves 12)
1 bottle claret (red Bordeaux wine)
1 wineglassful orange Curaçao
1 wineglassful brandy
Sliced orange
12 lumps sugar
6 cloves
600 ml (1 pt) boiling water

Heat the wine with the orange slices, cloves and sugar until nearly boiling. Add the boiling water, Curaçao and brandy. Pour into glasses and sprinkle grated nutmeg over the top of each drink.

THE BISHOP
(serves 12)
1½ bottles ruby port
50 g (2 oz) lump sugar
2 oranges
2 cinnamon sticks
Cloves
600 ml (1 pt) water

Prick one of the oranges all over with cloves. Place this in the oven at 180°C/350°F for about half an hour.

Pour the port into a saucepan and bring to boiling point, but do not allow to boil. Meanwhile, boil the water with the cinnamon sticks and the baked orange. Rub the sugar lumps against the skin of half of the second orange and place in a serving bowl with the juice of the orange. Combine the heated port and boiling water and pour into the serving bowl. Allow the cinnamon sticks to remain in the bowl, together with the orange 'hedgehog' for decoration.

Glossary of Wine and Drink Terms

—

Acidity	Mainly in the form of tartaric, citric, lactic and malic acid; in correct quantities it gives wine a refreshing, crisp flavour
Alcohol	The amount of potable ethyl alcohol (C_2H_5OH) in a drink obtained by fermentation and further increased by distillation
Aldeyhyde	Half-way stage between a wine and an acid
Almacenista	A spanish stockholder who makes and matures individual casks of sherry of high quality
Ampelography	The study of vine varieties and their behaviour in the vineyard
Ascorbic acid	More well known as vitamin C; used with sulphur dioxide to prevent oxidation in wine
Aspect	The way a vineyard is facing in relation to the sun
Atmosphere	The pressure inside a bottle of sparkling wine. One atmosphere equals 15 lb per square inch. Champagne has five or six atmospheres of pressure.
Bag-in-the box	An airtight bag usually holding three or ten litres (5.2 or 17 pints) of wine. The bag is made of layers of impermeable plastic enclosed in a cardboard box from which a tap obtrudes allowing access to the wine; synonomous with certain Australian wines
Baumé	French scale to measure *must* weight in order to gauge the potential alcohol in a wine
Blanc de blancs	White wine made from white grapes
Blanc de Noirs	White wine made from black grapes

Blush wine	White wine with pale pink tinges, made from black grapes; originated in California using the Zinfandel grape
BOB	'Buyers own brand'; associated with the champagne firms who make champagne for clients to be sold under the client's own label
Bodega	Spanish wine cellar
Bonded	Wines and spirits are bonded and kept in a warehouse under Government supervision until Customs and Excise duty is paid by the customer
Botrytis cinerea	The fungus which causes *pourriture noble* or noble rot to develop when climatic conditions are favourable
Cap	Mass of grape skins which surface to the top during the fermentation of red wine
Cask	Barrel usually made of oak used for fermenting and maturing wine
Centrifugation	Using centrifugal force to filter out dead yeast and other impurities in the making of wine
Chambrer	To bring wine, usually red, to room temperature
Chaptalisation	Addition of cane or beet sugar to enrich the *must* and secure a higher alcohol content
Château bottling	*Mise en bouteille au Château* guarantees authenticity
Clone	This is a strain of a particular grape species; for example, the classic Riesling grape has many clones
Commune	Wine parish or village
Congeners	Flavour and aroma agents which organic compounds impart to fermented and distilled drinks
Cork	*Quercus suber*; bottle stopper made from the bark of Spanish or Portuguese oak
Côtes	Hillsides where some vineyards are located
Cultivar	South African term for grape variety
Cuvaison	The length of time the *must* is in contact with the skins during the making of red wine. Also known as maceration.

Cuve close	Bulk method for making sparkling wine in a closed tank. Known also as the Charmat Method after its inventor Eugène Charmat (1907)
Cuvée	Blend of wines
Decanter	Glass container, often highly ornamented and of varying shapes
Decanting	The transference of a liquid from its bottle to the decanter to clear the wine of its sediment
Dégorgement	Champagne process to release sediment from the bottle
Eau-de-vie	Water of life, spirit
Estufagem	The heating or cooking process used in the making of Madeira
Eiswein	Intensely sweet wine made from frozen grapes in Germany, Austria and Canada
Éleveur	The 'bringer-up' of a wine in France; the proprietor who looks after a wine as it matures in a cellar
Esters	The combination of acids and alcohol which gives wine its bouquet
Filtering	The removal of dead yeast, solids and impurities from wine and beer to make them bright in appearance
Fining	The clearing of wine in cask or tank; fining agents include isinglass (the bladder of the sturgeon) and egg whites
Fine champagne	Finest Cognac brandy
Fine maison	Brandy of the house
Fusel oil	Toxic alcohol (not ethanol) found in spirits as a by-product of distillation
Gyropalette	Used in the champagne-making *remuage* process; these computor-controlled, hydrolically operated machines shake the sediment down into the neck of the bottle in preparation for the wine to be cleared by disgorging.
Hydrometer	An instrument that records the density of alcohol in a wine or spirit
Irrigation	Artificial means of watering vineyards
Laying down	Storing of wine in bottle

Lees	The sediment that falls to the bottom of the vessel when fermentation is completed
Macération carbonique	The fermentation of whole grapes in a sealed tank under a blanket of carbonic gas; this produces light, fruity wines such as Beaujolais Nouveau or the Italian Vino Novello
Malolactic fermentation	The lactic bacteria converts the harsh malic acid into softer malic acid; there is no increase in alcohol as a result of this secondary fermentation
Mousse	French term to describe the froth or bubbles in sparkling wine
Must	Unfermented grape juice
Mulled wine	Heated wine flavoured with spices; in Germany it is called *Glüwein*
Négociant	Wine handler, merchant or shipper
Oechsle	German system for calculating the specific gravity or *must* weight in order to estimate the potential alcohol of the grape juice
Oenology	The science of wine-making
Oenophile	A connoisseur of wine
Organic wines	Wine produced from grapes which have been grown without the use of pesticides, herbicides or chemical fertilisers
Pasteur, Louis	French scientist renowned for his work on fermentation and pasteurisation
Passe-tout-grains	A Burgundy blend of one-third Pinot Noir and two-thirds Gamay for making red wine
Pétillant	Semi-sparkling
Photosynthesis	This happens when the vine, using light energy absorbed by the green chlorophyll of its leaves, converts carbon dioxide and water into usable organic compounds such as carbohydrates
Phylloxera vastatrix	An aphid that feeds on the roots of the vine and kills it; the cure is to graft the European *Vitis vinifera* onto American root stock immune to the disease

Pruning	Removal of unwanted parts of the vine in order to regulate yield and quality. It is carried out in winter and spring
Punt	The dip in the bottom of a bottle; it strengthens and reinforces the bottle and, in the case of champagne bottles, stabilises the sediment after fermentation
Racking	Moving wine from one cask or container into another for the purpose of clearing the wine off its sediment
Refractometer	A hand-held instrument or optical device used to gauge the sugar content within the grapes while they are still on the vine; it helps to assess when the grapes are ready for gathering
Residual sugar	Natural sugar left in wine after fermentation
Rince cochon	Pigswill; using red Beaujolais instead of Aligoté as a base for Kir
Saccharometer	An instrument for measuring the sugar content in *must* or wine
Saccharomyces ellipsoideus	The most important wine yeast
Sommelier	A wine waiter or wine butler
Süssreserve (sweet reserve)	Unfermented, sterile grape juice added to give balance and sweetness to some wines before bottling
Tannin	Astringent acid imparted by stalks, pips and skins in the making of red wines; it is noticeable by a gum-drying sensation on the palate; it helps to preserve wine as it matures
Tastevin	Dimpled silver cup used by sommeliers to taste wine
Tears	Streaks or legs of wine that form on the inside of a glass as the wine is being drunk; they are an indication of a high alcohol and/or glycerine content
Vendange	The vintage or harvesting of the grapes
Vinification	The making of wine
Vintage wine	Wine made in a good year
Viscosity	When a wine is rolled around a glass, sometimes tears or legs form near the top of the glass and run back down into the wine; this indicates an unctuous, oily wine with a high level of alcohol and sugar

Viticulture	The cultivation of the vine
Vitis	The vine genus
Vitis vinifera	Wine-bearing vine; the species responsible for all the great wines produced
Wash	A fermented liquid destined to be distilled
Weeper	Wine that is weeping or leaking because of a faulty or dry cork
Yeast	Uni-cellular fungi found on the skins of grapes; these micro-organisms produce zymase, the enzyme which converts sugar into alcohol
Yeast autolysis	Dead yeast cells which fall to the bottom of a tank or bottle in the production of sparkling wines. It gives the wine a pleasing yeasty, biscuity bouquet

FURTHER READING

—

Anderson, B. (1992), *Wines of Italy*, London: Italian Trade Centre

Burroughs, D. and Bezzant N. (1987), *The New Wine Companion*, London: Heinemann

Clarke, O. (1985), *The Essential Wine Book*, London: Viking Penguin

Cousins, J. and Durkan, A. (1990), *The Student's Guide to Food and Drink*, London: Hodder & Stoughton

Doxat, J. (1971), *Drinks and Drinking*, London: Ward Lock

Dunkling, L. (1992), *The Guinness Drinking Companion*, London: Guinness Publishing

Durkan, A. (1971), *Vendange*, London: Edward Arnold

Fielden, C. (1994), *Exploring Wines and Spirits*, London: Wine and Spirit Education Trust

George, R. (1989), *The Wine Dictionary*, London: Longman

Hogg, A. (1985), *Everybody's Wine Guide*, London: Quiller Press

Jackson, M. (1988), *New World Guide to Beer*, London: Quarto Publishing

Jefford, A. (1988), *Port*, London: Merehurst Press

Lillicrap, D. and Cousins, J. (1994), *Food and Beverage Service*, 4th edn, London: Hodder & Stoughton

McNulty, H. (1985), *Liqueurs and Spirits*, London: Octopus Books

Prial, F. (ed.) (1992), *The Companion to Wine*, London: Mirabel Books

Stevenson, T. (1988), *World Wine Encyclopedia*, London: Darling Kindersley

Young, R. (1987), *The Really Useful Wine Guide*, London: Sidgwick and Jackson

INDEX

—